STUDIES IN HISTORY, ECONOMICS AND PUBLIC LAW

Edited by the
**FACULTY OF POLITICAL SCIENCE
OF COLUMBIA UNIVERSITY**

NUMBER 421

MACHINE POLITICS IN NEW ORLEANS
1897-1926

BY

GEORGE M. REYNOLDS

MACHINE POLITICS IN NEW ORLEANS
1897 – 1926

BY

GEORGE M. REYNOLDS, Ph.D.

NEW YORK
COLUMBIA UNIVERSITY PRESS
LONDON: P. S. KING & SON, LTD.
1936

To

A. McD. R.

CONTENTS

INTRODUCTION

MACHINE politics in various cities of the North and East has frequently been the object of intensive study and careful analysis. The present work, however, is the first to deal with this subject in connection with a Southern city. Machine politics in New Orleans invites the attention of the student because it affords a basis for comparing Southern methods with those of the North and East, while at the same time it discloses much that is unique and peculiar to New Orleans alone.

This work is primarily concerned with the Choctaw Club which was the dominant political organization of New Orleans, and with Martin Behrman who was the dominant political personality of that Organization. A study of this combination of machine and boss falls naturally into the period from 1897 to 1926. That these chronological limits are not arbitrarily chosen becomes apparent when one recognizes the significance of the disfranchisement of the Negro in 1897, and notes the political changes following the death of Martin Behrman in 1926, when Huey Long first came into prominence.

The Choctaw Club appeared at a most propitious time in New Orleans politics. Its rise to power must be studied in connection with the one-party system and the peculiar election machinery designed to disfranchise the Negro. The destruction of the Republican Party and the absence of effective opposition to the Machine are forces which must be considered. The writer has, therefore, given careful attention to the election machinery and has attempted to show how its operation has affected Machine control.

The study of the Machine leads directly to special treatment of Martin Behrman.   So transcendent was his role in New Orleans politics, and so completely was he an organization man that it is not strange that his biography should reveal much concerning the Choctaw Club.   In referring to Behrman as a " boss " and his organization as a " machine ", no disparagement is intended.   The inevitability and desirability of organization in politics cannot be denied.   The necessity for a spokesman, if not for a boss, is recognized. That politics in every large community will be " fixed " is conceded.   The point of interest to the average person is who are the " fixers ", and for whom is the " fixing " done. It is most unusual, however, for a boss to assume responsibility as well as power.   In this respect Behrman was distinctive in that he served not only as the leader of the Choctaw Club, but also as Mayor of the City.

Any adequate study of politics in New Orleans must take into account the unusual constitutional and legal position of the City with reference to the rest of the State.   The fact that New Orleans contained a fourth of the population of the State and that there was no other city of comparable size accentuated greatly the City-State political relationship. The exceptional needs and interests of the City of New Orleans have been consistently recognized by both the constitution and legislative law.   The Machine cannot, therefore, be studied as an organization separate and apart from State politics.   Consequently, much attention has been given to the place of the governor in City politics, and to the influence of the City Machine in State political campaigns and in the legislature.   No attempt is made, however, to evaluate the administration of any governor of the State.   Governors are discussed only in their relation to the Machine.

This book is in no sense a complete history of political events in New Orleans and Louisiana.   Chronological order is not strictly followed. Events are taken at random when they serve to illustrate the action of the Machine in any situation under discussion. When the proper sequence of events is violated, such violation has been deemed necessary in order to clarify some phase of the Machine's control. Politics in the period treated in this book was greatly influenced by the rise of powerful industrial and commercial forces. It has seemed advisable, therefore, to begin this study with a survey of the social and economic background of the period.

Little documentary material on New Orleans politics is available. Much dependence had to be placed on the newspapers for factual information. Since many of the motives and much of the work of a political machine are not revealed in the news, participants in the events and others in position to know the real objectives were interviewed. No printed material whatever was available on the organization, mechanics, customs and practices of the Choctaw Club. Information was obtained from men who at one time or another had been among its ruling elements; from newspaper men; and from others long familiar with the Organization. The author is therefore indebted to many citizens of New Orleans, and to a number of former State leaders for valuable information which has made this book possible. Because of the continued participation of most of these men in public affairs, the writer does not reveal their names. He is glad to respect the confidence given him under the circumstances, and takes this method of thanking them.

It may be added that the writer is fully conscious of the weakness of the negative evidence referred to in the chapters dealing with the Machine in its relation to business, vice and irregular election practices. Where there was conflicting testimony on men and events such testimony was weighed in the light of its apparent relationship to past or future considerations. It is hoped that reasonably fair conclusions have been reached.

The faction known as the Choctaw Club of Louisiana has been referred to at different times in New Orleans as "Choctaws", "Regulars", "Ring", "Machine", and "Old Regulars". The first four names have been used more or less throughout its history; the latter name came into usage to distinguish the Regulars from the "New Regulars", a faction organized in 1922.[1]

The author wishes to acknowledge his appreciation to Professor A. W. MacMahon and other members of the Faculty of Political Science of Columbia University for their many helpful suggestions and criticisms of this work. He is indebted to Professor Charles W. Pipkin, of Louisiana State University, Professor Bryant Davidson, of Centenary College, Mr. A. W. Newlin, of New Orleans, and Mrs. Amanda McDonald Reynolds for valuable assistance so generously given.

NEW YORK CITY,
JUNE, 1935.

NOTE.—After the completion of this manuscript, but prior to its publication, Senator Huey P. Long, of Louisiana, was assassinated on September 8, 1935. Some references and allusions to him and the future of Louisiana politics are therefore no longer applicable.

---

[1] When any of these names, or the word organization, is used to refer directly to the Choctaw Club the term is capitalized.

CHAPTER I

SOCIAL AND ECONOMIC BACKGROUND

Down the center of New Orleans' far-famed Canal Street, on each side of a double car line, extend two rows of ornamental lamp posts so placed to provide a great white way and to light artistically the historic route of Mardi Gras parades. Inscribed on each post is the following: " French Domination, 1718-1769 "; " Spanish Domination, 1769-1803 "; " Confederate Domination, 1861-1865 "; " American Domination, 1803-1861, 1865——— ". Thus the City Fathers have laconically indicated all along the street of Rex, Comus, and beautiful Creole Mardi Gras queens, the sweep of over two hundred years of New Orleans' rich history. Thus are suggested the varied racial and national influences that have created this most interesting of American cities; thus is the native, as well as the casual visitor, reminded of the social, economic and political influences that have played a part in shaping her past and present. One is reminded that although now American, now politically like many large cities, the material out of which her pattern of life has been woven was of such a nature that it has undoubtedly left its distinctive mark on the City and in many subtle ways influenced the thinking, habits, customs and ways of its citizens.

Crossing Canal Street to the Vieux Carree, one finds oneself almost in another world. Here is preserved concrete evidence of Spanish and French influence on New Orleans. Here one can roam for hours through narrow streets, visit picturesque Spanish patios, view old grilled iron French balconies, see old churches, stroll by the Pantabula, wander through historic Jackson Square, visit the Ancient Cabildo, and eat rare French Creole food. If one listens, French and Spanish may be heard, mingled with the more recently acquired Italian. It is not difficult to appreciate, to admire, the physical remains and effects of New Orleans' varied and colorful past.

When the observer turns to discover and evaluate the results of these influences on recent political history, the difficulties become great. New Orleans has clung tenaciously to her traditions. Those born and bred in Vieux Carree, who had struggled against the floods of the Great River and whose ancestors before them had been a part of New Orleans' life and tradition, often resented the outsider as a leader. Colonel Ewing, who fought his way to power in the fifteenth ward and later shared the stage as one of the bosses, never quite overcame the fact that he was not a native. This tolerant City with its cosmopolitan moral standards presents an atmosphere that might better be termed unmoral than immoral. It has had to oppose the forces in the state that would impose rural, political, or moral standards unsuited to its peculiar tastes and habits. Sensing its own individuality, deeply rooted in the past, the City has sought to preserve its way of life, which it considers good. The traditions, the subtle influences of Spanish and French background, have had their conscious and unconscious effects. To ferret out and relate all these influences to the politics and life of New Orleans is not within the scope of this work, but it is impossible not to feel their potency in any study of the politics of the past thirty years.

The period with which this study deals begins with the organization of the Choctaw Club of Louisiana (the Regular Democratic Organization of New Orleans) in 1897, and ends with the death of its leader, Martin Behrman, in 1926.

A general survey of the social and economic forces in Louisiana and New Orleans during the era will serve as a broad background for the later discussion of the methods used by the Choctaws in the acquisition, consolidation and exercise of political power.

In addition to being settled by the Spanish and French, New Orleans, in common with other parts of the country, received a large number of immigrants from Germany, Ireland and Italy.[1] The Germans and Irish began arriving in 1850. They quickly adapted themselves to their new environment, and by the time the wave of Italian immigration started in 1880, were taking an active interest in politics. They never formed a separate racial group as did the Italians. The names, Fitzpatrick and Kruttschnitt, the former a mayor and boss, and the latter the president of the Constitutional Convention of 1898, are reminiscent of the Irish and Germany ancestry of some of New Orleans' leading politicians.

For the most part, the immigrants from Italy were of the lower classes, poor and illiterate. By 1890 there were 7,767 foreign-born Italians in the City.[2] The Italian population was 16,560 in 1900; 18,581 in 1910; 21,818 in 1920; and 24,011 in 1930.[3] No wide-awake machine could ignore such

---

[1] *United States Census Reports*, 1850-1910, *passim.*

[2] *Eleventh Census 1890*, " Population " p. 705.

[3] *Twelfth Census 1900*, " Population ", vol. i, p. 800; *Thirteenth Census 1910*, " Population ", vol. i, p. 784; *Fourteenth Census 1920*, " Population ", vol. iii, p. 928; *Fifteenth Census 1930*, " Population ", vol. iii, pt. i, pp. 71 and 72. There was a higher proportion of Italians in New Orleans than in other large southern cities. In 1930, for example, Atlanta had only 509 out of a total population of 270,366; Dallas had 1913 out of a total population of 260,475; Houston had 4931 out of a total population of 292,352; Cincinnati a city outside the south about the same size as New Orleans, had 7432 out of a population of 451,160; New Orleans stood far ahead of these cities with 24,011 out of a total population of 458,762. *Fifteenth Census 1930*, " Population ", vol. iii, pts. i and ii, *passim.* The United States Census Reports for 1900, 1910 and

a susceptible group and the Choctaws made the most of their opportunities.   Using the tactics of ward politics everywhere, the Machine through personal contact, friendliness, charity, jobs, and general helpfulness, quickly won these new-comers to its support.   Their presence and the desire of the Machine to use their vote have left their mark on the laws and constitutional provisions relating to suffrage.   In the Constitution of 1879 and in subsequent election laws, men of foreign birth were granted the right to vote, provided they had declared their intention of becoming citizens.[4]   This arrangement continued until 1898 when citizenship was required as a condition of suffrage.   Special provision was made, however, exempting the illiterate foreign-born voter from the educational and property tests required in the Constitution of 1898.[5]

Probably the strongest force in determining the course of politics in Louisiana since 1861 has been the large Negro population.   Constitutional disfranchisement in 1898 successfully ended the Negro's active participation at the polls but did not do away with the possibility of his return.   It is well to note that the Democrats have not been negligent in keeping alive the Negro question since it helps that party to remain dominant in Louisiana.   The " Regulars " in New Orleans were defeated in the city election of 1896 by a combination of Republicans, Reform-Democrats, a few Populists, and the Negro.   The Choctaw Club, the successor to

1920 reveal similar proportions.   The Reports for 1930 state that 13% of the foreign white stock in the urban population of the United States was Italian and for the whole country 11%.   The Italian population of New Orleans was 23% of its total foreign white stock in 1930.

    [4] *Constitution of 1879*, art. 185.

    [5] *Constitution of 1898*, art. 197, sec. 5.   The newspapers ridiculed the Convention for making special provision for the illiterate " Dago " voter. It was generally recognized that the Italian vote was controlled by the Machine.   *New Orleans Times Democrat*, Feb.-May, 1898, *passim*.

the old machine, was therefore glad to help disfranchise Negro voters at the Constitutional Convention of 1898, which was called for that purpose. Exclusion of the Negro from politics has remained a "commandment" of that organization. A review of the part played by the Negro in the political conflict between various parties and factions in Louisiana before his disfranchisement in 1898 will help to place the Choctaw Club in its proper setting and characterize the atmosphere in which it has operated for so long.

Reconstruction in Louisiana, after the brief period of presidential control under Lincoln and Johnson, developed into one of the most violent struggles in the south.[6] The first attempt at reconstruction in Louisiana was made according to the plan outlined in Lincoln's proclamation of 1863, which provided that when ten per cent of the voting population of any Southern state, as determined by the election laws in force before the war, had taken the oath of allegiance to the United States, a new state government might be formed.[7] Louisiana took advantage of this proclamation. A constitutional convention was called for 1864 under the tutelage of General Banks, who was in charge of the federal military district at the time. The Constitution of 1852 had based representation on total population. This had enabled the planter class, among whom most of the Negroes lived, to secure representation far in excess of its voting strength.[8] To avoid the inequalities of this provision, the legislature

[6] For a detailed account of reconstruction through 1868, see Ficklen, "Reconstruction of Louisiana," *Johns Hopkins University Studies in Historical and Political Science*, vol. xxviii (Baltimore, 1910). For a complete history of reconstruction, see Lonn, *Reconstruction in Louisiana* (New York, 1918); Lewinson, *Race, Class and Party* (New York, 1933), has a brief account.

[7] McDonald, *Documentary Source Book of American History* (New York, 1926), p. 470.

[8] *Constitution of 1852*, art. 8.

in calling the convention of 1864 stipulated that representation should be based on white population only.   No effort
was made to allow the Negro to participate in the election
of delegates.   The plan was adopted also because it would
give New Orleans more nearly its proper share of delegates
since the proportion of Negroes to whites in the City was
much less than in the country districts.[9]   A majority of the
delegates at the convention were therefore from the City
and the poor white sections of the country.   In an effort to
make permanent their advantage over the " Bourbon " class,
one of the early acts of the convention was the adoption of
a provision basing representation in the legislature on the
number of qualified electors.[10]   When the question of Negro
suffrage arose, it was favored by the planter group and
opposed by the poor white majority.   The planters believed
they could control the Negro vote and saw in Negro suffrage
an opportunity to restore their lost influence.   The poor
whites also thought the planters would control the Negro
vote if granted and hence opposed the plan.[11]   The constitution as finally adopted granted suffrage to white males
only, leaving the question of Negro suffrage to the legislature.[12]   President Lincoln, in a letter to Governor Hahn, had
urged the granting of limited Negro suffrage.   The dominant group in the convention refused to respond to this plea.[13]
The distinct cleavage among the whites at the convention was
indicated by a speech near its close in which the delegates
were praised for emancipating the state from " Bourbon "
control.   The speaker indicated he felt this was as impor-

[9] Ficklen, *op. cit.*, p. 74.

[10] *Constitution of 1864*, art. 10.

[11] *Debates, Constitutional Convention of 1864*, pp. 143, 161, 501 and 502.

[12] *Constitution of 1864*, arts. 14 and 15.

[13] Lewinson, *op. cit.*, pp. 37-39. A similar attitude prevailed in Alabama, *ibid.*, pp. 37-38.

tant as the emancipation of the Negro slaves by President Lincoln.[14]   The constitution was adopted by a popular vote of 6,836 to 1,566.[15]

The convention had adjourned, subject to the call of the president.   The radicals among the Republicans in the state, who soon got the upper hand, sought to reconvene it in 1866 in order to grant the Negro the vote.   Although they failed to secure support from Washington, it was called for July 30, 1866.[16]   When the convention met in New Orleans, a riot resulted in which one member and several Negroes were killed and many wounded.   No further effort was made to continue the convention.   This trouble helped to hasten the congressional program of reconstruction.[17]

Radical Congressional reconstruction plans were imposed on Louisiana in the Constitution of 1868.[18]   Suffrage was granted to all male citizens who had been residents of the state for one year and of the parish in which they claimed the right to vote for ten days.[19]   To add strength to their control of the state, the radical Republicans then proceeded, under article 99, to disfranchise many Democrats who had belonged to the Confederacy by requiring a very distasteful loyalty oath before they could regain the vote or the right to

[14] *Debates, op. cit.,* p. 190.

[15] Ficklen, *op. cit.,* p. 89.   It should be recalled that part of Louisiana at this time was not under Federal control and that many people stayed away from the polls to express their displeasure of the existing situation. Congress did not admit Louisiana to the Union under this Constitution.

[16] For full account, see Ficklen, *op. cit.,* pp. 170-178.

[17] President Johnson stated that the radicals instigated the trouble to spur their program, Ficklen, *op. cit.,* p. 175.

[18] Ficklen, *op. cit.,* pp. 199-215.   Louisiana was readmitted to the Union after the adoption of this Constitution.   There were many Negro delegates at the convention.

[19] *Constitution of 1868,* arts. 25, 26 and 98.

hold office.   These provisions served to put the Republican party in complete control of state and local governments.[20]

As the Republican rule, supported by Negro votes, became more radical, corrupt and ruthless, the whites united in the Democratic party to overthrow it.[21]   At first they sought to enlist the Negro in their party, but finding this hopeless, they drew the color line.   Secret organizations sprang up among the Democrats, with the one aim of restoring white supremacy.[22]   Louisiana resisted Negro suffrage because the Negro population was in the majority until 1900, and because most of the Negroes had been won to the support of the Republican Party.[23]

After closing their ranks against the Negro, the Democrats were aided in their struggle for power by factional quarrels in the Republican party.[24]   The active revolt against the Republican Party started in the state campaign of 1874.[25]   In New Orleans the Democrats had ordered several cases of rifles to use to insure a fair election.   The arms were to arrive by boat.   Governor Kelly heard of the

[20] The Constitution was ratified by a vote of 51,737 to 39,076. Ficklen, *op. cit.*, p. 201. Henry C. Warmoth was elected Governor in 1868.

[21] Lewinson, *op. cit.*, p. 51.

[22] Among them were the Knights of the White Camelia and the Ku Klux Klan, Ficklen, *op. cit.*, p. 215.

[23] The relative Negro and White populations of the state were as follows: 1870, White — 362,065, Negro — 364,210; 1880, White — 454,954, Negro—463,655; 1890, White—558,305, Negro—560,192; 1900, White—729,612, Negro—650,804; 1910, White—941,086, Negro—713,874; 1920, White—1,096,611, Negro—700,257. *The U. S. Census, 1870-1920, passim.* The White population of New Orleans far exceeded the Negro population during the same period.   The population in the City averaged about three whites to one Negro.   In 1910 there were still 25 out of the 61 parishes where the Negro was in the majority. *Thirteenth Census, 1910,* "Population", p. 771.   The state was 43 per cent Negro. *Ibid.*

[24] Lonn, *Reconstruction in Louisiana*, chs. iv-viii; Lewinson, *op. cit.* p. 53.

[25] Lewinson, p. 55; Lonn, *op. cit.*, ch. xiii.

plan and on September 14, the day the rifles were to arrive, sent the metropolitan police to the Canal Street docks to seize them. The Democrats, however, were already there and well armed. A fight took place in which forty persons were killed and a hundred wounded.[26] The Democrats were victorious and the Republican government collapsed. The Democrats then installed John McEnery as governor. However, Governor Kelly was reestablished in a few days under protection of federal troops and McEnery was forced out. Shortly after this occurrence the election took place. First reports indicated a majority of the legislature elected were Democrats, but by some queer process, the Governor's Returning Board reported a majority of Republican legislators elected.

Undaunted, the Democrats continued the struggle through the election of 1876. The Republicans were using every means possible to hold the presidency of the United States, and their success depended on their control of several southern states. The election was one of the hardest fought in the history of the state. Both sides claimed victory—the Democrats by an 8,000 majority. Nevertheless, the Republican Returning Board certified a Republican victory by 1,000 votes.[27] Two state governments were set up in New Orleans. Civil War appeared imminent.[28] After the decision in the presidential contest between Hayes and Tilden, federal troops were withdrawn as a part of the compromise and the Republican government disappeared.[29] Governor Francis T. Nicholls had been the successful Democratic can-

[26] This incident is recalled because of the lasting impression it made in New Orleans. A monument was erected on the spot where the fight took place. Each year the victory of September 14, 1874, is observed by special ceremonies at the monument.

[27] Lewinson, *op. cit.*, pp. 55-60; Lonn, *op. cit.*, chs. xviii and xix, *passim.*

[28] *Ibid.*

[29] Lewinson, *op. cit.*, p. 55; Lonn, chs. xx and xxi.

didate and now entered on his duties as the sole governor of the state.

The problem of the Democratic party now was to disfranchise the Negro and adjust the conflicting interests of the whites. Disfranchisement of the Negro was complicated not only by the Federal Constitution, but also by the fear among the poor, illiterate white men, that, in taking the vote away from ignorant propertyless Negro by the imposition of educational and property tests, they too might lose the vote. The task of compromising the conflicting interests was to prove great and was delayed two decades, due to agrarian unrest and the growth of populism in the Eighties and Nineties. This break in white solidarity was to bring the Negro back into politics. The use made of his vote was to affect the result of the struggle between the white elements for control of the government.

A convention controlled by the Democrats was held to revise the distasteful constitution adopted in 1868 under Republican domination.[30] Although the convention, in its desire to disfranchise the Negro, felt itself blocked by the 14th and 15th Amendments of the Federal Constitution, some progress was made toward this end. Residence requirements in the parish and precinct were raised; the legislature was instructed to impose a poll tax; and registration changes were authorized.[31] These provisions, together with subsequent legislation and unequal administration of the registration laws, served to disfranchise many of the Negroes. In some sections the Negro was roughly treated and terrorized. The system of determining representation in the legislature on the basis of total population was restored.[32]

[30] *Acts of Louisiana,* 1879, Extra Session, no. 3.

[31] *Constitution of 1879,* arts. 185, 186 and 208.

[32] *Constitution of 1879,* art. 16.

The Constitution of 1879 stringently limited the powers of the legislature. The convention, remembering the excesses of reconstruction legislatures, inserted a clause which prohibited the general assembly from creating any debt or issuing any bonds in behalf of the state except to repel invasion or repress insurrection.[33] Special and local legislation was also rigidly limited.[34] Lotteries were continued but it was provided that they should cease to operate after January 1, 1895.[35] The Constitution outlined detailed taxes for many purposes. The powers of the governor were extended. This was particularly true of his appointing power.[36]

The division among the whites, which had been evident in the constitutional conventions of 1864 and 1879, was greatly accentuated by the Populist movement. Slowly gaining momentum in the Eighties and Nineties, the Populist party in Louisiana faced the Democrats with such formidable opposition through a fusion with the Republicans in the elections of 1892, 1894, and 1896 that the Negro was brought back into politics. The laws designed to keep the Negro out were swept aside and the Negroes were again voted in droves.

High prices after the Civil War had stimulated the growth of cotton to the exclusion of other crops. Price declines in cotton, beginning about 1875 and continuing through the Eighties, reached their lowest in 1894 when cotton sold for 4¾ cents a pound.[37] Low cotton prices naturally hurt the

[33] *Ibid.*, art. 44.

[34] *Ibid.*, art. 46.

[35] *Ibid.*, art. 167. This was the date on which the charter of the Louisiana Lottery Company was to expire. All lotteries by this Constitution were required to pay the state $40,000 annually for the privilege of operating. Attention is called to the lottery because it was the major issue in the election of 1892.

[36] *Ibid.*, arts. 58-79.

[37] *Yearbook of U. S. Department of Agriculture,* 1895, p. 536.

small business man as well as the farmer, since cotton was the chief money crop.

The Farmers' Alliance, therefore, found conditions favorable when it spread into Louisiana from Texas in 1876.[38] Its purpose was to educate and organize the farmer. By 1888 the movement had grown to considerable strength in the hill sections of north and west Louisiana, which was the region of the small farmer. The movement never gained much headway in the cotton plantation areas of the bottoms, in the sugar growing district or in the cities.[39]   The organization was an influence in politics by 1888, but not as a separate party. The farmers were still Democrats. They supported the Democratic candidate who seemed most favorable to the policies of the Farmers' Alliance.[40]

The first steps toward organizing the People's Party in Louisiana took place in Winn Parish during the Congressional elections of 1890.[41]   Because the candidate supported by the Winn Parish delegation was tricked out of the nomination in the Democratic nominating convention, they bolted and organized a People's Party Convention. A Farmers' Alliance organizer from DeSoto Parish was nominated as the People's Party candidate. Although he was defeated

[38] White, "Populism in Louisiana," *Mississippi Valley Historical Review*, vol. v, no. 1, p. 4; Hicks, *The Populist Revolt* (University of Minnesota Press, 1931), p. 111.

[39] Reports of the Secretary of State bear out this statement. The Populists never elected a member to the Legislature from New Orleans and only rarely from the plantation parishes.

[40] White, *op. cit.*, pp. 5-7. The DeSoto Parish Farmers' Alliance in 1898 adopted a platform in which it advocated sale of public lands only to small farmers, no trading in futures of agricultural products, abolition of convict labor leasing system, and free coinage of silver. DeSoto Parish is located in northwest Louisiana on the Texas line.

[41] *Ibid.*, p. 7. Winn Parish is the birthplace of the present Senior Senator from Louisiana, Huey P. Long. The parish was a stronghold of Populism throughout the Nineties. Senator Long was born in 1894.

by the Democratic candidate, the event served to start the new party on its way. During this campaign two newspapers began publication to foster the new party.[42]

A series of events in the Nineties helped to promote Populism. The overflows of 1891 and 1892,[43] the panic of 1892, the drought and an epidemic of disease among the stock in the spring and summer of 1896[44] added many recruits to the party.

In 1892 the party had a full ticket in the field in Louisiana. In general the Louisiana party adopted the aims of the national party. It desired also reform in the apportionment of representation in the state nominating conventions and in the legislature. Under the prevailing system, the Negro population was counted in calculating representation but did not vote. This tended to give the whites in the black parishes an undue amount of influence not justified by their actual voting population. The Populists charged that because of this, the governor, in order to build up his political influence, favored these sections and the cities in the matter of appointments.[45]

More important than the Populist movement in the state election of 1892 was the lottery issue. The Constitution of 1879, it will be recalled, had provided that after January 1, 1895, the lotteries were to cease operations.[46] In 1888, Samuel D. McEnery had been elected governor and had started the levee system. In 1890 the lottery companies offered to support the levee system and a fight was begun to

[42] *Ibid.*, p. 8. The papers were the *Winn Parish Democrat* and the *Comrade* both published at Winnfield by H. L. Brian, who later became chairman of the State Central Committee of the Populist Party.

[43] *New Orleans Times Democrat*, Sept. 1, 1892.

[44] *Ibid.*, Sept. 15, 25 and 29, 1896.

[45] White, *op. cit.*, pp. 7 and 8.

[46] *Cf. supra*, p. 10.

amend the constitution and renew the lottery charters before
they were scheduled to expire.   The governor and the legislature to be elected in April, 1892, would be largely responsible for deciding the issue.[47]   The controversy split the
Democrats and a bitter factional struggle ensued.   Because
the lotteries proposed to support his pet project, the levees,
Governor Samuel D. McEnery, came out for the lotteries
and was nominated by the Regular, or Pro-lottery Democratic faction.   Murphy J. Foster was nominated by the
Anti-lottery League, which was also made up largely of
Democrats.[48]

The Republican Party in the state was split; the Leonard
and Warmoth factions both claimed to be the official party
and each had a candidate for governor in the field.   With the
Populist candidate, this made five aspirants for the office.
The real contest, however, was conceded to be between the
two Democratic factions.

The result of the voting on April 19th was a victory for
the Anti-Lottery ticket, headed by Foster.   The People's
Party candidate, R. L. Tannehill, received 9,792 votes and
carried the parishes of Catahoula, Grant, Vernon and Winn.[49]
This vote did not indicate the real strength of the Populists
because the lottery issue overshadowed all others.   The
Farmers' Alliance in many parishes had combined with the
Anti-lottery Democrats.[50]   The Populists elected one state
Senator and two representatives.   The Regular (Pro-
lottery) Democrats carried the City of New Orleans for both
its state and city candidates.   The election was particularly

[47] Fortier, *History of Louisiana*, pp. 220-225 (New York, 1904) ; White,
op. cit., pp. 9-10; *New Orleans Item*, Oct. 30, 31, 1922, " Behrman Tells "
(this is Martin Behrman's autobiography written for the *Item*).

[48] White, *op. cit.*, p. 7.

[49] *Report of the Secretary of State*, 1894, pp. 178 and 179.

[50] White, *op. cit.*, pp. 7 and 8.

acute in New Orleans as it involved a factional struggle for control of the city government as well as the state lottery issue.[51]

Following the state election, the various factions and parties began preparing for the presidential election in the fall. The fusion between the Anti-lottery Democrats and the Populists had ended with their victory. The Populists sent a delegation to the national convention of the party in Omaha in the summer of 1892.[52] There was a rumor of fusion between the Republicans and Populists of the state for the presidential election in the fall. The press gave much attention to the Populist movement during the summer of 1892, bringing out its growth and strength in the hill parishes of the North and West. The state election in Arkansas, which involved a fusion of the Republicans and Populists, was watched with interest in Louisiana. Although the Arkansas Democrats won, it put a scare into the faction torn Democrats of Louisiana who feared similar tactics there. They visioned a Republican-Populist victory unless their own breach could be healed. The Democratic papers all urged that the party, split by the lottery fight, get together.[53]

True to the fear of the Democrats, a fusion agreement was worked out by the Republicans and the Populists on October 20, 1892, a few days after the Leonard and War-

[51] Lewinson, *op. cit.*, p. 77. The Regulars imported forty cases of rifles for the election. The Anti-Lottery forces expected to be "counted out" in New Orleans by the Regulars, who controlled the election machinery and had made threats to use force to get a fair count. Men familiar with this election say the count in New Orleans was unfair to the Anti-lottery faction while in many country parishes the Anti-lottery people "counted out" the Pro-lottery faction. The Negro vote was used extensively by both sides.

[52] White, *op. cit.*, p. 8.

[53] *New Orleans Times Democrat* and *Times Picayune*, July, Aug. and Sept., 1892. Especially July 4, Aug. 16 and Sept. 3.

moth Republican factions had come to an understanding.[54] The arrangement between the two parties provided for a combined electoral and congressional ticket with the understanding that there was no agreement to work together after the election.   Each party furnished half the candidates.[55]

In the campaign, the Populists advocated a break in the solid south and urged the Louisiana voters to join the toiling masses of the north, east, and west in their effort to overthrow the corrupt old parties of monopoly and vested wealth. The people were urged to regard the " Negro menace " as a creation of Democratic imagination.   The Democrats, having largely compromised their differences, won the election. Cleveland received 87,922 votes, Harrison, 13,282, and Weaver, the Populist candidate, 13,281.   The Democrats also elected their entire congressional slate.[56]

The fusion of the Republicans and Populists lasted through the congressional election of 1894 and the state election in the spring of 1896.   This combination divided the whites and brought the Negro back into politics with all the force possible.   Except for some participation in the elections of 1888 and the bitter lottery fight of 1892, he had been largely excluded since 1879.[57]   Both sides began to court the Negro voter and the fear of Negro domination returned.[58]

[54] White, op. cit., pp. 7 and 8. New Orleans Times Democrat, Oct. 20-21, 1892.

[55] Ibid., p. 10.   In a statement to the public announcing the fusion, the Populist denounced the old parties, monopolies, and wealth, and declared the fusion was made to get a fair deal for both parties from the hands of the Democrats, who controlled the election machinery. The Republicans simply announced they had made the agreement, against a common enemy, to secure a fair election.

[56] Report of the Secretary of State, 1892, pp. 176-177.

[57] White, op. cit., p. 12.

[58] New Orleans Times Democrat, Apr. 4, 1896.

The Democratically controlled legislature voted a suffrage amendment in January, 1896 to be submitted to the people at the state election in April. The act proposed educational and property tests for voting, its object being to deprive the Negro of suffrage. Although just as guilty in corrupting the Negro voter as the opposition, the Democrats announced the proposed suffrage amendment as the leading issue of the campaign and declared they would support the ratification.[59] It was, however, too late to keep the Negro out of the election. The flood gates were already open. The rising agrarian unrest of the Nineties, factional quarrels in the Democratic Party, and the formidable threat of the fusion forces so frightened the Democratic politicians that they went into the market place for Negro votes just as the opposition was doing.

The City election in New Orleans was on the same date as the general state election. To the consternation of the Democratic politicians, the professional and business interests of New Orleans, led by a few reformers, took this occasion to make an effort to break the machines' control of the City. To do this, they organized the Citizens' League.[60] The Citizens' League was joined by the Republicans and with the aid of the Negro vote succeeded in electing their candidate for mayor.[61]

In the state election in some quarters, the Populists took the offensive. In St. Landry Parish they took charge of the parish seat and went through the process of registering the Negroes. The Democrats retaliated by spreading terror among the Negroes. State troops were sent to keep order.[62]

[59] White, op. cit., p. 13.

[60] New Orleans Times Democrat, Apr. 2, 1896; New Orleans Item, "Behrman Tells," Oct. 31, 1922.

[61] Ibid., Oct. 31 and Nov. 1, 1922.

[62] Lewinson, op. cit., pp. 77, 78; White, op. cit., p. 14.

The election was the most disorderly ever held in the state. There were charges of fraud, coercion, stuffing of ballot boxes, in fact every known election crime.[63] Voting took place April 21, 1896, and resulted in the reelection of Governor Murphy J. Foster, the Democratic candidate, over John W. Pharr, the fusion candidate of the Republicans and the Populists, though not by the usual large Democratic majority.[64] The strength of the opposition was more evident in the election of the legislature. Out of thirty-six senators and ninety-eight representatives, the Populists elected eighteen and the Republicans thirteen. There were two Independents and two independent Democrats elected. The Citizens' League elected nineteen members from New Orleans. Thus out of 136 members of the general assembly, there were 54 members in opposition to the regular Democrats.[65]

Although Foster had been declared elected, the fusionists disputed the returns. They thoroughly believed there had been a false count and were determined to seat Pharr at any cost. Both sides bitterly declared they would never give in to the other. The Pharr group thought its best chance for

[63] *New Orleans Times Democrat*, Apr. 8, 10, 23, 25, 28, 1896. Lewinson, *op. cit.*, p. 79; White, *op. cit.*, p. 15. Participants in the elections in New Orleans told the author that each party escorted its Negro supporters to the polls under armed guards to prevent the opposition from intimidating them and keeping them away. Similar tactics were used in other parts of the state. Each party openly marked the ballots for its Negro allies.

[64] *New Orleans Times Democrat*, Apr. 22, 23, 1896.

[65] *Report of the Secretary of State*, 1894-1896, pp. 6-13. The Populists elected were from the Parishes of: Winn, St. Landry, Catahoula, Natchitoches, Sabine, Union, Jackson, East Baton Rouge, Claiborne, Lincoln, Grant, Vernon, and Arcadia. Most of these are located in north and west Louisiana. A heavy Populist vote was cast in the Florida parishes. No large city is located in any of these parishes. The City of New Orleans elected no Populists at this or any previous election. See *Reports of Secretary of State*, 1890-1896.

a fair deal was before the newly elected legislature, which was scheduled to meet in May. After much discussion, both parties finally agreed to submit the matter to that body. The Pharr group requested a count of the ballots. Armed supporters of both sides were present in Baton Rouge. In this contest in the legislature, the Citizens' League members from New Orleans split, some supporting Pharr and the others Foster.[66] After hearing the Pharr supporters, the general assembly, by a small majority, decided it had no authority to go behind the election returns.[67] True to the prediction of former Governor McEnery, who had stated before the election that the politicians would not have the courage to give more than lip service to the proposed suffrage amendment, it was defeated.[68] In this election Martin Behrman received one of his two defeats in politics. He was a candidate for the legislature from the Fifteenth Ward in New Orleans on the " Regular " slate.

Political events of the Nineties had indicated that when the whites were bitterly divided neither side could trust the others not to buy the venal Negro vote. The Negro could hardly be blamed for the conditions which had developed; he was ignorant, had no political background, and needed the money. The fault lay with the conflicting white groups who were his corrupters. The Republican party had enfranchised the Negro purely for political reasons in the days

[66] The Citizens' League was made up of many Democrats, as well as Republicans. The League Democrats had split the ticket in New Orleans, voting the state Democratic ticket and the reform ticket in the City.

[67] A brief account of the contest may be found in White, pp. 14-16. Full account, *New Orleans Times Democrat*, Apr. 22-May 17, 1896.

[68] For McEnery's statement and the result of the vote see *New Orleans Times Democrat*, Apr. 13 and 25, 1896. He stated the Negro was again dominant in Louisiana politics and hence the politicians would fear to actively support the proposed change which was intended to deprive the Negro of his vote.

of reconstruction, and with the power thus obtained, had imposed Negro rule on the South.   The bitterness engendered by this caused blame for past wrongs to rest not only on the radical Republicans, but also on the Negro.   Had Negro suffrage been gradually granted under southern leadership instead of being imposed from the outside, the problem that faced the South in 1896 might have been avoided. The disgraceful election of 1896 brought a demand for immediate action.   All the white elements felt that constitutional changes to eliminate the Negro vote were necessary to avoid a recurrence of such an election.   As the situation had developed it seemed best to take the Negro vote off the market and leave only the white electorate with its comparatively small venal vote to be traded in on election day.   The Negro had been selfishly used throughout his career as a voter and his vote was now to be sacrificed because of the conflict of the white elements for it.

It was in pursuance of this general sentiment that the legislature on July 7, 1896, passed a bill proposing a vote of the people for January, 1898, on the question of holding a constitutional convention in February, 1898.[69]   The resolution provided that if the people voted to hold the convention, it was to have authority to adopt a constitution without submitting it to the people for approval.   At the same session, and related to the convention bill, the Assembly passed a new registration law and a new election law.[70]   Both these laws became effective immediately and it was hoped by means of the new registration law to cut down the Negro vote before the election on the question of holding the constitutional convention.   It was also hoped by the new election law to

[69] *Acts of Louisiana*, no. 52, of 1896.   The act stipulated that the convention was to make no changes in the levee system, the lottery laws, the bonded debt, or the terms of office of present state officials.

[70] *Acts of Louisiana*, nos. 89 and 137 of 1896.

eliminate some of the evils of the elections of recent years. Both these bills contained some of the reforms demanded by the Populists.[71]

Early in the summer attention was focused on the presidential election. Bryan had been nominated by the Democrats. The Republican-Populist fusion agreement had come to an end at the close of the state campaign in the spring. The way was thus open for the Louisiana Populists to make an agreement with the Democrats, as was being done in many other states. The Populists in southwest Louisiana were the first to declare for Bryan. The group in north Louisiana was still bitter against the Democrats over the state campaign. On September 25, 1896, an agreement was reached. The Democrats promised a fair election and each party was to name half of the electors of the state.[72]

Senator Caffery of Louisiana, on Bryan's nomination, had gone with the Gold-Democrats and was permanent chairman of their Indianapolis Convention.[73] On his return to New Orleans, he came out for Palmer and sought to organize the state and City in his behalf. For this he was roundly denounced by the country Democrats.[74]

Another interesting angle of this election was that the sugar planters and sugar interests generally supported the Republican ticket, fearing that if Bryan and a Democratic Congress were elected, the tariff on sugar would be repealed.[75] The Republicans sought a fusion agreement with

[71] *Acts of Louisiana*, nos. 89 and 137, of 1896, particularly act 137.

[72] *New Orleans Times Democrat*, September 16, 24, 25, 26, 27, 1896. Having voted with the Republicans in the state election, the Populists now voted with the Democrats in the national election.

[73] Stanwood, *History of the Presidency* (Boston, 1928), p. 55.

[74] *New Orleans Times Democrat*, Sept. 21-25, 1896.

[75] *New Orleans Times Picayune*, Oct. 8 and 27, 1896; Hicks, *The Populist Revolt* (Minneapolis, 1931), p. 340.

the Gold-Democrats but were turned down.[76]   The election results were 77,175 votes for Bryan, 22,037 for McKinley, and 1,915 for Palmer.[77]   The elections of 1896 were the last in which the Republicans made any real fight and also the last in which the Negro voted in large numbers.

Into this flamboyant political scene, a new factor was injected when the Choctaw Club of Louisiana was chartered on March 12, 1897.   The Crescent Democratic Club had been the "Regular" Democratic organization in New Orleans for a number of years prior to its being discredited in the state lottery election of 1892.   John Fitzpatrick had been elected mayor by the "Regulars" in 1892.   Shortly after, the Crescent Democratic Club went out of existence and Democratic leadership in the City fell into the hands of Fitzpatrick and three powerful ward leaders, Messrs. Houston, Davey and Mauberret.   These men, without formal organization, were in charge of Democratic politics until the Choctaw Club was organized in 1897.   Their defeat in the City election in 1896 and the impending constitutional convention had indicated the need for stronger organization and leadership.   The Democrats of New Orleans, therefore, had double inspiration to create a stronger organization—to regain control of the City government and to assist in the general effort to eliminate the Negro voter. These two objectives were related.   Many "Regulars" felt the Negro had been the deciding factor in the election of Mayor Flowers over their candidate in 1896.[78]   Another condition favoring the new organization was the gradual break-up of the Citizens' League following the split in the legislature over the Foster-Pharr contest.

[76] *New Orleans Times Democrat*, Oct. 3, 1896.

[77] *Report of the Secretary of State*, 1898, p. 480.   The large Republican vote was due to the sugar vote and to many business men who feared the election of Bryan.

[78] *New Orleans Item*, Oct. 31, 1922, "Behrman Tells."

Far more important, however, was the fact that Governor Foster was recognizing the " Regular " Democrats in the matter of state patronage in the City and parish and not the Citizens' League. He was thus furnishing the very life blood for a machine struggling to be born. The " Regular " Democrats of course, had supported Foster in his race for governor. A new organization, even with some old faces, proved an immediate success. The " Reform " Democrats, who had voted with the Citizens' League in 1896, could now say, " The old machine is dead; we defeated it and now here is a new Democratic club that we can enter into, unite with the other Democrats, and help disfranchise the Negro." They were not deterred by the fact that the " big four " of the old machine, Fitzpatrick, Davey, Houston and Mauberret also joined.

Professional politicians organized the Choctaw Club and have always dominated it. This may explain its long and successful control of the City. Its avowed purpose, as expressed in the Charter, was " to add to the organized strength of the Democratic party in Louisiana." Although entitled, " The Choctaw Club of Louisiana," the organization has been wholly confined to New Orleans.[79] The Charter enumerates the purposes of the club as follows: 1. To uphold and advance Democratic principles; 2. to promote harmony, enjoyment, and literary improvements;[80] 3. to provide the convenience of a Club House.[81]

[79] A few men in other parts of Louisiana, for social or political reasons, belong to the Club. Former residents of New Orleans often keep up their membership.

[80] One should not assume from this that the New Orleans politicians spent their evenings at the Club reading Shelley, Keats, Longfellow, or even DeMaupassant and Balzac.

[81] The charter is on file in the office of the Clerk of the Civil District Court, New Orleans.

Among the charter members, besides the "big four," were Martin Behrman, destined to rise to leadership in the organization; H. C. Ramos, perhaps more famous as the concocter of the renowned "Ramos Gin Fizz" than as a politician; Robert Ewing, then a young newspaper man and later a powerful ward leader and newspaper publisher; Charles Rosen, a prominent lawyer and later a bitter foe of the organization; and George W. Vandervoort, a newspaper reporter and secretary to the Chief of Police.[82]   Several members of the New Orleans' Dock Board were also charter members of the Club.   Thus, from the very beginning, the Dock Board was closely associated with the Choctaws and became a prolific source of nourishment for the Machine.

The early strength and rapid growth of the new organization is indicated by the fact that a majority of the Orleans Parish delegation at the Constitutional Convention of 1898 were charter members of the Choctaw Club.[83]   Its remarkable influence from the beginning may be attributed largely to the patronage with which Governor Foster endowed it, the elements of the former machine brought in when the Club was organized, the political experience of its members and the disintegration of the opposition.   Foster recognized the fact that the Choctaws were the coming political power in New Orleans and, having his eye on the United States Senate, won the organization to his support by naming as many leaders of the new machine as possible to state jobs.[84]

[82] *New Orleans Item*, Nov. 2, 1922, "Behrman Tells." Governor Foster and former Governor McEnery were made life members. There were 137 charter members.

[83] *Report of the Convention of 1898*, published by the Democratic State Central Committee (New Orleans, 1898).

[84] Martin Behrman was named one of the seven Orleans Parish assessors by the Governor. See *New Orleans Item*, Nov. 2, 3, 1922, "Behrman Tells."

In its earliest years, the Choctaw Club represented the Democratic party in New Orleans as a whole rather than merely a faction as was the case in later years.

The election on the question of holding the constitutional convention was held January 11, 1898, and resulted in a vote of 36,178 for the convention to 7,578 against it.[85] The delegates elected to the Convention were, with two exceptions, Democrats.[86] It was regarded as a family meeting of the Democrats. The major business was to disfranchise the Negro. Other important issues related to education and the judiciary.[87]

To illustrate the predominance of the Negro question in this convention, one need only refer to the opening address by President E. B. Kruttschnitt and a resolution adopted by the convention. In his address, the President said,

In the first place, my fellow citizens, we are all aware that this convention has been called by the people of the State of Louisiana principally to deal with one question, and we know that but for the existence of that one question this assemblage would not be sitting here today. We know that this convention has been called together by the people of the state to eliminate from the electorate the mass of corrupt and illiterate voters who have during the last quarter of a century degraded our politics.[88]

One of the first resolutions adopted was offered by C. J. Boatner, which read in part: " Be it resolved—That no ordinance or proposition intended to become a part of this constitution, nor any resolution, motion, or order referring to or concerning any provision in the Constitution, shall be

[85] *Report of the Secretary of State*, 1898, p. 145.

[86] *Official Journal, Louisiana Constitutional Convention*, 1898. See Appendix, Official Roll. The two exceptions were a Populist from Winn Parish and a Republican from Irbeville Parish.

[87] *Official Journal, Louisiana Constitutional Convention*, 1898, p. 9.

[88] *Ibid.*, p. 9.

considered by this convention until the report of the Committee on Suffrage and Elections shall have been made to, and finally acted upon, by this convention." [89]

The convention was agreed that the Negro must be disfranchised but there proved to be considerable difference of opinion as to the method to be adopted. The real problem was to disfranchise the Negro without violating the federal constitution and at the same time not take the vote away from the illiterate whites. Some members of the convention favored a strict educational test and a poll tax requirement. Some were willing to see the ignorant white man also disfranchised, but these were undoubtedly in the minority. Martin Behrman, in commenting on the plan offered by Dr. Bruns of New Orleans, a reform Democrat, brought out his own political wisdom. He said Dr. Bruns simply made up his mind on what was best and did not consider whether it was politically possible. Bruns, he said, would not give up any details to get over his main idea as any wise politician knows he must. He failed to see, added Behrman, that people wanted all the Negroes off the registration rolls and as many whites as possible put on.[90]

C. J. Boatner proposed an " understanding clause " in place of the " grandfather clause." This plan would have given the registrars of voters much discretionary authority and it was feared some poor whites might thereby be disfranchised and therefore was voted down.

The convention finally adopted a suffrage provision containing educational and property tests and requiring the payment of a poll tax. The article also contained the well known " grandfather clause " for the benefit of the ignorant whites and illiterate Italians.[91] The former were especially

[89] *Official Journal, Louisiana Constitutional Convention,* 1898, p. 12.
[90] *New Orleans Item,* Nov. 8, 1922, " Behrman Tells."
[91] *Constitution of 1898,* art. 197, especially sec. 5.
These provisions will be discussed in detail in Chapter III. There was

valuable to the country politician and the latter to the City Machine. The newspapers of the state were critical and ridiculed the suffrage proposals being discussed at the convention and even opposed the plan finally adopted.[92]

Martin Behrman, commenting on this convention, stated in 1922 that he " regarded it as the most important political business in which he had ever had a hand." [93]   He believed that any organization to oppose the Democrats would bring the Negro back into politics.   The registrars, he said, would register those they could control and two elections with strong opposition to the Democrats would mean a repetition of 1896.   It was his belief that until the Fourteenth and Fifteenth Amendments were repealed there could not be two parties in the south.   He pointed out that there were many Republicans in the south who would vote that ticket if it were not for the Negro.   Behrman also stated he believed the south would oppose abolition of the electoral college and substitution of direct popular election of the president because of the fear that such action would bring the Negro vote into elections in presidential years.[94]

Under influence of the reform elements in the convention, a provision was put in the constitution, making the governor

considerable opposition to the poll tax requirement as being aimed at the poor.

After the United States Supreme Court in 1915 declared the "grand-father clause" unconstitutional (*Guinn and Beal vs. U. S.*, 238 U. S. 347, and *Myers vs. Anderson*, 238 U. S. 368), the Constitutional Convention of 1921 adopted an "understanding clause." *Constitution of 1921*, art 8, sec. 1.

[92] *New Orleans Times Democrat*, Feb.-May, 1898, especially May 10, 1898.

[93] *New Orleans Item*, Nov. 8, 1922, "Behrman Tells." The Negro vote was less important in New Orleans than in the state. In 1896 there were 48,492 white voters and 14,174 Negro voters. In the state outside of New Orleans, there was a small majority of Negro voters: White, 115,596; Negro, 116,168. *Report of the Secretary of State*, 1896.

[94] *New Orleans Item*, Nov. 5, 1922.

ineligible to succeed himself.[95]   Separate dates were set for the New Orleans City election and the quadrennial state election.[96]   This was aimed at the interplay of state and city politics.   The reformers wanted to separate the state election from the " contaminating conduct " of the city elections. In this they failed to realize that the machine controlled the parish election machinery and that the same hands officiated at both.   The Constitution of 1898 was not submitted to the people for ratification.

As the election of 1900 approached, the outlook for the Democrats was bright.   Although the Populist and Republican parties still existed, most of the Populists had remained with the Democratic Party after the Bryan campaign of 1896.   The Convention of 1898 had taken away the chief support of the Republicans and had, together with certain election laws, met the objections of the Populists relating to representation.   The Citizens' League in New Orleans had lost its power.   In short, the Democrats had liquidated their enemies, combined with their friends, and purged the electorate.   Although the Populists and the Republicans fused again in 1900 and brought out Donalson Caffery as their candidate for governor, he received only 4,938 votes.   He failed to carry a single parish; even Winn, stronghold of Populism, went Democratic.[97]   W. W. Heard was elected Governor with the support of the Choctaws.   Every member elected to the legislature was a Democrat.[98]   The Populists never put another ticket in the field in Louisiana.

[95] Constitution of 1898, art. 5.

[96] Ibid., art. 8, secs. 9 and 10. The separation of the City and state elections proved to be no blow to the Machine. It secured the election of its candidate for mayor and governor in 1900.

[97] Report of the Secretary of State, 1900, p. 380.

[98] Ibid., p. 564.

In the city election the Choctaw Club had no difficulty in naming its candidates to office. The reform administration had not been a success. The Citizens' League was a fusion organization and the various elements soon fell out. As many of the members were Democrats, they had joined the Choctaw Club when it was organized. In selecting " Regulars " to the constitutional convention in 1898, the voters had indicated they were through with the Citizens' League. Since Republican strength had been eliminated by Negro disfranchisement, there was little hope that the Citizens' League could again win the City Hall. The influence of these factors, together with the patronage furnished by Governor Foster, assured the defeat of Mayor Flowers and the election of the Choctaw candidate, Mr. Capeliville.[99]

In 1900, then, the Choctaw Club had its first taste of real power. Two of its objectives had been achieved; it had helped disfranchise the Negro and had captured the City government. It had also " added to the organized strength of the Democratic party in Louisiana and provided the convenience of a club house." A friendly governor had been elected with its support. Politically all seemed bright. A machine which desired to remain in control of the City and have great influence in the state must, however, make terms with other forces, principally economic in character. The nature of the population, industrial and agricultural interests, reconstruction debts, the peculiar topography of the City— all were important factors which had to be considered by the machine. A survey of these forces will add color to the political background already reviewed.

In 1900 Louisiana had a population of 1,381,625 and New Orleans, of 287,104. In 1930 their respective populations were 2,101,593 and 458,762.[100] From 1900 to 1930 there

---

[99] *New Orleans Times Picayune*, Nov. 4, 1899.

[100] *Abstract U. S. Census,* 1900 and 1930.

was a slow but steady shift of population from the country to the city. In 1900 the state was 73 per cent rural and 27 per cent urban; in 1920, 65 per cent rural and 35 per cent urban; in 1930, 60.3 per cent rural and 39.7 per cent urban.[101] While the country population still outnumbered urban population during this entire period, the two were becoming more equal, and when one considers that a higher proportion of the country population was Negro and hence had practically no political or economic power, the trend is even more pronounced. It must not be assumed, however, in viewing the Louisiana political scene, that the interests of the urban centers were identified in politics and that Monroe, Shreveport, Alexandria, Lake Charles and other larger towns joined with New Orleans politically. None of the cities and towns of Louisiana has become so powerful commercially or industrially as to be independent of the dominant agricultural, lumber, oil, gas, or other interests that surrounds it. This in part explains the lack of development of common urban interests between New Orleans and other cities of the state.[102] These facts, together with the difference in size, traditions, history, and racial influences, have thrown the other cities with the country against the " unmoral, boss-ridden " metropolis of the South. In politics there was always evident the

[101] *Abstract, U. S. Census*, 1900, 1920 and 1930. (Rural and urban populations were as follows: 1900—1,015,337 and 366,288 respectively; 1920—1,170,346 and 628,163 respectively; 1930—1,268,610 and 833,532 respectively. Urban as used here means towns of over 2500 population.

[102] The wide difference in the population of New Orleans and the other cities also brings out this point. In 1900, New Orleans had a population of 287,104; Shreveport, 16,013; Baton Rouge, 11,269; Lake Charles, 6,680; Alexandria, 5,648; Monroe, 5,428. *Twelfth Census*, 1900, "Population", p. 645. In 1910 New Orleans had grown to 339,075; Shreveport to 28,015; the others mentioned above to a little over 10,000 each, except Baton Rouge, which had a population of 14,897. *Thirteenth Census*, 1910, p. 601. In 1930 their populations were: New Orleans, 458,762; Shreveport, 76,653; Baton Rouge, 30,729; Monroe, 26,028; Alexandria, 23,025; Lake Charles, 17,791. *Fifteenth Census*, 1930, p. 990.

cleavage of country versus city, which meant not urban versus rural populations but rather metropolitan New Orleans against the rest of the state.[103] This alignment would have been a rather simple formula, but factional strife within New Orleans and particularly that within the country groups have greatly complicated the situation. Temporary and unstable alliances between the various country and City factions have been common. The interplay of state and City factions has greatly affected the New Orleans Organization, its leaders and its policies.

Industrially, the city and the state made much progress from 1900 to 1930. The value of the state's industrial products increased from $121,181,683 in 1900 to $685,037,000 in 1929.[104] The number of wage earners increased from 42,210 in 1900 to 87,345 in 1930.[105] Railroad mileage was increased from 2,824 miles to 4,772 between 1900 and 1928.[106] In 1930, of those gainfully employed in the state, 26 per cent were in industry, 13 per cent in transportation, and 16 per cent in trade.[107] In 1900, 217,125 horsepower of electric energy was used in manufacturing, and by 1927 its use had risen to 415,582 horsepower.[108]

[103] The respective population of New Orleans as compared with the rest of the state was: 1900—287,104 and 1,094,521; 1920—387,219 and 1,411,290; 1930—458,762 and 1,644,831. *Abstract U. S. Census*, 1900, 1920, 1930.

[104] Of this amount 1,111 corporations in 1929 produced $640,727,282. In 1900, 468 corporations produced $68,717,621 of the total of $121,181,683 of manufactured products. *Twelfth Census*, 1900, vol. iii, pp. 331 and 759; *Fifteenth Census*, 1930, vol. iii, p. 203.

[105] *Abstract U. S. Census*, 1900 and 1930 pp. 331 and 758 respectively.

[106] *Statistical Abstract of U. S.*, 1928, p. 394.

[107] *Fifteenth Census*, 1930, vol. iv, p. 616. (The balance were largely in agriculture.)

[108] *Abstract of U. S. Census*, 1900, p. 758, and *Abstract of U. S. Census*, 1930, p. 824.

The eight leading industries of the state in the order of the value of their products in 1900 were: (1) sugar and molasses refining; (2) lumber and timber products; (3) cotton seed oil and cakes; (4) bags (cotton); (5) rice, cleaning and polishing; (6) foundry and machine shops; (7) planing mills; (8) railroad shops.[109] In 1920 sugar and lumber were still the leading products. Oil refining had replaced cotton seed in third place; cotton seed products were fourth; and rice cleaning and polishing was fifth. Food preparation was now sixth; cotton bags had dropped from fourth to seventh place and baking was eighth. These were closely followed by shipbuilding and products of foundries.[110] By 1930 oil refining in the state had replaced sugar as the leading industry. The order then according to the value of the products for the eight leading industries was: oil, sugar, lumber, rice, cotton seed, paper, and alcohol.[111] After these came baking, bags, construction, and coffee roasting.

It may be seen from the above facts that the most notable industrial development in the state was the growth of the oil industry. Production of oil and gas is centered in North Louisiana.[112] Several large refineries are located in that section. The largest refinery, that of the Standard Oil Company of Louisiana, however, is in Baton Rouge. The largest gas fields are near Monroe in the north central region. This also is the center of the carbon black industry. The state produced only 4,310,000 barrels of oil in 1900; while in 1928 the yield was 821,847,000 barrels.[113] An important

[109] Twelfth Census, 1900, " Manufactures ", pt. ii, pp. 297-301.

[110] Fourteenth Census, 1920, " Manufactures ", vol. ix, p. 507.

[111] Fifteenth Census, 1930, " Manufactures ", vol. iii, p. 208.

[112] Since 1926 fields have been discovered in Central and Southwest Louisiana. The development in the oil industry has occurred almost entirely since 1900.

[113] Statistical Abstract of U. S., 1930, p. 780.

development occurring from 1920 to 1930 was the growth of the paper industry in North Louisiana. The industry was located in this section of the state to be near the supply of pulp wood as well as the natural gas fields.

While the industrial, financial, and commercial life of the state was growing, the agricultural interests were also undergoing changes and increasing in value. The number of farms increased between 1900 and 1930 from 115,969 to 161,445.[114] The value of the farm products in 1900 was $72,667,302; while in 1930 it was $149,750,498.[115] The chief farm crops were cotton, sugar, rice, sweet potatoes, and corn. In 1900 approximately 58 per cent of the farms were operated by tenants; while in 1930, 66 per cent were operated by tenants.[116] The land-owning class has been well represented in the legislature. The sugar-producing area has determined the vote of the United States Senators on tariff policies and of the four Congressmen whose districts produce or refine sugar.[117]

In New Orleans, in 1900, there were 1,524 manufacturing establishments with 19,473 wage earners making $7,645,967. Products manufactured were valued at $63,514,505, which was approximately half the value for the entire state.[118] In 1930 in New Orleans, 786 establishments employed 22,592 wage earners at a wage of $21,120,099, together with 3,591 salaried workers at $8,917,326. Products of these factories were valued at $148,388,315.[119]

[114] *Abstract, U. S. Census*, 1930, p. 291. (The average acreage per farm decreased from 95 to 57 acres.)

[115] *Abstract, U. S. Census*, 1930, p. 250.

[116] *Ibid.*, 1900 and 1930, pp. 288 and 295.

[117] Sugar is refined or produced in the 1st, 2nd, 3rd, and 6th Congressional Districts. There are eight districts in the state.

[118] *Abstract, U. S. Census*, 1900, p. 373.

[119] *Fifteenth Census*, 1930, "Manufactures", vol. iii, p. 203.

The leading industries in New Orleans in 1900 were, according to value of the products: sugar and molasses refining, bags, rice cleaning and polishing, foundries and machine shops, baking, clothing, malt liquors, and lumber.[120]   In 1920 the following was the order: sugar, bags, rice, food preparations, baking, tobacco products (cigars and cigarettes), coffee and spice (roasting and grinding), foundries.[121]   The order was only slightly different in 1930: sugar, bags, baking, coffee roasting, rice, food preparations, railroad repair shops, and clothing.[122]   One of the most potent influences in New Orleans has been the shipping of both river and ocean cargoes.   Located one hundred miles from the Gulf and having excellent harbor facilities, the port has grown remarkably in the past three decades.   In 1900 imports were valued at $17,490,811; and exports at $115,858,764; while in 1929 imports were valued at $208,431,000 and exports at $384,-570,000.[123]   The state-owned and operated docks have been important in the interplay of state and City politics.[124] Banking, the cotton exchange, and rice and sugar exchanges have also been extremely important factors in the commercial life of New Orleans and have reflected their power in the politics of the state.[125]   The largest cotton exchange in the world, sugar interests that are concentrated and very articu-

[120] Twelfth Census, 1900, " Manufactures ", pt. ii, p. 307.

[121] Fourteenth Census, 1920, " Manufactures ", vol. ix, p. 508.

[122] Fifteenth Census, 1930, " Manufactures ", vol. iii, p. 209.

[123] Statistical Abstract of U. S., 1900 and 1930, pp. 135 and 500 respectively. The peak years were 1919 and 1920, with $712,380,000 of exports and imports being the largest figure.

[124] The Parker-Sullivan Machine defeated Behrman and the Regulars in the mayor's race of 1920 by the liberal use of patronage on the docks. It was humorously said at the time that there were so many workers on the docks that it was impossible to get them out of the way so the ships could be unloaded. See infra, chapter VIII.

[125] Bank deposits in New Orleans in 1910 were $2,991,128,000 and in 1927, $4,165,757,000.

late, and the banking concerns whose financial interests extend into surrounding states and into the islands of the Caribbean, have not hesitated to use and be used by the New Orleans Machine. They have been particularly strong in influencing the position of the Orleans delegation in the state legislature on questions affecting their particular interests. They have demanded and received great consideration in settling the problems of taxation and business regulation in the state.[126]

The number of employees in the industries in the state and City does not correlate with the value of their products. In 1929, for example, oil products of the state were valued at $166,611,627 and employed 2,858 workers in their manufacture. The lumber interests in the same year employed 39,241 workers to manufacture merchandise valued at $121,-996,611.[127] Lumber comes first in the number of employees and is followed by construction, oil, sugar, food products, baking, cotton seed, and alcohol.[128]

During the entire thirty years under consideration, the bulk of the industrial output was produced from sugar cane, rice, cotton, forests, and oil. Manufacturing then was absolutely dependent on local raw materials. With the exception of the oil and lumber industries this tended to intensify the conflict between the producers of the raw materials and the manufacturer. Sugar growers frequently found themselves at odds with the American Sugar Refining Company which had a monopoly on refining in the state. In the state legislature the producers were able to force regulation on the great monopoly.[129] On the question of tariff their interests also were not at one. The growers wanted a tariff on raw

---

[126] *Infra*, chapter VI.

[127] *Fifteenth Census*, 1930, "Manufactures", vol. iii, p. 210.

[128] *Ibid.*

[129] *Infra*, chapter VI.

sugar while the refiners did not. The refiners wanted a tariff on refined sugar to which the growers did not object. The conflict over policies in Washington was generally settled by pooling interests and both supporting the imposition of a tariff on raw and refined sugar.[130] The rice growers felt the polishing mills did not pay enough for their product and the cotton grower was sure he did not get enough for his raw cotton and seed. The conflict was less notable in the oil and lumber industries. In these industries the big companies to a large extent owned the forests and the oil wells. The small logger and independent oil operator, however, often felt the pinch of centralized control in these fields. The pipe lines which gathered the oil were controlled by the oil monopolies and were often accused of " squeezing out " the independent producer by refusing to carry his oil or by excess charges.[131]

As industry in the state and City expanded and grew, it characteristically developed corporate organizations and concentration of financial control. This is shown by the fact that in 1900 only about fifty per cent of the state's manufactured goods were produced by her 468 corporations; while in 1930 over ninety per cent was produced by 1,111 corporations.[132] Particularly influential have been the great lumber interests. Owning both mills and vast timber lands, they controlled the raw materials as well as manufacturing. Ordinarily they were located in sparsely populated areas. As they represented the dominant economic interest of the

[130] Taussig, *The Tariff History of the United States*, Seventh Edition, pp. 306, 310-315, 409, 447. (New York, 1923), *Encyclopedia of Social Sciences*, vol. xiv, p. 451.

[131] *Louisiana Public Service Commission vs. Standard Oil Co. of Louisiana*, 154 La. 557; *New Orleans Times Picayune*, Mar. 26, 1919; *Report of Louisiana Public Service Commission*, 1923, Order no. 123 of May 5, 1923, no. 41; *ibid.*, 1926, Order no. 433 of Dec. 16, 1926.

[132] *Supra*, p. 41, note 104.

parish and employed large numbers of men, it was not difficult for them to control the parish government.   Their chief
political needs were a sympathetic assessor and friendly representatives in the legislature.   Ordinarily they had these
and were therefore able to exercise influence locally as well
as on measures in the legislature relating to taxation, labor
and the regulation of industry.   The fact that the industry
was widely scattered over the state and that its control was
in the hands of a few large companies made it especially
influential.

Another powerful interest was that of the sugar producers
and refiners.   The producing area is centered in the so-called
" sugar bowl " lying in the parishes immediately west and
northwest of New Orleans.[133]   Much of the cane is grown
on large plantations.   A comparatively small number of mills
convert the cane into raw sugar.[134]   The process of refining
sugar is absolutely dominated by the American Sugar Refining Company.   The plants of this Company are located in
and near New Orleans.   The sugar industry is old, well
established, and control is highly concentrated all along the
line.   It is, therefore, very articulate in making known its
desires, both in the state legislature and in Congress.[135]
Financially, New Orleans is bound by a thousand ties to the
whole sugar industry.   The United States Senators have
always voted for a tariff on sugar because of the great influ-

[133] The chief sugar producing parishes are: Ascension, Assumption,
Avoyelles, West Baton Rouge, Iberia, Irberville, Lafayette, Lafourche,
Point Coupee, St. James, St. John the Baptist, St. Martin, St. Mary,
Terrebonne, and Vermillion. *Fifteenth Census*, 1930, "Agriculture ",
Southern States, p. 1243.

[134] There are about seventy such mills—some owned by the planters,
some by the big sugar refiners and others are independent of both.
Fifteenth Census, 1930, " Manufactures ", vol. iii, p. 208.

[135] *Supra*, p. 45. Although there is concentration of control there is
conflict of interest within the industry between the growers and refiners
as previously indicated.

ence of the City and the sugar growing parishes in elections. In addition to controlling the votes of the Senators, the sugar interests as stated before have been able to control the votes of four of Louisiana's eight Congressmen. These four come from districts where sugar is either grown or refined.

The general principle of railway regulation was firmly fixed in the Constitution of 1898.[136] However, since the Constitution authorized the legislature to extend the duties of the Public Service Commission, the railroads were active in state politics but were by no means as influential as the other major interests of the state.

The growth of New Orleans naturally involved the development of great utilities in the City. The development, with the exception of the water supply, was carried on by private companies and hence involved public regulation. Supervision of the utilities serving New Orleans was tenaciously held to by the machine-controlled City government. Every effort to put them under the control of the State Public Service Commission was defeated.[137] After the discovery of gas in North Louisiana the struggle for a natural gas supply for the City was notable. There was some indication that politics and the company supplying artificial gas kept natural gas out of the City for years and thus kept rates high and their investment intact.[138] The light, gas, telephone and street railways services were early associated with large national operating companies and later with the great holding concerns, such as the Electric Bond and Share, and the American Telephone and Telegraph Company. Utility rates, particularly electric, have been notoriously high in New Orleans, which is further indication that perhaps the regulating body, i. e., the City government, has been extremely

[136] *Constitution of 1898*, art. 283.

[137] *Infra*, chapter VI.

[138] *Infra*, chapter VI, p. 155.

liberal with the utility companies, and it is not to be supposed that they in turn have been niggardly with the Choctaw Club.[139] The conflict between public and private interests in the operation of utilities and transportation both in the state and in New Orleans, plus the desire of the political organization in New Orleans to retain control of City utilities, have furnished a background of several struggles in constitutional conventions and the legislature.

Along with the growth of industry in Louisiana, there was a slow growth of unionism and social legislation. The unsatisfactory employers' liability acts were replaced by a fairly comprehensive workman's compensation act in 1914.[140] The fact that the state has been more agricultural than industrial during the period has made proper and advanced labor legislation difficult. Cheap labor, partly due to the presence of the Negro, has been a factor in the development of industry. The semi-feudal character of the lumber towns and the disorder and rush of oil and gas booms have not tended to promote labor organization. In New Orleans the unions of the building trades, railway, and street car workers were strong. Textile and dock workers have made some progress toward unionization in more recent years. In all political campaigns candidates made an effort to win the labor vote even though it was never a decisive influence.[141]

Besides the influences outlined above, the political machine had to deal with other factors of great importance that tended to limit its activities and diminish the spoils of office. Among these were reconstruction debts and the political heritages which reconstruction government passed on in the

[139] *Infra*, chapter VI, p. 142.

[140] *Acts of Louisiana*, 1914, no. 16. For operation of the law, see *Tulane Law Review*, Feb., 1933, "Administration of Workmen's Compensation Laws in Louisiana," Gladys Vonan.

[141] For labor record of Choctaw Club, see chapter VIII, p. 212.

form of constitutional restrictions.   Another was the peculiar topography and geographic location of New Orleans.
In the City alone, the corrupt reconstruction government increased the debt from $9,930,096.25 in 1868, to a peak of
$22,041,378.60 in 1876, with an interest rate on the new
part of the debt as high as ten per cent.[142]   From 1876 until
1900, the debt remained practically stationary.   Since 1900,
in common with other cities, it has grown steadily, reaching
a total of $56,822,000 in 1930.[143]   While the City debt was
piling up, the state carpet-bag government was increasing
expenses ten times the normal amounts and adding $57,-
000,000 to the state debt.

The peculiar topography of New Orleans has created difficult and expensive drainage, sanitation and flood problems.
The City is shaped much like a saucer.   A large portion of
it is below sea level, the high-water mark of the Mississippi
and the normal level of Lake Pontchartrain.[144]   It is not
an uncommon sight to look down Canal Street toward the
docks and see a ship which appears to be several feet above
the street level, and in fact is.   The average rainfall in
New Orleans is 57.4 inches and the maximum recorded is
85.4.   Frequently three inches of rain will fall in an hour.
and nine inches in twelve hours have fallen.   When one
realizes that every drop of rain that falls in the City must

[142] Phillips, *History of the Bonded Debt of the City of New Orleans,*
1822-1933 (New Orleans, 1933), pp. 24-25.

[143] In 1930, with the exception of Newark and Cincinnati, New
Orleans had the largest debt of any city in her population range.   In
1908 forty per cent of the tax. receipts of the City went to meet debt
service.   The debt, in 1908, was the largest of any city in the United
States of the same population.   In 1926, thirty-seven per cent of the
City's revenues went to debt service.   *Financial Statistics of Cities,* U. S.
Department of Commerce, 1908, pp. 244, 299; 1926, p. 96; and 1930, p.
250; Phillips, *op. cit.,* p. 24.

[144] This lake was formed from a part of the sea which escaped the
filling-in process of the river.

be pumped out, the magnitude of the problem becomes apparent. In fact it was not until two centuries after the founding of the City that this problem was finally solved.[145] The topography of the City, plus the heavy rainfall, have necessitated the building of canals under the streets, the largest of which is twenty-five feet wide and nine feet deep. These canals lead to eight pumping stations, their daily capacity being seven billion gallons. Add to this the fact that the sewage must also be pumped out of the City through a separate system and the further limitation on the "pickings" of the Organization is readily apparent.[146] In 1908, twenty per cent of the City budget was used for drainage and sanitation, which is ten to fifteen per cent higher than the proportion expended in most cities for this item.[147] Out of the total governmental expenses of $33,177,633.00 in 1930, $8,111,196.00 was expended for drainage, sewage, and levee purposes.[148] The debt problem for drainage and sanitation expenses may tend to explain why most of the political leaders and ward bosses of New Orleans died poor. At least these items form an important part of the background against which the leadership and the Organization operated.

Conditions for the growth of machine politics were not all so inhospitable as those just enumerated. Control by a few was not a new thing. The French and Spanish domination had left its influences. Likewise, the political control by the old landed aristocracy was as common to Louisiana as to the rest of the south. Following the Civil War, a

---

[145] Even in 1927, after all the precautions had been taken, it was necessary to blast the Poydras levee below New Orleans to save the City from the great flood of that year and the City had to pay to the Parishes of St. Bernard and Plaquemine $5,000,000 in damages.

[146] The fact that both coal and oil to furnish the power for pumping have to be imported adds to the expense.

[147] *Financial Statistics of Cities*, 1908, p. 89.

[148] *Ibid.*, for 1930, p. 500.

small group of Republicans ruled by dominating the Negro voters.   The Republican-Negro combination was then over-thrown by insurrectionary methods of the former ruling minority, who later convinced the majority of the whites of the desirability of " lily white " politics.   In addition to the above influences, New Orleans had long been accustomed to a well organized political machine.

Reconstruction deeply affected the legal basis of Louisiana and New Orleans government.   The Constitution of 1879 is basic to subsequent constitutions.   The people feared the possible return of Negro rule and therefore severely limited the power of the general assembly.   Much of the power was reserved for the people.   Such drastic tax limitations were imposed as to render impossible proper educational facilities and needed public improvements.   The Constitutions of 1898 and 1913 were glorified amendments of that of 1879.[149] The purpose of the Convention of 1898 was to disfranchise the Negro and that of 1913, to refund the state debt.[150] Because of the distrust of the general assembly, much legis-lation is found in the constitution, and many items with ref-erence to the City of New Orleans are a part of the document. It is often necessary, to get a needed revision, to have the entire electorate of the state vote a constitutional amend-ment affecting only New Orleans.   Thus is the interplay of state and New Orleans politics accentuated.   It might also be noted that the governor, through his control of patronage

[149] Long, *Compilation of the Constitutions of Louisiana* (Baton Rouge, 1930).

[150] Marr, "Historical Review of Constitutions of Louisiana," *Pro-ceedings of Louisiana Bar Association*, vol. xiv, 1912. Also Gronest, " The Constitutional Convention of 1913", *Southwestern Political Science Quarterly*, vol. iv, no. 4, March, 1924; Kernan, " The Constitutional Con-vention of 1898 and Its Work," *Proceedings of Louisiana Bar Association*, 1899.

in the Parish of Orleans, had a position of large influence and power in the affairs of the City.[151]

Briefly, then, Martin Behrman and the ward bosses of the Choctaw Club with whom he shared the stage of political power in New Orleans from 1897 to 1926 found varied and powerful influences with which they had to deal. The population of New Orleans, largely Catholic, was subtly influenced by a historic past. The City was a rapidly growing seaport of cosmopolitan complexion and desired no legal inhibitions on its morals or way of life. There was a fairly distinct cleavage between metropolitan New Orleans and the rest of the state, which was broken frequently by the interplay of state and City factions within the Democratic party. The City and state experienced marked industrial growth related closely to the products of the soil. Oil and gas were suddenly thrust into the picture with their vast economic power. Corporate growth and consolidation, utility expansion with its attendant problems, and a growing labor consciousness gradually forcing social legislation on semi-feudal industry, were characteristic of the epoch. The situation was further complicated by reconstruction debts, a state constitution written in fear of Negro rule, and a difficult engineering problem due to lack of natural drainage. There was also a religious cleavage.[152] These forces set the limits within which the game of politics must be played.

It was the task of Behrman and his colleagues to adjust the conflicting demands of the varying economic and social

[151] See chs. vii and ix, *passim.* The Constitutional Convention of 1921 was urged by Governor Parker as essential to his efforts to end boss-rule in New Orleans. It is significant that in order to make the desired changes in New Orleans government, it seemed necessary to rewrite the state constitution. There was much the legislature could not change. *House Journal,* 1920, p. 336.

[152] New Orleans and south Louisiana are largely Catholic; while central and north Louisiana are largely Protestant. See chapter IV.

interests and to harmonize them into a coordinated machine. They had to get from the governor and the legislature what New Orleans desired and give in exchange no more than was necessary. They had to prevent state interference in the City when interference was not desired, and be forever vigilant lest the governor dominate the local scene through an alliance with a local reform faction seeking to overthrow the so-called bosses. To satisfy all partially, to alienate none, and to keep always fresh and vigorous the root of their political power, the precinct organization, by watering it with as much patronage as possible—these were the tasks to which they devoted themselves so long and so successfully.

CHAPTER II

LEGAL POSITION OF NEW ORLEANS

STRUCTURE OF CITY GOVERNMENT

WHEN the Choctaw Club first won control of New Orleans in 1900, the aldermanic form of government was in effect and continued until 1912 when it was replaced by the commission form. The City had operated under aldermanic government since the original incorporation in 1805. In 1896 the reform administration of Mayor Flowers secured a new charter from the legislature.[1] It contained a number of improvements over the charter of 1882, including civil service, better financial control and improved coordination of administration.[2] The reformers hoped that the change would help to keep the machine out of the City Hall and failing that, prevent it from entrenching itself. Their hopes proved illusory. The charter they had written contained several provisions which fostered organization control. The powers of the City government were vested in a mayor, council, and a number of boards and commissions. The division of the City into wards and municipal districts was retained. From each ward, depending on its population, one or more councilmen were to be elected. The charter specified a councilman must have been a resident of the City for five years and of his ward at least one year. The division of the City into municipal districts was continued because state law provided for the election of an assessor and a tax collector from each of the districts. The plan of electing

[1] *Acts of Louisiana*, 1896, no. 45.
[2] *Ibid.*, 1882, no. 20.

the councils by wards fostered a local rather than a City-wide outlook among its members. The salary was too small to attract men of unusual ability and the chief business of councilmen soon became that of securing all the patronage and improvements possible for their particular wards. Since smaller political units are more easily controlled than larger ones the divisions provided in the charter encouraged machine politics. The council was vested with general legislative and administrative power.[3] The charter instructed the body to create six departments as follows : controller, treasurer, public works, police and public buildings, city engineer, and city attorney. The mayor was authorized to appoint, with the consent of the council, all department heads except the treasurer and controller who were elective officials. Heads of departments were permitted to attend council meetings and participate in discussions concerning their departments, but had no vote. They were empowered to appoint subordinates with the advice and consent of the council from the list of eligibles furnished by the civil service commission.[4] The mayor was given general executive authority and the veto power which might be overriden by a two-thirds vote of the council. He had the right to remove officials, whom he had appointed, without the consent of the council. The charter also provided that no money should be paid from the City treasury except by check signed by the treasurer, the controller and the mayor. Particularly influential in delivering the City into the hands of the Machine was the provision requir-

---

[3] Included were the powers to regulate utilities, grant franchises and prepare an annual budget. Control of utilities by the City government was tenaciously held against attempts of the legislature to place it under the state Public Service Commission. *Infra,* chapter VII.

[4] Removals by department heads were controlled by the civil service law, which provided for review by the civil service board. If this body considered the cause of removal insufficient, the employee had to be reinstated.

ing confirmation of appointments by the ward-elected council. Even though employees had to be on the civil service lists before being eligible for appointment by department heads, political considerations played a part. A councilman could easily suggest to the department which of those on the list he would vote to confirm. " Senatorial courtesy" worked in the New Orleans City council as well as in Washington.[5]

In common with the practice followed in many other cities, as the functions of government had expanded and as new problems arose, New Orleans had created a number of administrative and advisory boards and commissions. No attempt was made in the new charter to combine, integrate or abolish these boards. All were recognized as presently constituted, and a civil service board was added. Of particular importance to the politicians were the Board of Police Commissioners,[6] the Board of Fire Commissioners,[7] the Board of Civil Service Commissioners [8] (created by the charter), the Board of Liquidation of the City Debt,[9] and a board established in 1899, the Sewage and Water Board.[10] The laws establishing these boards had sought to make them independent of politics by giving the members long terms which would overlap those of the appointing authorities. The new charter sought to safeguard them further by extending civil service requirements to all employees of the boards.

Police courts, always a valuable machine asset if under its control, were continued by the new charter. The judges of these courts were to be elected for terms of four years.

[5] For full discussion of the distribution of patronage, see chapter VII.

[6] *Acts of Louisiana*, 1888, no. 63.

[7] *Ibid.*, 1894, no. 83.

[8] *Ibid.*, 1896, no. 45, art. 6.

[9] *Ibid.*, 1880, no. 133.

[10] *Ibid.*, 1899, no. 6.

The mayor, with the advice and consent of the council, was authorized to fill vacancies that might occur because of death or resignation. Any organization that could control elections, therefore, could make use of these courts.[11]

The provision in the new charter establishing a Board of Civil Service Commissioners gave promise of improving public service.[12] It was the intention to make the commission independent. The mayor was instructed to appoint "three discreet persons," with the consent of the council, for terms of twelve years, who would constitute the Board of Civil Service Commissioners.[13] The salary of the members was fixed at $3,000 a year and the City council was to furnish the necessary operating budget. No person engaged in politics during the previous four years was eligible for appointment as a commissioner. The duty of the Board was to inaugurate and administer civil service in all branches of the City government. It was authorized to appoint a chief examiner, hold competitive examinations, keep a list of those qualified and make rules for promotion on the basis of merit and seniority. Examinations were to be practical and to test the applicant's fitness for the place sought. Heads of departments were required to select persons to fill vacancies only from the list of eligibles. Removals could not be made except for cause and were subject to review by the Board. Political contributions by civil service employees were forbidden. The district attorney was required to prosecute, at the request of the Commissioners, any one violating any part of the civil service law.

It is interesting to note that after the Choctaw Club took charge of the City all these boards were reorganized by state

[11] For discussion of political uses of police courts, see Ch. v, p. 113.

[12] *Acts of Louisiana*, 1896, no. 45, art. 6.

[13] The mayor was authorized to remove members of the Board provided he reported his reasons to the council.

law—the Civil Service Board in 1900, the Sewage and Water Board in 1902, the Police Board in 1904 and the Fire Board in 1910.[14] The Board of Liquidation of the City Debt was not touched.[15] The common purpose of these reorganizations was to give the mayor and the council more control of the boards. This was accomplished mainly by eliminating the overlapping term feature of the old laws, decreasing the number of members, and centering appointment and removal powers in the mayor and council.[16]

The most interesting and significant reorganization occurred in connection with civil service. Because of its importance in the development of Machine rule, the revision will be discussed in detail. Perhaps the best evidence that the civil service provisions of the Charter of 1896 were at least hindering Machine rule is the fact that shortly after the City and state elections of 1900 an act was passed by the legislature revising the article of the charter relating to civil service.[17] The Choctaw Club had just carried the City election and a friendly governor had been chosen. The Civil Service Board, appointed in 1896, still had eight years to serve. It seemed best to the Choctaws to revise the law rather than have the mayor remove the members appointed by the Flowers reform government; more than a change in the personnel of the Board was desired.

A new board was created, composed of the mayor as chairman, the treasurer, the controller and two citizens appointed

[14] *Acts of Louisiana*, 1900, no. 89; 1902, no. 111; 1904, no. 32; and 1910, no. 58.

[15] It has been made a part of the Constitution (Act 110 of 1890).

[16] The reorganization of the Sewage and Water Board was an exception in some respects to the general plan outlined above. This Board was enlarged and long terms were continued. Members of related agencies of the City, parish, and state were added and their appointment vested in the mayor. This enabled him to control a majority of the Board.

[17] *Acts of Louisiana*, 1900, no. 89.

by the mayor with the advice and consent of the council. The requirement that the appointed members be non-political was dropped.   This gave the mayor complete control.   The provisions relating to classification, examination, promotion, dismissal, political contributions and enforcement were left substantially the same.   The real " joker " in the new law was incorporated in Section 9, which read: ". . . The Board shall within thirty days after the induction into office of each new municipal administration, hold a general examination of all applicants for positions in the classified service and within ten days after the result of such examination shall be made known to the appointing officers, all lists of eligibles in existence prior to such general examinations shall become null and void.   *In every such general examination all persons either holding or desiring to hold positions in the classified civil service shall be obliged to participate.*"   In addition to the above section which went a long way toward nullifying one of the principal aims of civil service, Section 29 enumerated a long list of exempt positions.[18]   Still another section authorized the Police, Fire, and Sewage and Water Boards to name their own examiners and fix their own rules for promotion.

The boards under the old laws tended to decentralize administration in the City government.   This type of organization violated the modern principles of integration and responsibility of city administration without gaining the sought after advantages of non-political control.   This was particularly true in the period after reorganization.   The

[18] The following were exempt: chief clerks, secretaries, cashiers, stenographers, receivers of public money, attorneys, engineers, surveyors, doctors, chemists, electricians, superintendent of the Fire Alarm System, officers of the council, street laborers, carpenters, drivers, watchmen, porters and janitors.   Confederate veterans of "good record" were exempt from examinations and might be appointed without reference to the law.   In 1924 a new list of exemptions was made (Act 111 of 1924).

appearance of independent board control was kept up without its substance. As the Machine gained power in the City, the lack of integration was bridged by its dominance of all agencies. The lines of effective authority extended from the mayor to the boards. It is not to be inferred that the reorganization of some of these boards was not in the interests of efficiency, but attention is called to the matter to show how the laws relating to City government were changed to serve the ends of politics. From this standpoint, centralization of power in the hands of the mayor, who owed his election to the Machine, and the elimination of long terms on the boards were significant changes.

Reform elements in New Orleans began agitating for a change from the aldermanic to the commission form of government in 1910. An organization known as the Citizens' League was effected to crystallize public sentiment and to secure the passage of the necessary legislation. At the session of the legislature in 1912, a proposed charter was introduced which had been drawn under the auspices of the Citizens' League. It was the belief of the reformers that the Choctaw Machine held its power because of the practice under the old charter of electing the City council by wards. It was felt by this group that the commission plan was less adapted to machine control and would promote efficiency. Machine representatives in the legislature fought the proposed charter. Mayor Behrman, however, sensing that there was real demand for change, had a commission charter drawn which omitted some of the more drastic reforms proposed in the one sponsored by the Citizens' League. Because of the influence of the Choctaw Club in the legislature and with the governor, its proposed charter was passed and later adopted.[19] The substitution of a small commission council elected at large for the ward-elected council did not change

19 For full account of this incident, see chapter VII, p. 193.

political control as the reform elements had hoped.[20] Although no officials were now elected by wards, their importance as units for political organization remained.

The commission charter vested executive, administrative and legislative powers in the mayor and four commissioners.[21]   The term of office of these officials was fixed at four years.   Five departments were established: Public Affairs, Public Finance, Public Safety, Public Utilities and Public Property.   The mayor was designated to administer the Department of Public Affairs.   He was charged with general oversight of the other departments, boards and commissions. He was also named as *ex-officio* member of each board, commission or other body created by the charter or by any ordinance.   No veto power was given the mayor.   At the first regular meeting after election, the commission council was directed, by majority vote, to assign the commissioners to specific departments.   The council was authorized to change these assignments at any time it appeared that the public service would be benefited thereby.   It was also authorized to appoint by majority vote a number of City officials.[22] The Charter required that all other persons engaged in any department of the City government, except day laborers, should be chosen in accordance with the rules governing the classified service.

The commission council was instructed to make an annual budget.   The charter required that twenty per cent of the estimated revenues be reserved by the council for public

[20] *Ibid.*, The Citizens' League had included in its proposed charter proportional representation features which, if adopted, might have weakened machine control.

[21] *Acts of Louisiana*, 1912, no. 159.

[22] These were: city attorney, judges and clerks of recorders courts, auditor of public accounts, chief engineer of the fire department, superintendent of police, superintendent of public health, city engineer, city chemist and city notary.

improvements and not under any circumstances be appropriated for current expenses. The Boards of Police, Fire, and Civil Service Commissioners were recognized as presently constituted with some slight adjustment in membership to conform to the change in City government. These alterations in no way affected the fundamental control of the boards as previously outlined. The Fire and the Civil Service Boards in fact became mere committees of the commission council, the non-city official members being dropped entirely from membership.[23] Other boards and commissions of less importance in politics were continued as under existing law.[24]

The Recorders (Police) Courts were put under control of the commission council, judges being named by this group and were subject to removal by it.

The charter established initiative and referendum. The power of initiating petitions, however, was so involved that the provisions have never been used.[25] The charter also contained extended sections relating to taxation, paving and public improvements, opening streets and other miscellaneous matters. Recall of city officials was provided in the State Constitution.[26]

PECULIAR CONSTITUTIONAL AND LEGAL POSITION
OF THE CITY

To those familiar with the Constitution and Laws of Louisiana, the expressions " the City of New Orleans ex-

---

[23] *Acts of Louisiana*, 1912, no. 159, secs. 17 and 20.

[24] In 1934 there were a total of thirty-six boards and commissions performing city functions. In addition there were two parish boards and twelve state boards of primarily local concern. Most of these were in existence in 1912.

[25] *Ibid.*, sec. 34. Thirty per cent of the registered voters must sign a petition for either initiative or referendum.

[26] Constitutions of 1898, 1913 and 1921, arts. 223, 223 and 9. This provision has never been used in New Orleans.

cepted " or " the Parish of Orleans excepted " are well known.   The specific exceptions indicated by these words together with many provisions both in the constitution and statutes applying exclusively to the City or Parish are indicative of its peculiar legal position.   The boundaries of the City and Parish are coextensive.   The exceptions and special laws have grown up through many years of constitutional and legislative changes.

The peculiar problems of New Orleans may be realized more fully if it is recalled that up to 1920 it was the only City in the state that had a population of more than forty thousand.   Its tasks of government have been vast, intricate and complex compared with those of the smaller cities. Its political power has been great—so great that it has had both advantages and disadvantages.   The City has been strong enough to get much of what it wanted in the way of exceptions and special laws but because of its size there have been many efforts, some successful, to curb the influence of its controlling machine.

Several factors, therefore, have entered into the development of the special legal and constitutional position of New Orleans.   The fact that her needs were different has undoubtedly been the greatest.   Governors, constitutional conventions, and general assemblies have willingly and wisely recognized this.   On the other hand, the governor and the legislature have made efforts to curb the power of the Machine by imposing special restrictions on the City.   Because of this the Machine made a practice of seeking to preserve its power by incorporating much legislation relating to the City in the state constitution.   The habit of putting City legislation in the constitution began in 1879, when there was still fear of Negro rule, and has continued for the reason just stated.   Such action made it difficult for an unfriendly governor and general assembly to take away powers from

the local government.[27]   Constitutional amendments require
a vote of the entire electorate.   The whole state, therefore,
has frequently voted on matters relating solely to New
Orleans.   Constitutional legislation has not always been an
unmixed blessing.   A much desired change or an unwanted
reform may be prevented or imposed by a powerful governor who has the legislature and a majority of the electorate
supporting him.[28]   The interplay of state and City politics
has been greatly accentuated by the desire of the City
Machine for a favor or the desire of some state faction to
impose a reform.

It has always been the admitted purpose of the Orleans
delegation in the legislature and constitutional conventions
to have enacted the kind of legislation and constitution that
the Machine and the business interests wanted.   It also
sought to prevent the passage of measures objected to by
these forces.   The Choctaw Club has been the unifying force
which has enabled the delegation to deliver its strength with
the most telling effect.   With twenty-five out of one hundred votes in the House of Representatives and nine out of
thirty-nine in the Senate, and with excellent political leadership directing, it is little wonder that the Machine has been
able to secure a special legal position for the City and has
sacrificed so little of its own power in return.   A brief
survey of the constitution and some of the statutes will serve
to illustrate the unique position of the metropolitan
community.

[27] See message of Governor Parker, June 18, 1920. *House Journal,*
1920, p. 336.

[28] Governor Parker used his power in this way in the Convention of
1921, and Governor Long, in more recent years, has used both the legislative and constitutional methods of controlling the City. The regular
and special sessions held in 1934 and 1935 passed several laws transferring
powers formerly exercised by the City to the state. At these sessions
Senator Long was in complete control of the legislature. His state
machine was functioning perfectly.

Article VII of the Constitution of 1921 provided for the state judiciary. A Supreme Court and District Courts of Appeal were established. The article then described the organization and defined the jurisdiction of the District Courts, " the Parish of Orleans excepted ". Beginning with Section 75 and extending through Section 96 the organization, nature and jurisdiction of the courts of the Parish of Orleans were detailed. A Court of Appeals, a District Court, divided into criminal and civil divisions, two City Courts and a Juvenile Court were established; and the qualifications of judges for the Recorders Courts were defined. These sections also provided for sheriffs, clerks, attorneys and other court officers. A judicial expense fund under the control of the district judges was provided.[29] The peculiar court needs of New Orleans were similarly provided for in the Constitutions of 1879, 1898 and 1913.[30]

In 1908 a law was passed by the legislature providing that the registrars of voters in all parishes except Orleans were to be elected by the police juries (county board). The act stipulated that the registrar in Orleans should be appointed by the governor.[31] Under the influence of Governor Parker, who desired to make permanent all possible state control over New Orleans, the above provision was incorporated in the Constitution of 1921.[32] The legislative act had been designed to curb alleged registration abuses of the Machine and such was Parker's purpose in 1921. It was not very effective, however, in limiting organization control, either as a legislative act or a constitutional provision, when the governor and the Choctaw Club were on friendly terms.

[29] Constitution of 1921, art. 7, sec. 95. Fees collected by court clerks and certain parish officials constituted the fund.

[30] Constitutions of 1879, 1898 and 1913, arts. 130, 132 and 132, respectively.

[31] Acts of Louisiana, 1908, no. 98.

[32] Constitution of 1921, art. 8, sec. 17.

At the suggestion of the governor, other provisions to safeguard registration were incorporated in the same constitution. A state Board of Registration composed of the governor, lieutenant governor and speaker of the house of representatives, with the power to remove any registrar in the state and to supervise registration generally was created.[33] Shortly after the convention a law applying to the entire state was passed, providing for a new registration of voters and designed to eliminate fraudulent names from the registration rolls.[34] The law also directed that a police canvass of voters in each precinct in New Orleans be made and that two special investigators be employed to uncover registration frauds in the City.[35]

Another attempt to bring about permanent reform in New Orleans was made in 1921 when the following civil service clause was inserted in the constitution. " The legislature shall provide for civil service in municipalities having a population of 100,000 or more, and for the recognition and adoption of the merit system in the employment or appointment of applicants; and shall provide against the discharge of employees or appointees without good and sufficient cause ".[36] Governor Parker had pledged true civil service for the City in his successful campaign against the bosses in the election of 1920.[37] Colonel Sullivan, the manager of the Parker faction in New Orleans, was strengthening his machine which an effective civil service law would have made

[33] *Constitution of 1921*, art. 8, sec. 18.

[34] *Acts of Louisiana*, 1922, no. 122.

[35] The Parker faction controlled the police in New Orleans at this time. It was, therefore, willing for the police to make the canvass. Had the Choctaws been in power a check by the police would not have been adopted.

[36] *Constitution of 1921*, art. 7, sec. 15.

[37] *New Orleans Times Picayune*, Sept. 5, 1920.

difficult.   Hence, the innocuous provision quoted above was the Parker-Sullivan fulfillment of that election pledge.   The legislature never acted and the old civil service law which was in charge of a committee of the commission council remained in force and was administered to serve the ends of politics.   The episode reveals the effects of the interplay of state and City politics on the fundamental law.[38]

The constitutions of 1898, 1913 and 1921 provided for the election of seven assessors for the Parish of Orleans, one to be elected from each municipal district.   In addition to acting as assessors in their districts, the group constituted the Board of Assessors of the Parish.[39]   In other parishes of the state there was only one assessor and the police jury served as the board of review.   Prior to 1908, the Parish of Orleans had also seven state tax collectors elected in the same manner as the assessors.   In 1908 a constitutional amendment combined the seven offices into one.[40]

Another provision relating only to New Orleans is found in all constitutions beginning with that of 1898, which assured to the electors the right to choose their own public officials.[41]   It was incorporated in an effort to prevent the legislature and the governor from taking over the selection of any City officer and is stark testimony of the struggle that has gone on between factions in the state and City.[42]

It may be seen from these references to the constitutions that New Orleans holds a peculiar position in the funda-

[38] For full discussion of the City-state relations see chapter VII.

[39] *Constitutions of 1898, 1913, 1921*, arts. 309, 309 and 14.

[40] *Constitution of 1898*, art. 309; *Acts of Louisiana*, no. 25, 1907, Extra Session; *Constitutions of 1913 and 1921*, arts. 309 and 14, respectively.

[41] *Constitutions of 1898, 1913 and 1921*, arts. 319, 319, and 14 respectively.

[42] There are a number of other provisions in the constitutions limited to or excluding New Orleans, but the ones given were more closely related to politics than the others.   See *Constitution of 1921*, especially art. 14.

mental law. Some of the articles relating to the City reflect the unquestioned particular needs of the one metropolis. Others bring out the conflict that has gone on for a long time between rural and urban standards and ways of life. Still others reflect either the efforts of the Machine to retain, or the efforts of another faction to take away, powers held by the City government. This has all tended to lengthen the constitution by cluttering it with much that should have been statutory law.

On examining the statutes of Louisiana one is struck by the fact that there are so many laws that apply exclusively to New Orleans and further that there are many laws which specifically except New Orleans from their operation. So extensive are the special laws and exceptions that one author in compiling the laws of the state uses the abbreviations " O. E." and " N. O." in his index to denote by the former that the reference does not apply to the Parish of Orleans and by the latter that it applies only to that Parish.[43] It is not essential to this work to make a detailed analysis of these various laws, but it is well to note the general subject matter with which they deal. Much of the special legislation for the City has related to the charter, elections, registration, special boards and commissions, and assessment.[44] The laws excepting New Orleans from their operation have concerned such things as changes in the general laws governing parishes and cities,[45] registration,[46] courts,[47] taxation and assessment.[48] One of the chief reasons for the prevalence of the

---

[43] Marr, " Revised Statutes of Louisiana " (1915 and 1926).

[44] *Ibid.*, Acts no. 167 of 1916; no. 152 of 1898; no. 98 of 1908; no. 58 of 1910; no. 32 of 1904; no. 78 of 1906; no. 170 of 1898.

[45] *Ibid.*, Acts no. 161 of 1894; 204 of 1912; 160 of 1918; 61 of 1920; 285 of 1908.

[46] *Ibid.*, Act 98 of 1908.

[47] *Ibid.*, Acts no. 58 of 1888; no. 83 of 1921.

[48] *Ibid.*, Acts no. 170 of 1898; 78 of 1906; 102 of 1921.

expression, " the Parish of Orleans excepted," was that country representatives found that by excepting the City from a proposed law it was much easier to get it passed. The City delegation seldom opposed and often supported laws which the country wanted, provided the City was not affected.[49]   With a fairly equal division of the country votes on a particular measure its enactment or defeat depended on the position taken by the solid block of New Orleans votes. The Orleans delegation was always suspicious of any law that did not except the City, especially if it smacked of political or moral reform.

Statutory stipulations like the many provisions of the constitution itself reflect both the unique needs of a great City and also the factional struggles that have resulted from the attempt of the state to subdue politically potent New Orleans.

[49] See chapter VII.

CHAPTER III

The Election Machinery and Party Organization

CONSTITUTIONAL PROVISIONS

THE suffrage and election laws of Louisiana beginning in 1898 were designed to exclude the Negro from the polls and perpetuate the Democratic party in power. Not only did the Democrats use the laws of the state to achieve these ends but they also designed party machinery and rules with the same objects in mind. The party was successful through these methods in establishing its complete dominance of state and local politics. To possess the right to use the Democratic party label assured election to any candidate. This made the control of party machinery crucial. The real contests, therefore, in Louisiana and New Orleans politics were between the factions of the Democratic party in the primary. The faction in control of the party organization had a tremendous advantage over its opposition.

During the period from 1897 to 1906, important changes in the election laws were being made. During the same interval, the Choctaw Club was becoming the dominant faction in New Orleans politics. The Organization therefore had a part in creating the election machinery which was to prove so useful to it. Designed primarily to establish white supremacy, the new laws and party rules also established Democratic supremacy and thereby the supremacy of the leading faction of that party. The Choctaw Club demonstrated the difficulty of dislodging the group in control of the election machinery, party committees, and patronage. It was largely due to the Organization's grip of these instruments that it was able to retain its hold on the City government without interruption from 1900 to 1920.

The suffrage and election articles of the Constitution of 1898 were basic to all subsequent constitutional and statutory changes. This constitution set up the following suffrage provisions: residence in the state two years, in the parish one year and in the precinct six months; the voter must register personally and demonstrate his ability to read and write; if unable to read and write he might qualify to vote provided he owned property valued at $300 on which all taxes were paid; a poll tax of one dollar per year must be paid and the voter must be able to present receipts for his poll tax for the two years preceding the year in which he expected to vote; he must be a citizen of the United States; a " grandfather clause " was included for the illiterate whites unable to qualify under the educational and property clauses, provided they registered before September 1, 1898; the illiterate foreign-born voter who had become naturalized before January 1, 1898, was also exempted from the property or educational tests.[1] An examination of these provisions readily shows that they were aimed at the known weaknesses of the southern Negro. To a greater degree than the whites, he was illiterate, propertyless, careless, and moved about a good deal. Furthermore, neither he nor his grandfather had voted prior to January 1, 1867. It was therefore very difficult for him to qualify to vote.

These stringent requirements in no way weakened the New Orleans Machine. In fact they proved a boon. The precinct leaders of the Machine saw to it that their supporters registered and paid their poll tax and in every way com-

---

[1] *Constitution of 1898*, arts. 197, 205 and 210. The poll tax requirement was not to be effective until immediately after the general election of 1900. The privileges of registering under the " grandfather clause " and " foreign voter clause " were extended by a constitutional amendment in 1912. *Acts of Louisiana*, 1912, no. 24.

plied with the new law. Exemption of the foreign-born voter from the educational and property tests had saved the " Dago " vote which the Organization controlled. On the other hand, many of the potential supporters of the opposition, the more cultured if less politically minded clientele of the " silk stocking " reformers, failed at times to attend to these important details and were unable to vote in the City election.[2]

Article 202 of the Constitution of 1898 enumerated certain classes of persons who could not qualify to vote under any circumstances.[3] Section 8 of this article assured voters immunity from arrest during attendance on elections except for cases involving treason, felony, and breach of the peace. The two latter offenses were common among the Negroes. All the constitutions since 1898 have provided for voting the straight ticket by means of marking the party device at the top of the ballot.[4] Because the Democratic primary was the decisive election, this provision was of no great importance. It did, however, tend to weaken occasional movements to split the ticket at the general election when there was dissatisfaction with the Democratic nominees.

The Constitution of 1913 made no significant changes in the suffrage and election provisions. Two events happening prior to 1921, when the constitution was again revised, caused some notable changes relating to these subjects. The so-called " grandfather clause " had been declared unconstitutional by the Supreme Court of the United States in a case

---

[2] *New Orleans Item*, Nov. 19, 1922, " Behrman Tells ". Behrman lists the failure of his " silk stocking" opponents to pay their poll tax as an important factor in his election as mayor in 1904.

[3] Included were those guilty of crimes involving a penitentiary sentence, inmates of charitable institutions and the insane. A like provision is found in the constitutions of 1913 and 1921.

[4] *Constitutions of 1898 and 1913*, art. 212; *Constitution of 1921*, art. 8, sec. 15.

originating in Oklahoma.[5] A substitute had to be found that would, like the old device, include the poor illiterate white voter and exclude the Negro voter. In 1916, John M. Parker had run for governor on the Progressive ticket and had polled over 40,000 votes. Some politicians in Louisiana feared the development of a permanent party opposed to the Democrats and in consequence the return of the Negro. These fears proved unfounded before the convention met; nevertheless Negro disfranchisement was strengthened. The second important factor was that the same John M. Parker, now the Democratic governor of the state, had promised in the City election of 1920 to destroy the influence of the New Orleans Machine. The Parker forces dominated the Convention of 1921. The primary purpose of such convention, according to Parker, was to complete the destruction of bossism in New Orleans.[6] The tasks relating to suffrage then seemed to be to mend the damaged fence against the Negro and strike at false registration, floaters, voting dead men and other evils charged to the Choctaws.

The property qualifications were dropped, along with the " grandfather clause ", in the revised suffrage provisions of 1921. The educational test remained the same except that even though a person could read and write he must also be of " good character and shall understand the duties and obligations of citizenship under a republican form of government." [7] The registration article further stated that in addition to ability to read and write, " said applicant shall also be able to read any clause in this constitution or the Constitution of the United States, and give a reasonable interpretation thereof." The illiterate voter must have not only " good character ", but also a " good reputation." He must be

[5] *Guinn and Beal vs. U. S.*, 238 U. S. 375 (1915).

[6] *House Journal*, 1920, p. 336.

[7] *Constitution of 1921*, art. 8, sec. 1.

" attached to the principles of the Constitution of the United States and the State of Louisiana, and shall be able to understand and give a reasonable interpretation of any section of either constitution when read to him by the registrar, and he must be well disposed to the good order and happiness of the State of Louisiana and of the United States and must understand the duties and obligations of citizenship under the republican form of government." [8] The same article also provided that a person must be able to establish that he is the identical person he represents himself to be when registering or voting. The registration form also required the age of the voter in years, months and days. It may be seen that these changes were designed to exclude the Negro by unequal administration. The Negro who could read and write might now be excluded because his character was not pure or because he did not " understand " the duties of republican citizenship or because he failed to given an interpretation of the constitution that seemed " reasonable " to the registrar.[9] This was indeed " progress." Under previous constitutions a Negro who could read and write or who owned property could qualify. This same Negro could now be deprived of the vote. The provision applying to illiterate voters was subject to even wider variations in interpretation. A Negro might have a " good character " but he could be excluded if he did not have a " good reputation." [10] If he passed both these tests, the " reasonableness " of his inter-

---

[8] *Ibid.*

[9] The author has registered and voted in Louisiana for a number of years and was never called on to prove his " good character " or interpret the Constitution.

[10] There is no reported case of a blemish ever being found on the character or reputation of an illiterate white voter either in the City or the country. White voters also seemed to have understood thoroughly the duties of republican citizenship, and their constitutional interpretations to have been " reasonable."

pretation of the constitution depended on the registrar of voters who was seldom a constitutional lawyer of any note. Attention is also called to the fact that it would be possible to interpret these provisions so as to exclude persons of radical persuasion. In a period of " red baiting " any one, white or black, who held economic ideas at variance with those of the ruling clique might, because of shortage of " character ", " lack of attachment " to the principles of the constitution or because of indisposition toward " the good order and happiness " of the state or nation, be deprived of his vote. The possibilities in this connection have never been used.

A number of these provisions were important to the New Orleans Machine. In preserving suffrage for the illiterate country voter, it was also kept for the illiterate foreign voter of the City. The section requiring that the voter be able to prove himself the identical person whom he represents himself to be was aimed not only at the Negro but also at the use of " floaters " and false registrations in which the Machine was supposed to be indulging with a good deal of flagrance. Included in the Constitution of 1921 was a provision against altering or fraudulently issuing poll tax receipts or paying the poll tax of another. These were offenses likewise attributed to the Choctaw Club.

Some important election regulations which had formerly been provided for by statute were incorporated in the Constitution of 1921. An article authorized the governor to appoint the registrar of voters for the Parish of Orleans, while in other parishes the selection was left to the police jury.[11] The same article made the Board of Registration, composed of the governor, lieutenant governor and speaker of the house, a constitutional body. This Board, as under the statute, was given authority to supervise registration and

[11] *Constitution of 1921*, art. 8, sec. 18.

to remove any registrar in the state. A completely new registration of the voters of the entire state was ordered. Governor Parker, under these provisions hoped to " purify " the electorate at its source by controlling the gate through which it entered the primary as well as the general election. All political activity of whatever character was limited by the constitution to legally registered and qualified voters.[12] Hence these regulations would also affect the selection of party committees. Similarly a part of the Corrupt Practices Act of 1912, providing against the buying or selling of votes, was incorporated.[13] A person guilty of offering a reward for giving or withholding a vote was forever barred from the right of suffrage and from holding any office of trust or profit under the laws of the state. This provision was of very little importance as such crude methods of carrying elections in the City had largely given way to more refined and subtle methods.[14]

The constitutional changes of 1921 avowedly designed to end Machine control in New Orleans were proved by later events to be no match for an effective City Organization and therefore no hindrance to the return of the Choctaw Club to power in 1925. If New Orleans was to have alternation of power in the City Hall, laws alone could not achieve it; a permanent well organized opposition to the " Regulars " would seem the only answer to the problem. For reasons

---

[12] *Ibid.*, sec. 4. It is obvious that these registration provisions were aimed at the New Orleans Machine where accusations had been recently made of irregularities during the campaign of 1920. *New Orleans Times Picayune*, Sept. 1 and 2, 1920.

[13] *Constitution of 1921*, art. 7, sec. 23, taken from Act 213 of 1912.

[14] It is not intimated that the venal vote did not exist. Better organization, the use of patronage, subtle hints from the police and the use of assessment had become by 1920 more important influences than direct purchase of votes.

which will be discussed later, the Parker faction could not furnish this essential need.[15]

The constitutional method was effective in eliminating the Negro vote.[16]   After 1906 the "white primary" rule of the Democratic party made his exclusion even more complete.   Should a cleavage arise among the whites, similar to the Populist movement of the Nineties, there is nothing inherent in the constitution or the primary law to prevent the use of the potential Negro vote if those administering the laws desired.[17]   The constitutional efforts to crush the strength of the City Machine have failed.   The Organization seems impervious to this form of restraint.   Realistic politicians among the Choctaws tapped new sources of power or devised means to defeat the restraints.   Reform groups in power found their own devices inconvenient.   For one reason or another those that proved a real hindrance to machine methods fell into innocuous desuetude.   The chief reason why Negro disfranchisement was effective and efforts to disinherit the machine failed was that in the former case there was a sincere desire on the part of all factions to be rid of the Negro voter; while in the latter case there was no such universal desire to be rid of the Machine or its sources of power.

ELECTION LAWS

Shortly after the Constitutional Convention of 1898, the general assembly passed a new general election law.[18]   Nominations were still made by conventions in Louisiana; so the

[15] For further discussion of this point, see ch. viii.

[16] The number of Negro voters in 1896 was 129,760.   In 1900 it had fallen to 5,380.   *Reports of the Secretary of State*, 1896 and 1900.

[17] It would of course be very difficult for the faction not in power to register and vote the Negroes.   For a detailed discussion, see Lewinson, *Race, Class and Party* (New York, 1932), especially ch. ix.

[18] *Acts of Louisiana*, 1898, no. 152.

law also laid down rules covering the nominating process. The provisions of this law gave the Democratic party almost complete control of the election machinery.

The law established in each parish a Board of Supervisors of Elections. In Orleans Parish, the board consisted of a president to be appointed by the governor, the registrar of voters and the civil sheriff.[19] The board was required by law to appoint three election commissioners and one clerk for each precinct in the parish, not more than two of whom should be of the same party. In Orleans Parish such commissioners and clerks were to be selected from a list of not less than six names furnished by each party or nominating body. The officials selected by the board must represent, as far as practicable, all political parties authorized to make nominations.[20] Each party or nominating body was entitled to appoint a watcher for each precinct, such watcher to be commissioned by the board. Watchers were allowed to take no part in the conduct of elections. The police was authorized to keep peace at the polls under orders of the Board of Election Supervisors and precinct commissioners.[21] Persons violating the peace, however, must be allowed to vote before being taken to jail. Each party was also allowed one challenger at each poll. In case a voter was challenged, it was the duty of the election commissioners to decide on his

[19] In other parishes the board consisted of the registrar of voters who was elected by the police jury, a second member appointed by the police jury and a third member appointed by the governor.

[20] After 1900, since the Republicans had candidates on only a few occasions, this provision was of little importance. In practice Democrats were selected for these posts in most instances.

[21] The election officials were given control of the police with the idea of preventing those in control of the City from using them for political purposes. The futility of such a provision is evident when it is realized that the party in control of the City Hall was also in control of the election machinery of the Parish of Orleans. The same criticism might be made of the use of peace officers in the country parishes.

eligibility. Voting booths were required in cities of over 50,000 population.

The part of the general election law concerning nominations was of particular interest since the Democratic nomination was tantamount to election. It authorized party nominations by convention, caucus or meeting. A party was defined as a body that had cast twenty per cent of the entire vote in the election.[22] It was further provided that nonparty nomination might be made by filing nominating papers when signed by the required number of qualified electors.[23]

Several changes of importance were made in the general election law of 1898 when it was revised in 1916.[24] These were concerned chiefly with the rules governing the formation of new parties and the use of party labels on the ballot. When voters to the number of one thousand desired to form a new political party and had nominated candidates, they were required to write in the certificates of nomination that they were candidates for party recognition under the party name specified by them in their nominating papers. On fulfilling these conditions, the law required that the name of the proposed party be printed on the official ballot over that of the nominees. If, in the election following, any one of their candidates received as many as ten per cent of the votes cast in the entire state, the persons signing the nominating papers were to be recognized as a lawful political party.[25] In

[22] The percentage was lowered to ten in 1900 (Act 132).

[23] For state offices, 1000; parish offices, 100; ward offices, 25 electors were required to sign such petitions. By a law passed in 1908 no person registered as a member of a political party was permitted to sign nonparty nominating papers. In checking such petition the registrar was instructed not to count such a signature. The law also stipulated that nominating papers must be filed before the first primary was held. Minority parties must therefore make their nominations prior to knowing the results of the major primary.

[24] *Acts of Louisiana*, 1916, no. 130.

[25] This meant the new party must cast between 3,000 and 4,000 votes to secure legal recognition.

another section, a blow was struck at minority groups who desired to nominate by filing nominating papers instead of by primary election. The law forbade such groups to use their party emblem on the official ballot above the name of their candidates even if they had received ten per cent of the vote at the preceding general election. The only designation allowed in such case was " nominating papers."

These new regulations undoubtedly discouraged minority parties and were particularly objectionable to the Socialist party. A minority party had the choice of attempting to become a legally recognized party or of merely listing the nominees under the indefinite designation, " Nominating Papers." If it chose the former course and was successful, the primary laws required that its nominations be made by direct primary. Such an arrangement was of course objectionable to a disciplined party like the Socialists since there was chance of " impure " elements filtering in who might capture the party machinery. If the latter course was chosen, there was little opportunity of building up its following since it could not identify its candidates by a party label. If the minority group had polled less than the ten per cent it might use its party label on the ballot, but the minute it began to gain strength, it either lost the use of its label on the ballot or must nominate by direct primary.

Another provision of the law helpful to the dominant party was the so-called " assistance " clause. A disabled or illiterate voter had the right to ask and secure assistance from the election commissioner of his choice. The ballot must be marked, however, in the presence of a second commissioner. This was particularly important to the New Orleans Machine whose followers included a large block of illiterate foreign-born voters.[26]

---

[26] An " assistance " clause had been included in the primary law of 1906 (Act 49). Its use was of course more important in the primary

The first primary election law was passed in 1900.   After that year the importance of the general election decreased and that of the nominating process increased.   Before the enactment of state laws on the subject, primaries had been used by the Democratic party in selecting members to party commitees and delegates to party conventions.   After the Convention of 1898, which had destroyed the voting strength of the Republican party, it became increasingly obvious that the nominating process of the Democratic party was of paramount importance in Louisiana politics.   Since the general election was fast becoming merely a rubber stamp for the Democratic nominating convention, the demand for nominations by direct primary grew.   The law passed in 1900 did not make nominations by primary obligatory.[27]   It simply authorized a party polling ten per cent or more of the vote at the last general election to nominate by direct primary. The proper party committees were empowered to call the primary and conduct it.   Since the decision to hold a primary rested with the party managers who thought their control was safer in the convention, but few elections were held under this law.[28]   The law did, however, contain a number of provisions relating to party rules and party committees that were of some importance in the primaries conducted to elect delegates to conventions.   State Central, District, and Parish Committees were authorized to adopt such rules and regulations for the conduct of primaries as they might see fit, not inconsistent with the law, " and provided further that these rules shall have the effect of law."   The rules of local

than in the general election. For further discussion on the political importance of the " assistance " clause, see chapter VII.

[27] *Acts of Louisiana*, 1900, no. 133.

[28] A few local elections were held in accordance with the law but no election in New Orleans and no nomination of state candidates were made by this method until after the compulsory law of 1906 was passed.

committees were made subject to revision by the State Central committee. The party committee calling a primary was authorized to set forth in the call the qualifications required for voters " in addition to those laid down in the constitution and election laws." It was under the legal sanction of this clause that the Democratic party, by resolution, limited voting to white men in the primary. Any person voting in one primary was prohibited from participating in the nominations of any other party or from signing nominating papers. The law required the unit of government concerned to pay the ordinary expenses of the election. The Democratic candidates for state and city offices nominated in 1904 were the last to receive their nominations from a convention. The increasing conclusiveness of Democratic nomination made the direct primary inevitable.

In 1906 an act was passed requiring all nominations of political parties by direct primary.[29] The matter was no longer optional with the party leaders. Practically all the provisions of the earlier law were incorporated in the new, with many additions which tended to centralize and magnify the importance of party organization. A party was defined as any organization whose candidates received five per cent of the vote at the preceding general election.[30] The power to prescribe voting qualifications in addition to those laid down by law was lodged exclusively with the State Central Committee. This sheared the local committees of power they had previously held subject to being overruled by the state body. Party affiliations must be declared at the time of registration and none but those registered as party mem-

[29] *Acts of Louisiana*, 1906, no. 49.

[30] The Act of 1900 had fixed ten per cent. " Defining a political party as one that shall have cast a designated percentage of votes is not granting special provileges." *State ex. rel. Labonne vs. Secretary of State* (121 La. 374).

bers might take part in the party primary.[31]   Candidates were required to give proper notice and pay the entry fee to the party committee a certain number of days before the election. The law required the election of all party committees at the primary.[32]   The use of official ballots with a detachable numbered slip was obligatory and election officials were instructed to detach the number without viewing the ballot just before it was cast.   The purpose of the slip was to insure that the ballot cast was the identical one given to the voter. It was hoped by this device to stop the "endless chain" practice by making vote buying too uncertain to be useful. Under the new law the buyer could not be certain how the seller had voted since he could not vote a previously marked ballot.[33]   Sample ballots were furnished and might be used by the voter as a guide in marking his ballot.   Illiterate and disabled voters were allowed to receive assistance in marking their ballots.

Precinct election commissioners for the primary were to be selected by the party committee at a public drawing, fifteen days before election, from names of electors submitted by each local candidate or candidate for state office.   The names submitted by the candidate were to be placed in a box and thoroughly shuffled.   The person drawing the slips on

31 *Ibid.*, "This does not violate secrecy of the ballot."

32 Ward leaders in New Orleans always ran for a place on the State Central Committee.   A ward leader failing of election was displaced as leader by the successful candidate.

33 The "endless chain" was explained to the author by one who served as a "repeater" on many occasions.   An official ballot would be slipped to the precinct worker before the poll opened and properly marked for the Machine candidates.   The "repeater" or venal voter was then required to go to the poll, cast the previously marked ballot and return to the worker with the unused ballot before being paid fifty cents, a dollar, a dime, or whatever the current price happened to be.   The process was then repeated.   This method prevented the seller from double crossing the purchaser.   It was a method of enforcing a code of fair competition.

which the names were written was to be blindfolded, and the law required that the slips be identical in size and shape. The three persons whose names were drawn first were to serve as election commissioners, the next two as clerks and the remaining as watchers. It was hoped under this plan to give all contending factions representation in every precinct.

The law of 1906 established the existing committees as the legal machinery of the party.[34] It vested in the State Central Committee authority to direct and order how subordinate and local committees should be organized and constituted and to fix their number, terms of office, and time of election.[35] Voters were forbidden to participate in more than one primary or nomination. To discourage party members dissatisfied with the results of a primary from organizing and nominating candidates by petition, the law forbade any one voting in a primary from later becoming a candidate in the general election in opposition to the nominees of the primary. A run-off primary was required between the two highest candidates in case no one received a majority in the first election.[36] Practices made illegal by the law included buying of votes, repeating, fraudulent counts and police interference with the voter.[37] These apparently reflected the evils then common in state and City politics.[38]

[34] The State Central Committee consisted of one member from each of the wards of the Parish of Orleans, one member from each of the other parishes and three members at large from each congressional district.

[35] The Choctaw Club completely controlled the Orleans Parish Democratic committee. It was composed of one member from each ward.

[36] In the state election, if the candidate for governor had received a majority, then the candidates for the other state offices having the greatest number of votes were declared elected regardless of whether they had a clear majority.

[37] Only one policeman was allowed at each poll and he was to be under orders of the election officials only. As in the case of the general election law previously described, this was so designed to keep the faction in the City Hall from using the police to influence the voter.

[38] The primary law of 1906 was revised in 1916 by Act 35. Few

In 1922 during the administration of Governor John M. Parker, the primary law was revised.[39]   In general most provisions of the law of 1906 were continued.   An effort was made further to insure party regularity.   The law made it a misdemeanor to participate in a primary of a party different from the one the voter had claimed to be a member when registering.   The law ordered the following pledge printed at the bottom of all primary ballots: " By casting this ballot I do pledge myself to abide by the result of this primary election and to aid and support all the nominees thereof in . the ensuing general election."

These two regulations, together with a continuation of the provision of the law of 1906 which forbade a voter in a primary from running against the nominees, completely discouraged any deflection from the fold of the Democratic party.   The provision for the use of the ballot with the detachable numbered slip was continued.   This device, it should be noted, was not required in the general election law.   Further evidence is thus afforded that there was no real contest in the general election and hence no need to guard against certain election abuses common in the primary. The Democratic primary was the election which determined not only factional control within that party but also dominance in the personnel of government.

There were some sections of the 1922 primary law applicable by specific limitations or by implication to New Orleans. Each precinct in the City was required to have on election day a poll list containing the name of the voter, the serial numbers of his registration and poll tax receipts and the

changes of importance were made. A slight revision was also made in 1912 which barred persons from the primary who refused to give their party affiliations at the time of registration.

[39] *Acts of Louisiana*, 1922, no. 97.

number of his ballot.[40]   Minute regulations concerning assistance to illiterate voters were indicated.   The selection
of police for use at the election and their assignment to specific voting precincts were placed in the hands of the parish
board of election supervisors.[41]

Louisiana passed a Corrupt Practices Act in 1912.[42]   The
law was made applicable to both primary and general elections.   Because of an adverse court decision in 1921, the
law no longer applied to primary elections.[43]   It was there-

[40] A provision of the registration law was changed in 1921.   The
proper parish authorities were instructed to furnish the registrars of
voters with notices of deaths, persons sent to the insane asylum, and
persons convicted of crime, in order that their names might be struck
from the registrar's rolls.   Officials failing to supply this information
were subject to fine (Act 212 of 1912).   This change in the law seems
to have been aimed at the good old New Orleans custom of voting dead
men and idiots.   The " Regulars " did not believe in denying the faithful
their vote even after death or when reason had fled.   Their opponents
even contended that they preferred both these types.   It is also alleged
that in voting a " floater " they had no scruples against using the name of
a former opponent, who if alive or sane would have cast his vote against
the Organization.

[41] During the City election of 1920 in which the Machine was defeated,
there had been charges of police interference with the voter.   The law of
1922 sought to minimize this evil by taking selection and assignment of
police away from the City Hall.   Such arrangement was of course futile
when the Machine also controlled the Parish election board.   Events at
a recent election indicate how this might be overcome.   The use of police
by the Choctaws to influence voters was feared in the congressional
election in September, 1934.   Senator Long called 2,000 National Guardsmen to New Orleans to counteract police influence.   Due to their presence
in the City ready for duty at the polls, the Choctaw and the Long factions came to an agreement under which no police and no National
Guardsmen were to be near any polling place.   The police could be of
no use if their influence was to be balanced by a Guardsman.   A special
committee of citizens representing both factions equally policed the polls
on election day and kept perfect order.

[42] *Acts of Louisiana*, 1912, no. 213.

[43] *Wood et al. vs. Bateman*, 149 La. 290.   In the decision in this case,
the Supreme Court of Louisiana declared the Corrupt Practices Act

fore in effect, so far as the decisive elections were concerned, for only nine years. By the terms of the law, a candidate must name a treasurer to handle all campaign funds. A report by the treasurer must be filed in the case of candidates for states offices with the Secretary of State and in case of local candidates with the clerk of the court. Such reports must give detailed accounts of all sums spent. In the case of items of expense above five dollars the name of the person paid and the nature of the service rendered must be stated. Reports must be filed within five days after the primary and within twenty days after the general election. To insure that all accounts were included it was provided that all claims against candidates for money due must be presented within four days after the primary and within ten days after the general election; otherwise, such claims could not be the basis of a suit for collection. Any candidate paying a bill after filing his report was liable to penalities laid down for violations of the act. Those failing to file a report, if elected, were punishable by forfeiture of the right to take office and a fine; if not elected they were subject to a fine. Any person running for office must also file a statement of all monies spent by himself and his relatives on his

(No. 213 of 1912) had been superseded, in so far as its provisions applied to primary elections, by Act 35 of 1916. The latter act had revised the primary law of 1906. The decision rested on the repealing clause in Act 35 which declared that all laws and parts of laws on the same subject were repealed. The decision was made May 2, 1921. After 1921 therefore no Corrupt Practices Act existed so far as the primaries were concerned. Only such prohibitions as were contained in the primary law remained to inconvenience the politicians. These included the buying of votes, police abuses, stuffing ballot boxes, false counts, the use of floaters and the like, but did not include any reference to the amount of money a candidate might spend in the primary or to the making of reports on receipts and expenditures. Reports are still filed in accordance with the law of 1912 but since practically no money is spent by either candidates or the party, except in primary, the law is of little consequence. See note on next page covering specific reports.

candidacy. All statements, when filed, became public documents and open to inspection.[44] Non-elective office holders or those whose terms were not fixed by law were forbidden to make political contributions.[45] Public utilities and banks were forbidden to contribute to campaign funds.[46]

[44] Examination of the reports on file in the office of the clerk of the Civil District Court in New Orleans made in accordance with the provisions of the law indicate only a perfunctory observance both before and after the court decision of 1921. In 1916 Martin Behrman filed a statement covering the primary declaring he had made no promises of political appointment and had received no money from City employees. The affidavit added that a detailed account of his campaign receipts and expenses was attached. However, it could not be found. It was either lost by the clerk or never filed. In 1920 Behrman filed a statement covering the primary, showing receipts of $1950 and expenses as follows: newspaper advertising, $1950; bands and music, $297; printing and engraving, $626; miscellaneous, $5.00. Andrew McShane the successful candidate for mayor of that year, filed an affidavit to the effect that he had received no contributions and made no disbursements in the primary campaign. In 1925, after the decision of 1921 previously referred to, Behrman filed a report showing he had spent $464 at the general election for newspaper advertising and had received no contributions. No record was found for the unsuccessful candidates of 1925 who were Maloney and McShane. It was clear that the filing of these reports was regarded rather lightly both by the Machine and by its opposition and was frequently never done. Since the law no longer applies to the primary the reports even if filed would give no clue to the amount or use of money in New Orleans elections.

[45] Violations of this section of the law have been notorious both on the part of City and state employees under pressure of their political superiors. Contributions of City employees are recognized as one of the chief sources of the Machine's war chest. Since the Corrupt Practices Act was declared in 1921 no longer applicable to the primary elections, the civil service law is supposed to protect city employees from solicitation. No effort has been made by either officials or employees to secure the observance of the law in this matter. It is simply ignored completely. There is no civil service law for state employees.

[46] Act 20 of 1915 amended this provision. Contributions from all corporations were barred. The corporation or any representative of it was forbidden to oppose or aid any issue or candidate in any election. Corporations might be required to file sworn reports concerning contri-

Other sections of the law forbade candidates to promise appointments prior to election or to agree to divide the official salary. All campaign literature must bear the name of the publisher. Candidates were forbidden to hire watchers or other agents at the polls. Twenty-five voters might contest election results on the ground of fraud before any district court.[47] If, however, the candidate was unaware of the violations or they were trivial or immaterial the result of the election remained unchanged. The costs of contesting an election must be borne by the side losing the suit and all contests must be filed within ten days after a primary and within thirty days after the general election.

There is little doubt that the Corrupt Practices Act has never been enforced. Both corporations and office holders make political contributions. It is also not disputed that unreported money is used for " current expenses " on election day to influence the venal vote not only in New Orleans but also in the country. The law itself discourages contests based on fraud charges in view of the fact that the names and number of the alleged fraudulent votes must be given in the charge and the loser in such a suit must pay the costs. In New Orleans where the Machine in the past has controlled

butions. Failure to file when requested subjected them to heavy fines. District attorneys were encouraged to ferret out violations by an offer of a special fee. A company failing to pay a fine was barred from access to the courts for any cause. The governor was authorized to direct actions against a suspected corporation. Stockholders were given the right to recover from the officers responsible any fine assessed for violation of the law. The corporation was also liable to a fine of $10,000 and forfeiture of its charter for violations. This law has not stopped contributions of corporations. They are now made openly through the officers and owners as individuals, or secretly by the corporation and never reported.

[47] " In contesting elections the number and names of the illegal votes must be given." *Thornhill vs. Wear*, 131 La. 479.

all branches of government there was little to be gained by bringing suit.[48]

CONCLUSIONS ON ELECTION MACHINERY

It now remains to point out more specifically how the constitution and election laws fostered the type of organization politics represented by the Choctow Club in New Orleans. The suffrage provisions of the constitution, together with their unequal administration, effectively consolidated the strength of the Democratic party and firmly entrenched the one party system. Not content with the reduction of the Negro vote by constitutional disfranchisement to a very minor role, the party completely eliminated it from the decisive election by means of the white primary.[49] This was possible under the laws which authorized the appropriate party committees to conduct the primary and which also required primary voters to have all the qualifications prescribed by law plus such qualifications as might be laid down by the party. The one-party system was established to exclude the Negro, but the internal party machinery designed to further this end was quickly seized and utilized by experi-

[48] Every judge and district attorney in the parish owed his election to the Machine. This at least had a psychological effect, if nothing more, on such officials when charges of fraud were brought against their own faction. The author was informed that no promises were ever demanded by the Choctaws of candidates for judgeships. Behrman always insisted on naming competent men to the bench. The Recorders Courts were, however, admittedly subservient to their political masters. Information is that a ward leader could get one of his friends released for anything short of murder.

[49] Frank R. Kent is undoubtedly correct in his view that the White primary is the most important factor in eliminating the Negro vote and that registration, poll tax and other devices are secondary. He lists as other factors selfishness of white Republicans, unfavorable white sentiment, the habit of not voting, and futility. Kent, *The Great Game of Politics*, p. 338. See also Meyers, *Politics in the South* (Dallas, 1934); Sait, *American Parties and Elections* (New York, 1927), ch. ii.

enced politicians to perpetuate their faction in power. The Choctaw Club beginning in 1900 controlled the election machinery of Orleans Parish. With a friendly governor at Baton Rouge, it secured the appointment of an Organization man to the office of registrar of voters and thus had charge of registration. In like manner the Club was able to have its candidate named as a second member of the board of election supervisors for the parish and since the criminal sheriff was the third member, the organization was in full control of the general election. The patronage involved in naming election officials and selecting polling places was used in the interest of the faction. More important still, the Choctaws always elected a majority of the members of the Orleans Parish Democratic committee who had the more significant duty of conducting the Democratic primary. Here again the committee's influence in the matter of election patronage was great and helped to keep the faction it represented in control. Also important was its power in the State Central Committee where the Club had seventeen votes out of a total of seventy-six. A further element of strength the Choctaws possessed was their influence with state authorities. They either controlled or had weight with all officials to whom election reports were made. It was necessary for the opposing faction to bring fraud charges before an Organization district attorney and in turn before a judge of like persuasion. Since frauds were difficult to prove and the loser in such actions had to pay costs there were few contests. The faction in the saddle, i. e., the Choctaw Club in New Orleans, thus became in the conduct of the primary, lawmaker, administrator, and judge as well as dispenser *par excellence* of election patronage. In New Orleans, if a man's vote was to be effective or if he desired to hold office, he must align himself not only with the Democratic party but also with the dominant faction, the Choctaw Club.

CHAPTER IV

MARTIN BEHRMAN, MAYOR AND CHOCTAW CLUB LEADER [1]

IN 1904 Martin Behrman, at the age of thirty-nine, was elected mayor of New Orleans and shortly after taking office was selected by the Choctaw Club as its leader. He remained its outstanding figure until his death in 1926. His leadership rested not only on his official position and the fact that he fitted into the condition of his day, but also upon the fact that he had already had sixteen years of political experience in the City. By persistent work he arose from the bottom of ward politics to a position almost unique in political life. Unlike such machine leaders as William Tweed and Richard Croker of New York, and Abe Ruef of San Francisco, he assumed responsibility as well as power. From 1904 to 1920, Behrman was mayor of New Orleans as well as the head of its ruling machine. Defeated in the election of 1920, he reorganized the Choctaw Club. In 1925 he was again elected mayor and became the sole master of the Organization.

In his story of his career, Behrman stated that he had his first experience in organization politics when, at the request of the leader of his ward (the fifteenth), he served as secretary of the ward campaign committee in the election of 1888. As a result of his work on this occasion, he was offered a place as deputy assessor by one of the men whom

---

[1] This chapter is based largely on personal interviews with Behrman's contemporaries, his autobiography published in *The New Orleans Item*, Oct. 22, 1922, to March 25, 1923, and the account found in Zink, *City Bosses in the United States* (Durham, 1931) ; and from facts contained elsewhere in this work.

he had helped to elect.   He accepted the offer and devoted
the remainder of his life to politics.[2]

Martin Behrman was born in New York City, October
14, 1864.   His parents, Henry and Fredrika Behrman, were
German Jews.   They moved to New Orleans when Martin
was only seven months old and made their home in the
French Quarter.   His father, a cigar-maker by trade, died
while Martin was still an infant, and his mother, a woman
of determination and energy, opened a bazaar in the Old
French Market to support herself and only child.   Martin
attended the German-American School and the St. Phillips
Public School where he learned to speak both French and
German.   When he was twelve years old, his mother died
and he was forced to go to work.

His first job was in a general store at a wage of fifteen
dollars a month.   His mother had urged him to get an education, and, remembering this advice, he attended night
school.   In a few years he secured a better position in
another store across the river in Algiers (a part of New
Orleans) and had to give up his studies.   From the time he
moved to Algiers until he entered politics in 1888, he was
in work that prepared him for his later political career.   As
a clerk in a general store and later as a partner in a store
which also served as the post office, he made many friends
who were to prove helpful in later years.   For two years
he was salesman for wholesale grocery concerns, which wid-
ened his contacts among the merchants of the City.   The
fact that he could speak French and German helped him to
make friends and increase his sales since many of the small
merchants in New Orleans spoke poor English.   Having
been thrown on his own resources at an early age, Behrman
developed self-reliance, the habit of hard work and an apt-
ness at meeting people.   Behrman felt that his early experi-

[2] *New Orleans Item*, Oct. 23, 1922, " Behrman Tells."

ences as a clerk and salesman were valuable to him in politics. He once remarked that he found getting votes not greatly different from selling merchandise.[3]

During Behrman's youth, the volunteer fire companies were centers of machine politics. As a member of the company in Algiers, he became acquainted with the leaders in his ward. They appreciated his energy, popularity, and ability as a salesman, and asked him to help in the campaign of 1888, the first in which he was old enough to vote.

In 1887, the year before he entered politics, he married Miss Julia Collins of Cincinnati, Ohio, whom he had met when she was visiting in the home of a former employer, John Lawton. Eleven children were born to the Behrmans, only two of whom survived infancy.[4] The family lived in a modest home in Algiers, and even after Behrman became mayor they never moved across the river to the more fashionable residential section of the City. He was always known as a " family man ", and there was never any scandal about his personal life. Mrs. Behrman's primary interest was her children and husband. She took no interest in politics even after the Choctaw Club organized a woman's division in 1920.

Behrman's entry into politics came at a time when Populism was gaining headway in the state. The Negro question was still a problem and was rapidly coming to the front again as economic issues began to break white solidarity.[5] As early as he could remember, Behrman had heard discussions of the evils of Republican rule supported by Negro votes. The New Orleans machine leaders had helped reestablish

[3] *New Orleans Item*, Nov. 5, 1922, " Behrman Tells."

[4] His son, Stanley, is head of a paving company in New Orleans. He succeeded his father, on the latter's death in 1926, as leader of the fifteenth ward. Helen May, his daughter, now deceased, became the wife of Nathaniel Bond, a lawyer, who was prominent in Choctaw Club politics.

[5] *Infra*, chapter I, p. 21.

white supremacy in 1876 and were doing all they could in the Eighties to reduce the number of Negro voters. His attitude toward the Negro voter and toward reformers who split the white vote was therefore greatly influenced by the discussions he heard around the stores and the fire house and by his own participation in the elections of the late Eighties and early Nineties.[6]

As deputy assessor from 1888 to 1892, Behrman lost no opportunity to make friends. He attributes some of his earlier successes to friends he made among the property owners whose assessments he had handled.[7] His work did not require all his time and he was able to build up a strong following in his ward before the next election. In those days, it was customary for the party to hold primaries in the wards to select delegates to the nominating conventions. Four days before the primary of 1892, Behrman organized a faction, printed his own ballots as was the custom, and succeeded in getting a majority vote of the ward for his candidates.[8] Behrman himself was one of those elected and he headed the delegation from the fifteenth ward to the convention. He threw the support of his faction to John Fitzpatrick, who was named by the convention as candidate for mayor. In the ensuing general election, Fitzpatrick was elected and Behrman became the recognized leader of the fifteenth ward. It was not until he actually sat in the City caucus with Fitzpatrick and the other leaders and had a hand in distributing patronage that he realized he was a power in politics.[9] As a reward for his work in the election he asked for and received the clerkship of the council committees on

[6] New Orleans Item, Oct. 23, 1922, " Behrman Tells."

[7] Ibid.

[8] These primaries were party affairs and no legal regulation was in effect.

[9] New Orleans Item, Oct. 22, 1922, " Behrman Tells." Behrman stated that most of the members of the caucus in those days had a business or a professional connection in which political influence might be valuable.

budget, public order and streets and landings. Behrman stated that he especially desired this work as he saw in it an opportunity to learn the details of City government.[10]

The state election had gone against the Machine and when Governor Foster took office, Behrman lost his deputy assessorship. In this election Behrman had sought membership on the school board from his ward and had been elected. He always took a great deal of interest in the development of the schools and supported increased taxes for this purpose in the City and State on many occasions.[11] His special interest in education, according to his friends, was his desire to make it possible for every child to have the advantages of at least a high school education, which had been denied him. He served on the school board for three successive terms. To supplement his income as committee clerk, he secured a job as solicitor for the Edison Electric Company, which he held until after the election of 1896. While clerk of various council committees, he learned that many things that are good and should be done by city government can not be done because the public is not able to see that they are good and worth the cost. He saw that often years of education and agitation were necessary to achieve some results, the wisdom of which the well-informed had understood years before. He also observed that after a thing is done, no matter how valuable it proves to be to the city, the authorities will be criticized on the methods used. Criticism, he learned, was inevitable in city government for both action and inaction.[12]

[10] *New Orleans Item*, Oct. 23, 1922, " Behrman Tells."

[11] *New Orleans Times Picayune*, Dec. 4, 1904; *Official Journal of Constitutional Convention*, 1898 and 1921.

[12] *New Orleans Item*, Oct. 22, 1922, " Behrman Tells." Behrman also stated in this connection that it was occasionally necessary to force through a regulation which a majority of the public did not understand or desire. He recalled the great opposition to the City ordinance requiring screens over cisterns, which was obviously in the interest of public health.

In 1896 Behrman ran for the legislature but was defeated, along with other machine candidates, by the Citizens' League. The " Regulars " had supported Governor Foster for reelection in 1896 and were recognized by him in the dispensing of state patronage in the City.   Behrman was named assessor of the fifth municipal district by Governor Foster.   For a short time after his appointment he continued to work for the Edison Electric Company but resigned because of criticism.   In his race for mayor in 1904 this dual connection was used against him, the implication being that while assessing the company's property he had been on its payroll. Behrman successfully proved that he had assessed no company property while in its employ.[13]   Although his conduct in this case was politically unwise, there was apparently no intention on his part of wrong-doing.   However, the fact that he was for several years an employee of the utilities may have influenced him when as mayor he had the responsibility of regulating them.   As a leader of the fifteenth ward, he became a member of the caucus of the Choctaw Club when it was organized in 1897.   He was the delegate from his ward to the Constitutional Convention of 1898.[14]   When Governor Heard was elected in 1900, with the support of the Choctaw Club, he reappointed Behrman assessor for another term of four years.

By 1904, Behrman had clearly demonstrated his ability as a politician and as a loyal Organization man.   He had been a ward leader since 1892; he had helped organize the Choctaw Club; he had made a favorable impression at the constitutional convention; and had been recognized with an important

[13] *New Orleans Times Democrat*, Oct. 26 and 29, 1904.

[14] Behrman's chief activities in the convention were his support of Negro disfranchisement, increased school funds, compensation for land taken for levee purposes and opposition to the provision forbidding politicians from accepting railroad passes. *Official Journal of the Constitutional Convention of 1898, passim.*

appointment by two governors. He was well known not only in New Orleans but in state political circles. At the State Democratic convention of 1904, he was nominated for state auditor, a position paying forty-seven hundred dollars a year. It was felt by some state leaders that his nomination was unfortunate because the country people would not vote for an " uncouth ward boss." Behrman campaigned with the other Democratic candidates endorsed by the Choctaw Club. He was a very poor speaker, but his plain, direct appeal won the country people to his support. The cry " beware of a ward boss " raised by his opponent was of no avail. The country voters could see nothing sinister in this man and he carried the country as well as the city. Soon after assuming office in May, he uncovered a shortage in state accounts. This prompt action assured his country supporters that they had made no mistake about his efficiency and honesty.

With the state election successfully behind, attention was now turned to the coming City campaign. In August, 1904, the Choctaw Club offered to support Charles Janvier for mayor at the Democratic nominating convention shortly to be held. For personal and business reasons, he declined to become a candidate. Because of the strength he had shown in the state campaign, the Organization then turned to Martin Behrman as " the only man on whom all the ward leaders could agree." An informal caucus was held at the offices of the New Orleans *Times Picayune* between former Governor Foster, Charles Janvier, Colonel Ewing and Behrman. These leaders offered to support Behrman for the nomination. He stated that he did not care to make the race as he had just been elected state auditor. However, after consultation with his wife and further urging by the leaders, he announced on August 24, 1904 that he would run. He was nominated by the Choctaw controlled convention.[15] The Choctaws anticipated no difficulty in electing Behrman mayor. Since its organization in 1897, the Club had had the benefit of state patronage to build up its strength. With this aid and a split in the opposition, the Organization had won the City election of 1900. Governor Blanchard, elected in May, 1904, had already indicated that he expected to cooperate with the Club.

It was not expected by the Choctaws that Behrman would be opposed but a new faction was organized as a result of Governor Blanchard's interference in local affairs in forcing his nomination for district attorney on the Machine. The faction was called the Home Rulers and was led by Page M. Baker, a wealthy publisher and leader of the " silk stocking " element in New Orleans politics.[16] Charles F. Buck was the candidate for mayor of the new faction.[17] The Home Rulers proved to be no match for the experienced, patronage supported Choctaws and Behrman was elected mayor and thus began his long service in that office.

[15] The Democratic Primary League had unsuccessfully attempted to get the parish Democratic committee to nominate candidates by direct primary under the optional law of 1900. *New Orleans Item*, Nov. 17, 1922, " Behrman Tells." Behrman was nominated at the convention by James O'Conner, known at that time in New Orleans as the " Gascon Calliope " because although Irish he had a French accent and was the Choctaw's most effective campaign speaker. It may be added that Mr. O'Conner served in Congress for several years and is now assistant attorney general of the state. He is one of the most colorful characters in Louisiana politics. *New Orleans Times Democrat*, Aug. 25, 1904.

[16] Behrman defined " silk stocking " politicians as those citizens who knew all about government from reading books and magazines but did not know where to go to file a complaint about garbage. They did not realize that the average voter was not interested in why the Roman Empire fell but were interested in water, sewage, police, parks and charity. *New Orleans Item*, Oct. 24, 1922, " Behrman Tells."

[17] For detailed account of this election see chapter VIII.

The characteristics possessed by Martin Behrman, which affected his success as a political leader, as revealed by statements of his friends and foes and by an analysis of his actions and policies on numerous occasions, may be grouped under certain broad categories. They concern: his general personal qualities; his ability in making contacts, political compromises, and as an organizer; his capacity to fit in with the social and economic forces of his day and age; and his power to anticipate and evaluate public sentiment in political affairs.[18]

Behrman was a man of great personal magnetism. He had a genial disposition, and although he had strong loves and hates seldom nursed a grudge. He was a good listener and had a marvelous memory for names and faces. He was generous and charitable. Having been poor himself, he could sympathise with poverty and his charity was presumably spontaneous and real. Although a German Jew by birth, he was of Catholic faith. There was no prejudice against people of Jewish blood in New Orleans politics and since the City was largely Catholic, his religion was probably a help.[19] Two characteristics which both the testimony of

[18] Compare with introduction by Merriam in Gosnell, *Boss Platt and his New York Machine* (Chicago, 1930).

[19] The lack of Jewish prejudice in New Orleans may be partially explained by the fact that the number of Jews in the City was small and because many of them were of the more well to do class. They took part in all phases of civic life and in general were good citizens. They adopted the southern political viewpoints, particularly on the Negro question and therefore eliminated that as a possible source of friction. A number of Jews have been elected to prominent political office. Since the City is predominantly Catholic there is naturally no prejudice against Catholics holding office. It would seem that Protestants might be discriminated against at the polls by the Catholics. Such is not the case. A number of reasons contribute to the absence of the religious question in politics. Among the more important are the cosmopolitan and tolerant character of the City, the prominence of many Protestants in business, finance, law, medicine and other callings, and the close relation between

men and events confirmed were that he was honest, carried out his promises and had the capacity to work long and effectively.   He was careful about making political promises, but once having committed himself, he would carry out an agreement regardless of the cost.   In 1920, while under Behrman's guidance, the Choctaw Club had pledged to support Colonel Stubbs of Monroe for governor.   During the course of the campaign, it appeared that Stubbs had no chance to win and Behrman was urged to desert Stubbs and switch Choctaw support to Parker.   This he refused to do and as a consequence lost all possibility of a compromise with Parker.   In the ensuing City election, Behrman was defeated through the efforts of Governor Parker.[20]   With reference to his capacity for hard work, all the leaders of the Club agreed that he worked harder at the job of politics than any other man in New Orleans.   He possessed a good mind and learned from everything.   A former governor who was a well-educated attorney said that Behrman had the best un-educated mind with which he had ever come in contact.   He had what may be called native ability; and with his force of will and rigid adherence to work he was the superior of most of his political contemporaries.   He deplored hypoc-risy, once remarking that " one of the most disgusting things

City and state politics.   The latter reason is probably the more important. The Central and Northern part of the state is Protestant while the South-ern part is Catholic.   Should the religious issue be drawn in City politics it might be reflected in the state, which as a whole is more Protestant than Catholic.   It is therefore the course of wisdom for the leadership in New Orleans to relegate religious consideration to the background. Behrman was always careful to seek to allay any evidence of religious feeling in politics either in the City or state.   One of his reasons for deciding to support Henry L. Fuqua, a tolerant Protestant, for governor in 1924 was to avoid a possible clash between the Klan and the Catholics. There were two other candidates, one a Catholic, and the other a Protes-tant, whom Behrman considered less tolerant than Fuqua.

[20] *Infra*, chapter VIII.

in public life is that you have to pretend to believe men whom you know to have lied to you. You have to get along with all kinds of people when you represent all the people." [21]

Behrman's ability to handle men, to organize and to compromise conflicting interests, were developed to a remarkable degree. His personal qualities were great assets in this work, as were his early training and experience. He was an excellent judge of men and studied carefully the strength and weakness of those concerned in politics and directed his appeal on the basis of his close analysis. He used tact and diplomacy in dealing with his subordinates, knowing when to be mild and when to be firm. Because of his ability to adjust dissension within the Machine, desertions were rare and only on one occasion affected the results of an election. He believed thoroughly in party organization and felt the factional quarrels of the Democrats should end with the primary. " Let's get together," was his slogan for the party, and whether he won or lost he was willing to give and take in order to secure party solidarity. His compromises with Governor Blanchard in 1904 and Governor Hall in 1912 illustrate his willingness to sacrifice in order to secure harmony.[22]

Having grown up in machine politics, he was convinced that the victors should have the spoils. He felt that unless his friends were named to office his administration would not receive wholehearted cooperation. He sensed that the average city ward leader was more interested in affairs in his ward than in state and national politics and by satisfying him in a large measure with patronage, he and a few other leaders were able to determine candidates and legislative policy with little interference from others. Members of his official family might differ with him and he gave their point of view

[21] *New Orleans Item*, Nov. 11, 1922, " Behrman Tells."
[22] *Infra*, chapter VIII.

every consideration. In 1912 during the first commission administration, Behrman and Commissioner Lafaye disagreed over paving contracts, and for a time it seemed there would be an open break. As Lafaye's policy developed, Behrman saw he was wrong and acknowledged his mistake. In the same administration he had a disagreement with Harold W. Newman, Commissioner of Public Safety, over policies in the police department, which resulted in the latter's resignation. In this case in addition to the difference concerning policy, Behrman believed Newman planned to run against him for mayor in 1916 and that he was using his office to build up his political influence. Because he considered himself the responsible head of the government, in general, he expected the other officials to defer to his judgment when no compromise seemed possible.

A. W. Newlin, a newspaper man and one of the shrewdest political observers in Louisiana, said of Behrman at the time of his death: " He developed with the situation." [23] He was referring among other things to Behrman's capacity to sense economic and social changes and to adapt the political methods of the Choctaw Club so as not to alienate powerful forces. Behrman very early in his career saw the advantage of securing the cooperation of business and in many ways tried to use the Club's power to achieve this end.[24] When the progressive movement appeared he sought to compromise the conflicting interests so as not to lose public support.[25] He aligned himself openly with the business and civic interests such as the Association of Commerce, Rotary, and other clubs, and continually consulted business and financial leaders on policies which affected their interests. His tendency to depend heavily on the advice of business leaders was prob-

[23] *New Orleans States*, Jan. 12, 1926.

[24] *Infra*, chapter VI.

[25] *Infra*, chapter VI.

ably due to the feeling of his lack of fundamental economic knowledge. He regarded business men as experts and was guided by their advice on business and labor legislation very much as he was guided in legal matters by lawyers. In many ways he was socially minded but too often supported private interests against the public welfare.[26] He regarded socialists as " thoroughly impractical people who did not realize you could not drive people to sudden change." [27] In his support of horse racing, toleration of gambling and prostitution and loose enforcement of Sunday laws, he was following the general feelings of his tolerant City. Although the political power of the Choctaw Club was continued and his personal leadership enhanced by the fact that he followed the dominant motifs of his day, in many ways New Orleans and the state suffered for lack of more enlightened policies and greater social vision.

A few examples will serve to illustrate Behrman's ability to anticipate and evaluate public sentiment and to take the necessary action to meet a given situation. When he became Mayor in 1904, the police force was under the domination of D. C. O'Malley, then publisher of the *New Orleans Item.* The public was disgusted with this unofficial control and one of Behrman's first acts was to break O'Malley's influence with the police. He effectively dramatized his victory by having O'Malley arrested.[28] When it became evident in 1912 that there was strong sentiment for efficiency and econ-

26 *Ibid.*

27 *New Orleans Item*, Nov. 21, 1922, " Behrman Tells." In this connection he pointed out how public ownership had grown and said in his youth, all public ownership was regarded as socialistic. " Socialists," he said, "are fighting human nature when they fight the capitalistic system. We all look forward to having money some day; hence the system will continue." Laborers, he argued, would not help support artists and painters. Here again his lack of education is evident.

28 *New Orleans Times Picayune*, May 2, 1925.

omy in City government, he saw to it that the first commission council was made up of business men.[29] In 1925 a spirit of progress and prosperity was abroad, he effectively translated it into a civic force by offering as his platform for election a vast program of public improvements.[30]

On several occasions he failed to anticipate public sentiment correctly. His position in the bitter school controversy in 1910, in the governor's race of 1912, and on the issue of a constitutional convention in 1915 are illustrative.[31] More notable was his failure to keep up with the course of public sentiment from 1916 to 1920. His vigorous fight to retain the restricted district of 1917 proved to be out of line with feelings developed during the War.[32]

He also failed to recognize the discontent developing in labor ranks in 1918 and 1919 and by opposing labor legislation lost much support.[33] His continued toleration of the more flagrant Machine abuses in connection with vice, elections, and economic interests were out of harmony with the spirit of the day. The people were for change and Behrman was offering none. His defeat in 1920 was certainly due in part to his failure to catch the trend of these years just as his victory in 1925 was fostered by the fact that he was correctly translating public sentiment into action.

Two newspaper comments on Mayor Behrman aptly summarize his qualities as a leader. The *New Orleans Times Picayune,* a fairly consistent opponent, wrote at the time of his election in 1925: "Of his purpose to govern well and lead wisely, we have no doubt. Of his sincere devotion to the well-being of his community there is no question. He

[29] *Infra,* chapter VIII.
[30] *Ibid.*
[31] *Infra,* chapter VII.
[32] *Infra,* chapter V.
[33] *Infra,* chapter VIII.

has great, if ill-balanced capacities and is above the average of his faction mates like peaks in a desert." [34]   The *New Orleans Item,* which had both opposed and supported him, said at the time of his death : " Beginning nowhere as politics goes, with only an inherent understanding of the motives of men for capital, a remarkable adaptability to conditions, coupled with unsparing attention to details and an indomitable perseverance made him at last, the most powerful single political leader in any of our Southern States and a figure of mark throughout the country. . . . In the end he enjoyed the good opinion even of those who fought him hardest." [35]

[34] May 4, 1924.
[35] January 12, 1926.

CHAPTER V

The Organization and Election Methods of the Choctaw Club

THE CHOCTAW CLUB

As indicated in a previous chapter, the Choctaw Club, when originally organized, was in fact the Democratic party in New Orleans and not merely a faction of that party. No division developed within the ranks of the party in the elections of 1900, the first in which the Choctaws participated. The elections of that year proved to be the last in which the Populists had candidates in the field. The constitution of 1898 and the subsequent election laws were completely undermining the voting strength of the Republican party. Bryan's campaigns for the Presidency had brought a union of Democrats and the Populists, which union had become permanent by 1904. The terms Democrat and voter had come to mean the same.

These forces, which enthroned the Democratic party, meant that such contests as were to occur in New Orleans and Louisiana politics would inevitably be between factions of the one dominant party. The lack of a division in the Democratic party of 1900 was due to the fact that the Republican and Populist parties again ran a fusion ticket and because the Democrats felt that intra-family quarrels must not be allowed to prevent the consummation of Negro disfranchisement. By 1904 the Negro vote had been reduced from over one hundred thousand to approximately five thousand. It was therefore natural, since the Negro voter was no longer a menace, that factions within the Democratic party should begin to appear. Such opposition as the Choctaws have had in New Orleans since the election of 1900

108

has been Democratic and the real contests have occurred in the primary election.[1]   Except on one occasion the opposing faction proved no match for the well organized professional politicians who guided the destinies of the Choctaw Club.[2]

The membership of the Choctaw Club from 1897 to 1926 was a good cross section of the citizenship of New Orleans. Men from all walks of life were represented—bankers, manufacturers, merchants, brokers, realtors, lawyers, doctors, carpenters, bricklayers, textile workers, gamblers, City and state employees, labor union members, and professional politicians. In number of members no particular economic class seemed dominant.   As the power and influence of the Organization grew, the more active adherents came to have a kind of a religious faith in the Organization.   Some undoubtedly observed more strictly the discipline of their chosen political Machine than that of their religion.   Power begets power, and a feeling grew up in New Orleans that the Choctaws were invincible.   This belief of course enhanced their power. Although the membership of the Organization was varied, control always rested with a few experienced politicians. These men garnered to themselves the political power of the City and then in turn "loaned or rented" this influence to any group powerful and articulate enough to command their attention.   The membership of the Club ranged from three to six thousand.   All City employees and officers were virtually obliged to belong.   Dues of one dollar per month were charged.   Club members had full access to the facilities of the club house owned and operated by the Organization. Members, not employees of the City, were often kept on the rolls even though they were behind with their dues; con-

[1] The Republicans have in some elections had candidates but their vote has been too small to influence the result.

[2] The one occasion on which the Choctaws failed to carry the City election for their candidates was in 1920. A full discussion of this election will be found in chapter VIII.

tinued support of the Club's political objectives in many cases was sufficient for those unable to pay the dues.   The governing powers of the Club were vested in seventeen directors who held their offices by virtue of being the leaders of the seventeen wards of the City.   These same men also constituted the official caucus of the Choctaw Club.

The headquarters of this famous political Organization are located at the corner of St. Charles Avenue and Lafayette Square in a quaint three-story building of the French architecture characteristic of New Orleans.   Large signs inform the most casual observer that here is " The Choctaw Club of Louisiana."   Inside of the building are well furnished offices, lounging, game and caucus rooms.   A few steps away, also facing Lafayette Square, is the City Hall, an ancient structure fronted with impressive Greek columns. At the top of the steps leading into the building the visitor is confronted with the sinister-looking muzzle of a small-bore naval gun, a world war memorial, the gift of a Republican Assistant Secretary of the Navy to his Democratically ruled city.   Between elections, both the Choctaw headquarters and the City Hall are quiet and uninteresting places to visit, with power seemingly located in the City Hall.   During elections, however, the situation is greatly changed.   The Club headquarters become the focal point of activity.   It is the center from which the campaign is directed.[3]   The City Hall no longer seems the residence of power; its only activities seem to be carrying out routine City functions and serving as a clearing house for political gossip.   Stenographers and clerks from City offices are busy day and night at the headquarters sending out campaign literature, telephoning and attending to numerous other tasks connected with a political campaign.   By day their time is paid for by the City and by night it is donated as a token of love to the

[3] Campaign headquarters are also maintained at one of the large hotels.

Organization to which they owe their daily bread. On a bulletin board is announced the schedule of ward and precinct meetings for the day. Loud speakers carry campaign speeches to the busy passersby and to the derelicts seeking rest on the cool green grass of Lafayette Square. Important as the campaign activity at the headquarters may seem it is not until the precinct and ward organizations of the Machine are studied that the real sources of its power and effectiveness is understood.

New Orleans is divided into seventeen wards and two hundred and sixty-two precincts. It should be recalled that since the aldermanic form of government was abandoned for commission government in 1912 no City officials have been elected by wards. Nevertheless the wards were legally the units for electing members to the State Central Committee of the party and to the general assembly. The old divisions on which party organization had been built were thus maintained. In 1924 wards had from nine to twenty-five precincts and the number of votes in a ward varied from three to ten thousand. The number of votes in a precinct ranged from one hundred and fifty to five hundred and fifty.

THE PRECINCT ORGANIZATION [4]

The precinct organization was the foundation on which the power of the Machine rested. As in any other city it

[4] The facts concerning the precinct and ward organization of the Choctaw Club were obtained by personal interviews with a number of men who had served or were serving as precinct or ward leaders. Because the precinct organization is the foundation of the Machine it will be discussed first, and will be followed by a description of the ward and city units. The hierarchy is thus treated in reverse order. Since there are a number of problems, such as patronage and the building up of majority control, which arise in each division, some duplication of discussion is inevitable in order to bring out the functions and work of each as its structure is presented. Attention is directed to the fact that the Choctaw Club is almost a complete duplication in its pattern of organization of machines of the north and east. See chapter IX for comparisons.

was the most important unit, its functioning spelled either success or failure at election time.   The ward leader selected the precinct leader whom he could dismiss at will.   He was selected because he had proved his worth as a political worker and because he controlled votes, the chief commodity in which the ward leader was interested.   As the agent of the ward boss all activities in the precinct centered around him. The ward boss demanded of his subordinates personal loyalty and a majority of the votes in the precinct at elections.   He was neither unduly curious nor critical about the means by which this end was achieved.   The precinct organizations were realistically built on patronage as were the ward organizations which ruled over them.   Each precinct leader held a small political job, usually with the City, but sometimes with the parish or state governments.   His salary was between $1,000 and $2,000 annually.   Because he held a political appointment he was able to devote a considerable part of his time to his duties as precinct leader.   His superiors, who were also Organization men, let him off from his official duties whenever necessary and it was a practice to excuse precinct captains regularly about the middle of the afternoon. During election campaigns all of their time was devoted to political activities.

The duties of a precinct leader in New Orleans were numerous and required the services of a man of energy and persistence.   His first task was to see that every prospective Machine voter in his precinct was registered and had paid his poll tax.   Each precinct leader furnished himself with a list of all prospective voters in his precinct and made a house to house canvass to assure himself that these legal requirements had been fulfilled.   His headquarters were located in a saloon, a drug store, an office, a fire house or other convenient place.   The leader made it his business to know every voter.   He learned the voter's profession, all about his family, his habits and interests, in fact any information about him that might be valuable in appealing for his support.   It was the job of the leader to make frequent rounds of his territory and to see that the proper City services were being furnished regularly to his people.   He arranged through his ward leader the contacts desired by his constituents at the City Hall.   He cut the red tape of government and mitigated the inconveniences of bureaucracy for those whose allegiance he sought to hold.   When new families moved into his precinct he immediately got in touch with them and rendered any assistance possible.   He was especially active among the foreign elements, helping them to adjust themselves to their new environment.   He was quick to report families needing charity to his ward leader, who would at once take the case up with the committee of the caucus in charge of the relief funds of the Organization.   The case would be investigated and if real need existed help would be extended.   The system of central control of charitable assistance was used to prevent precinct leaders from dispensing it too liberally and to minimize chances of intra-party graft.[5]

When one of his followers ran foul of the law, the precinct leader was always notified by family or friends of the person in trouble.   If the offense was not too serious the precinct leader ordinarily could obtain the person's release from jail through the intervention of his ward leader.   At least he could get the offender off with a small fine or a suspended sentence.   This was particularly true of cases of law violation within the jurisdiction of the police courts.   Precinct leaders were also active in getting jobs for those out of work.   These he secured through his ward leader.   The

[5] No evidence was found to indicate that public charity funds (i. e. from taxes) were taking the place of party funds; or that the Organization attempted to gain credit with the recipients of public funds by indicating it had influenced the City charity agency to grant the aid.   This is in contrast to conditions found in New York by some observers.

jobs for the most part were with the City, parish or state, but not infrequently the ward leader had influence with a public service company or other business and was able to secure work for Machine followers in private concerns. The precinct leader was continually doing small favors for small people and thus building up his following. He was the essential link between the average voter and the Choctaw Club. In most precincts there was a social club which was under the control of the leader. The clubs did not ordinarily have rooms but often gave entertainments in the ward club quarters.[6] In the more fashionable wards and precincts social clubs were more nominal than real. In such neighborhoods the traditional methods of ward politics were ineffective.[7]

Every precinct leader was fully aware of the paramount importance of the primary election. Since the general election amounted to a formal legal ratification of the decision reached at the Democratic primary, the whole strategy of party workers was designed to win this election. Not only was the possession of the government at stake but also control of the party machinery. Possession of party machinery is necessary to any city machine in any state but it was especially important to the New Orleans Machine because the mechanics of the election system used to disfranchise the Negro accentuated the control of the dominant faction within the Democratic party.[8] An analysis of how the precinct leaders in New Orleans built up and retained their majorities will go a long way toward explaining the continued control of the City by the Choctaws. Every precinct leader had a personal following of at least ten voters made up of his family, rela-

[6] Not all wards had club rooms. The facilities at the headquarters down town were available for social affairs.

[7] Practically every ward in New Orleans contained a large number of the poorer classes.

[8] See chapter III.

tives and close personal friends.   Since his faction controlled the Democratic committee, which conducted the primary, he was able to see that from three to five of the precinct election officials were of the Choctaw faction.[9]   These officials were paid by the City as a regular part of the election expense. Although nominally named by the candidate in the primary they were actually named by the faction supporting the candidate and hence the precinct leader controlled the choice in his district.   The leaders were all wise enough to select for these places men or women with several votes in the family. On an average, each person appointed could be counted on to deliver five votes.   About twenty votes were assured the precinct leader from this source.

The location of the polling place in most instances was worth five more votes.   Each office holder in the precinct, whether City, parish or state, was good for five votes.   The number of office holders in the precincts varied widely as patronage was not evenly distributed but averaged about ten to a precinct.   This meant fifty more assured votes for the Machine.   From the sources just mentioned the leader had available about eighty-five votes.   In addition he could count on the police and election day money to produce about twenty more.[10]   It may be seen that the Choctaw precinct leader had over one hundred votes of which he was absolutely certain before election day.[11]   In some of the larger pre-

---

[9] In a particularly hotly contested election the Organization sometimes named "dummy" candidates so as to have a chance to nominate more election officials. After such candidates had served their purpose in the process of choosing election officials the precinct leader would pass the word around that no one supporting the Machine was to vote for the dummy. For details of the method of choosing primary election officials, see chapter III, p. 84.

[10] For influence of police in securing votes, see *infra*, p. 131.

[11] This is higher than the estimate made for the country as a whole by Frank R. Kent. He estimated the average precinct leader controlled 65 votes through official prerogatives and patronage. Kent, *The Great*

cincts, the number of certain votes might go as high as one hundred and seventy-five.   In the average sized precinct of four hundred votes a leader controlled one hundred through his prerogatives and patronage.   To carry the precinct such a leader had to have two hundred and one votes.   The task then was to manage the campaign so as to get voluntarily one hundred and one more votes out of the three hundred remaining.   Compared to the task of the opposition, which ordinarily had no patronage on which to build up advance commitments, this was comparatively easy.[12]

Several precinct leaders told the writer that through a canvass of the voters in their precinct made a few days before the election, they could forecast the result within a few votes.[13]   Through the pre-election poll the leaders discovered any weakness in time to do additional work or secure enough election day money to turn the tide in their favor if it appeared to be going against them.   Whether the work of the precinct captain or the use of money could be made effective depended on the character of the voters, the strength of the opposing candidates and the particular conditions of a given campaign.   In a well-to-do part of the City there was little the leader could do if he found the opposition had won over a majority of the voters except to hope that enough

Game of Politics (New York, 1923).   The writer found that most precinct leaders in New Orleans averaged 100 controlled votes.   This may in part be explained by the one party system, the weakness of the opposing factions and by the fact that the Choctaws controlled City, parish and state patronage.   During Democratic administrations in Washington they also could count on federal patronage.

[12] When state patronage was in the hands of the opposition a more effective fight could be expected.   In 1920 Governor Parker organized an opposition faction to the "Regulars" and by the liberal use of state patronage succeeded in defeating them.   See chapter VIII.

[13] Robinson, *Straw Voting* (New York, 1934).   This writer cast doubt on the accuracy of pre-election canvasses made by political workers, p. 45.

of the opposition would fail to vote and thus enable him to win by default.

On election day the precinct leader had to spend the whole day at the polling place where he kept a careful check of each vote cast. The purpose of this check was to see that opposition voters were qualified and to prevent any chance of illegal voting by the other faction. It was also made to see that all those who had promised to vote for the Machine candidates actually came to the polls and cast their ballots. Machine supporters failing to vote by noon were called on by the leader's assistants; if they had not arrived by three o'clock, transportation was sent for them. The leader's task on election day was largely, therefore, to make sure that every supporter of the Organization voted. The precinct leader also had the disposition of election day money in his hands. He received whatever share of it the ward leader saw fit to give him and could use it in any way he thought wise. He was not required to make a report to the ward leader or to anyone else as to how he spent the money. No questions were ever asked if he carried his precinct, and seldom if he failed. A number of precinct leaders complained to the writer that the amount usually passed down to them from the top was small. Nearly all agreed that on occasions when they had failed to carry their precincts they could have succeeded if they had been given more money. Such funds as they had to use were spent on signs, transportation, assistants, drinks and other effective election day practices. The leader was careful to place his money where it would do most good. A member of a family with three or four votes in it was often employed as an assistant on election day or the family car was hired, thus assuring the leader of the vote not only of the worker but of the whole family. Bachelors and old maids were as greatly despised by precinct leaders in New Orleans as they are now disparaged (although for very different reasons) in Fascist Italy.

THE WARD ORGANIZATION

Ward leaders of the New Orleans Machine were its most powerful officials. Although nominally subject to the decisions of the caucus, they possessed almost absolute power in the administration of their wards. Until 1925 there was no boss at the head of the Choctaw Club to whom they owed unquestioned obedience and even had there been, sound political experience would have left the management of ward affairs wholly within their power. Before the passage of the primary law in 1906 ward leaders were selected at a primary election held by the Club. In order to become a ward leader a man must be elected president of the mother club [14] (the ward club) at a primary held for the purpose. If he were a successful ward leader he was seldom opposed and many held command for life and some were even strong enough to pass the office on to their sons. The ward leader was invariably a self-made politician and had shown his ability as a precinct leader or worker and perhaps later as a lieutenant of the ward leader. It was generally understood in a ward who was the second most influential politician and on the death or retirement of the leader the person so recognized was usually elected to the post. After the enactment of the primary law in 1906, ward leaders remained in power provided they ran and were elected to the Democratic State Central Committee. The election to ward leadership was thus transferred from the unregulated ward primary to a legalized state election. Technically of course the person elected to the state Committee was not running for ward leadership but party custom caused him to be so recognized. Also by virtue of Choctaw practice he became head of the mother club. If the leadership were being contested in an election, each candidate sought the support of the precinct

[14] Ward clubs were popularly called the mother club to distinguish them from precinct clubs.

workers.   Contests, however, were not numerous as the man who had proved his merit in political situations was generally unopposed.   After his selection he was introduced at the next meeting of the caucus as the leader from his ward. In theory the caucus had the right to accept or reject any leader selected by the ward but because he had demonstrated his ability to carry the ward in an election, rejection by the caucus never occurred.   If a ward seemed hopelessly divided and the selection of a man considered weak or unsuitable was likely to occur, Mayor Behrman, who was also head of the City Organization, and four or five of the more influential ward leaders would intervene and make a selection.[15] At the next meeting of the caucus he would be present and was invariably ratified by the group.

Almost without exception each ward leader held a City, parish or state position which often paid an annual salary of $3,000 or more.[16]   Before the change in the form of government ward leaders frequently sat in the City council as representatives of their wards.   In this capacity they were able to see that their bailiwicks were fairly treated in the matter of patronage.   After 1912, a number of leaders felt that concentration of patronage in the hands of the Mayor and Commission Council had enhanced unduly the power of ward leaders whom these officials chose to favor.

[15] Behrman and the chief leaders might make an outright appointment. On other occasions they might seek to assist a candidate they favored by helping him carry the ward at the election.

[16] The writer was informed that after 1912 more ward leaders received their appointments at the hands of the Mayor and commission council than before.   This enabled the City officials to have more control over them.   State and parish patronage was of course used for other purposes.   Occasionally a ward leader held no government job.   This was the case with Col. Bob Ewing, long the leader of the Tenth ward.   Although holding no public position himself Ewing undoubtedly held his ward leadership almost wholly by the use of patronage.   At one time he is said to have controlled about one-fourth of all City jobs.

Ward leaders were potent because they had under them from nine to twenty-five precinct organizations and because once established they were able to build up a strong following through favors and patronage. There was a wide variation, however, in the influence and power of the ward leaders. Behrman explains the greater power of some on the basis of personal traits, hard work, uneven distribution of patronage, and luck.[17] At different times, from 1900 to 1926, from four to ten outstanding ward leaders were the real masters of the New Orleans Machine. The others had little influence because their hold on their own wards was not great. This loose coalition of ward leaders, varying in number from time to time, collaborated on the basis of their realization of the necessity for union and solidarity and kept the Machine running effectively for many years. Martin Behrman was always a member of this powerful group. His personal qualities and the fact that he was mayor, made him the most influential, and he was recognized as the Organization's official head and spokesman.[18] As time went on he was deferred to more and more by the others.

The ward leader was a field commander and as such was considered responsible for all activities in his ward. As previously indicated he had authority to organize it and to select his precinct leaders and other assistants as he saw fit. Moreover, all the patronage dispersed in his ward must have his approval. He had the controlling influence in nominating candidates for party committees and for the state legis-

[17] *New Orleans Item*, Nov. 16, 1922.

[18] He was elected leader by the caucus after he became mayor in 1904. After that time his leadership was simply continued without further formal action of the caucus. Behrman established the custom of the mayor being named leader of the club. It has been continued since his death in 1926. However, later mayors have not possessed the power Behrman won for himself.

lature from his ward.[19]   As a member of the caucus his
statement often determined whether a candidate living in
his ward would receive the endorsement of the Choctaw Club
for the office he sought.   It was his duty to assist his precinct
leaders whenever they needed his influence with more important government officials.[20]   Before the elections ward
leaders always checked carefully the pre-election work in the
precinct to see that it had been well done.[21]   The ward leader
handled for his subordinates all major registration and poll
tax difficulties with the parish offices.   On the night before
the election he gave each of his precinct leaders whatever
election day expense money he thought they needed or that
he could spare from the amount which he had for use in his
ward.   He made no accounting for the money he received
from headquarters.   On election day the leaders were active
throughout their wards, helping the precinct leaders wherever
needed.

The ward leader's ability to deliver a majority vote for
the Organization candidates at elections of course rested on
the total strength of his precincts.   The average ward in
New Orleans in 1924 contained sixteen precincts with a
total of around 6500 votes.   In the discussion of the precinct
organization it was indicated that the typical precinct leader

---

[19] Each ward in New Orleans had at least one representative. The
larger wards had two or three. There were nine senatorial districts in
the City made up of from one to three wards. Nominees for the state
senate were chosen by a caucus of the ward leaders concerned and submitted to the City caucus for final approval.

[20] The ward boss might assist, for example, in getting the assessment
of one of the precinct leaders' followers " adjusted."

[21] One noted politician informed the writer that a successful ward
leader should live in the rear (the part furthest from down town) of his
ward so that he would have to come through it every day on his way to
town and thus keep in closer touch with what the people were thinking
and what his precinct leaders were doing.

controlled approximately one hundred votes.[22] The ward
leader therefore could count as fairly certain 1,600 of the
3,251 votes necessary to carry his ward. The task then was
to secure an additional 1,651 votes. Since in any election
the uncontrolled vote could usually be counted on to divide
almost equally between opposing candidates, the leader was
ordinarily successful. By extending this calculation to a
City-wide basis it may be seen that in the seventeen wards
the Machine controlled about 27,000 votes. There were a
hundred thousand votes in the City in 1924. The strategy
of the Machine in the City campaign was therefore to divide
the 73,000 uncommitted votes and rule.

A social club was maintained by many of the wards.[23]
The ward leader controlled this organization just as he did
the other political machinery of the ward. A number of
wards had their own club rooms with recreational features.
An appeal was made to the young people through athletic
programs, dances, and other social affairs. Dues were small
but people unable to pay were also welcome.

THE CITY CAUCUS—PECULIAR PLACE OF BEHRMAN

The City caucus of the Choctaw Club was made up of
the seventeen ward leaders. Martin Behrman, the leader
of the fifteenth ward, after his election as mayor in 1904,
was the spokesman of the Organization and was gradually
being recognized as its real head by governors, business men,
newspapers, and the public generally.[24] As late as 1912

[22] *Supra*, p. 116.

[23] Ward leaders with whom the writer discussed ward clubs did not
regard them as very important politically. Some felt the recreational
features helped. Only about half the wards had permanent club rooms.
Lack of money for quarters was given as the reason for their failure to
be more active.

[24] Behrman remained as leader until after his defeat in 1920. In 1921
he was replaced but again assumed the leadership with his reelection as
mayor in 1925.

although Behrman was more influential than before, he still shared the stage with Fitzpatrick, Ewing, Mauberret and a few of the other more powerful leaders. Behrman's dual capacity as ward leader and mayor undoubtedly had its influence in making him the real as well as the titular head of the Choctaws. He was no backroom boss and desired responsibility as well as power. This, no doubt, had its effect on those who dealt with the Machine. Their contact seemed more real since it was with not only the spokesman of the caucus but also the head of the City government. Such an arrangement seemed to carry double assurance of power. This, together with Behrman's personal charm and effectiveness in dealing with people, went a long way toward creating conditions favorable to the continuance of Choctaw power.

One of the chief tasks of the caucus was to select and endorse a complete ticket of candidates for every City, parish and state election. Ordinarily a preliminary slate was drawn up by Behrman and the chief ward leaders and then submitted to the entire membership of the caucus for final consideration. In choosing the candidates for minor places the caucus in most instances respected the wishes of the ward leader in whose territory the candidate voted. The selection of candidates on whom the entire City voted, however, was not so much influenced by the opinion of one ward leader. The caucus also decided which of the several candidates for governor, congress and other state and national offices the Choctaws would support.[25] In some cases men became candidates for these offices only after they were assured of the support of this powerful Organization. The caucus selected men for some of the major appointive offices which were considered of too great importance to leave to a ward leader.[26] As in the case of nominations, such appointments

[25] For discussion of considerations affecting these choices, see chapter VII.

[26] Patronage is discussed in detail in chapter VII.

were decided by Berhman and a few leaders and submitted to the caucus for ratification.

Majority vote controlled in all caucus decisions.   It was a standing custom that any ward leader remaining in the caucus was bound by its decisions.   Disputes between ward leaders, if not settled by Behrman, were settled by vote of the caucus.   Its decision was final.   Only in a few instances did a ward leader break with Behrman and the majority of the caucus.   Such action meant he was cut off from patronage, and would immediately be faced with the transfer of the allegiance of his precinct leaders to another leader selected and recognized by the caucus.   Except to the most daring the prospect of such an ordeal was enough to hold them in line.[27]   The caucus had authority to expel a member who was known to have gone over to the opposition or who refused to be bound by a decision of the caucus.   In the latter case a motion would be made to expel all those who refused to indicate that they would accept whatever decision the caucus made.   This was simply a move to bring into the open leaders suspected of disloyalty when bitter factional fights were in progress or impending.   Negotiations between the Choctaws and other factions were carried on by a committee of the caucus.   Sometimes these committees were given full powers and at other times they were required to bring the results of their conference back to the caucus for consideration.   The appointment of a committee of this type was used when a matter such as an alliance with another faction was in prospect or when the bitterness of the election

[27] Col. Ewing broke with the Machine in 1912 and 1920.   He believed the opposing faction in 1912 would win but his judgment proved wrong and after a time he returned to the Organization.   In 1920 he again broke and this time supported the Parker faction.   John Sullivan deserted in 1920 and Henry Maloney in 1925.

indicated that a neutral arbitration committee was necessary to insure peace at the polls.[28]

The position of the Orleans delegation in the legislature on major legislation was determined by the caucus. As was the case with nominations and major appointments, a few leaders made the decisions and the caucus ratified. In reaching decisions on legislative policy, the leaders were advised by the floor leader of the delegation and the more prominent legislators.[29]

Since the members of the City caucus were also members of the Democratic State Central Committee it was a practice to act as a unit on important political questions coming before the committee. If some matter arose unexpectedly in one of the meetings and no decision had been previously agreed on by the Orleans group they would either follow Behrman's lead or secure a temporary adjournment for the purpose of holding a conference.

The centralization and coordination of power in the caucus made the Machine's rule of the City more effective. It also enabled it to deliver the great political influence of the City with more telling effect in state governmental and political affairs.

That leadership of the precinct, the ward and the City Organization required a tremendous amount of work and nervous energy is brought out by Martin Behrman's state-

[28] On several occasions the Choctaws and the opposing factions agreed to make a committee of neutral citizens final arbitrators in election disputes when violence was threatened by either side. Such committees were of course extra-legal but their decisions were respected. The committee posted representatives at each polling place who made preliminary decisions in any disputes that might arise at the poll. If the representatives of the factions at the polls would not accept the decision, the dispute in question was carried at once to the central committee. Its decisions under the peace agreement were final.

[29] A full discussion of the state legislative practices of the Orleans delegation will be found in chapter VII.

ment: " If you want to be a precinct captain you have to work. If you want to be a ward leader you have to work much more. If you want to be a real political chief you must be on the job day and night. If you want to be mayor and at the same time leader of a big city organization and stay in office sixteen years, you have to do so much work that by the time you are fifty-eight years old, which I am now, the doctors will be telling you what you cannot eat and to avoid all strenuous excitement. That's what they are telling me now." [30] This was said two years after his only defeat and four years before his death. He was in the process of rebuilding the Choctaw Machine and at the same time acting as vice-president of a bank. Knowing, as he did, the tremendous strain of the dual capacity of boss and mayor, he was nevertheless making preparations to win the two places again. Politics was his whole life and his love of power and his zest for the game were not dimmed by his failing health. Behrman set a pace in the Organization which none of the leaders could equal but which had the effect of furnishing an excellent example for those ambitions to gain more power. Every precinct leader knew that the man at the top worked harder than anyone else in the Organization.

In 1920 after the adoption of the Nineteenth Amendment to the Federal Constitution the Choctaws duplicated completely their precinct and ward organization among the women. A City-wide caucus of the women ward leaders was also created. The organizations of the men and women worked in harmony though the two caucuses never met together. It was the practice of the women's caucus to endorse the candidates previously selected by the men's organization. In all matters of policy the action of the men was followed. Up to 1926 the influence of the women in

[30] *New Orleans Item*, Jan. 25, 1923, " Behrman Tells."

the matter of patronage was small. The men remained the referees, such patronage as the women secured being obtained through their influence with the City leader. The interest and influence of the women in New Orleans politics was on the increase at the time of Behrman's death. The Machine may find it necessary to yield them a larger share of power and make their participation in politics more real. So far their rewards have been limited to minor appointments.[31]

CAMPAIGN AND ELECTION METHODS

In a sense the Choctaw Club conducted its election campaigns the year round. Its effort to hold the allegiance of the voters never ceased. The activity of the precinct and ward organizations, although more intense at election time, was continuous. It may be accurately said that the Choctaw Club depended more on its daily work to win elections than on the short period covering the intensive campaign. Mayor Behrman believed, and rightly so, that elections were won more by what had happened before they occurred than by the noise and panoply of a short campaign. It was the precinct and ward organization based on patronage and control of the election machinery that elected Choctaw candidates. They knew that no amount of work during a campaign could match these forces. Campaigns, however, there must

[31] Only one woman candidate was given endorsement for office by the Choctaws during Behrman's time as leader and it was done in this instance to secure the support of a New Orleans newspaper for the Choctaws in the City election of 1925. The wife of one of the publishers wished to run for Congress. Behrman had the political Organization and her husband had a newspaper, the support of which Behrman needed. They, therefore, agreed to exchange favors. There was no indication that the participation of women in politics improved either the character of political methods or the quality of those holding public office. The answer of the women to this might be that it was due to the fact that they had so little voice in naming the nominees. Precinct leaders, however, informed the writer that women voted, for the most part, like their Choctaw men folks.

be and to balance activity of this sort on the part of the opposition, the Choctaws matched election rally with election rally throughout the City.   Their spell-binders sought to praise their own and denounce the opposition candidates with even more exaggeration than was forthcoming from orators on the other side.   On the closing night of a campaign the two factions held simultaneous rallies a few blocks apart on Canal Street, each striving to draw the largest crowd and surpass the other in showmanship.   As far as the Choctaws were concerned such efforts for the most part were regarded as stage play.   Frequently before their speakers arose at the last colossal night rally to boast of the record of their faction in the City Hall and to warn against putting any trust in the opposition, the leaders already knew, through the pre-election canvass, within a few thousand votes of what the result would be.

The Choctaws adopted every conceivable means of influencing the voter.   They sought newspaper support and on most occasions had at least one paper with them.[32]   The newspapers in New Orleans were extremely partisan.   Their owners and managers were for the most part active in politics and the papers changed front wherever it seemed wise financially, politically or personally to the owners.[33]   Partisanship was not confined to the editorial page and often the best editorials on the campaign were to be found in the news columns.   In addition to newspaper publicity the Choctaws used circulars, posters and moving pictures.   In his race in 1925 Behrman also used the radio.[34]

[32] There were two morning and two evening papers.   The morning papers were "The Times Picayune" and "The Tribune."   The evening papers were "The States" and "The Item."   "The States" was owned by Col. Ewing.

[33] For general comment on southern press see *Culture in the South*, Allen, "Journalism in the South" (Chapel Hill, 1934), p. 126.

[34] This simply illustrates Behrman's willingness to adopt new methods. The radio in 1925 was not regarded as being at all important in New

The campaigns were extremely personal since they were factional contests and represented no conflicting party principles. The opposition ordinarily chose the issues and the Machine defended its acts and boasted of its record of accomplishments. Martin Behrman and "bossism" were always the basic issues in any campaign. The stock cry of an opposing faction was, "Down with the bosses". With this as the invariable chorus they would point to mal-administration, failure to pave all the streets or alleged connection of the Machine with the "interests" and the underworld. The Machine would answer with evidence of its solid accomplishments in public improvements and the progress of the City under its rule. Denial would be made of any questionable relationships. Proof of the existence of wide-open vice conditions in the City seemed to have little effect on the fortunes of the Machine. Tolerance in this respect was desired by many, and the controlling business interests could not well break the working arrangement between vice and government without endangering their own close relationship. The attitude was prevalent that in a big city, machine rule was necessary, and if one faction did not control another would. The general feeling was that the Choctaws did a fairly good job and that the interests most vitally affected by politics could count on " fair " treatment by the leaders.

The Machine was accused of many irregular practices in elections. The accusers claimed more serious and widespread evils than were actually practiced. To say that the Organization as a whole, by concerted effort, stole elections by the use of stuffed ballot boxes, crooked counts, false registrations, floaters, and police coercion is far from true. Such practices were much more common during the days of

Orleans politics. In contrast with this many observers regarded Senator Long's use of the radio in the Congressional elections of 1934 as the decisive factor.

reconstruction and in the bitter struggles of the Nineties than under Choctaw rule. Their Organization was so effective that such practices were not necessary to insure control. Furthermore, the wiser leaders, among them Martin Behrman, knew that those who stole for them might also be induced to steal from them and hence, though tolerant, they did not encourage irregular practices. That election evils did exist in the precincts and wards, however, is not denied. Even the most loyal Choctaw admitted that no election was entirely free from some of the unfair practices claimed.

Because the Organization controlled both the City and parish and had so much influence in the state government the temptation to indulge in questionable methods was great, since there was little chance of being exposed. Poll tax receipt books were sometimes taken out of the parish office and given to precinct workers who then went around and collected for the tax and issued receipts.[35] There was some evidence that on occasions the registration rolls were padded. Registration under fictitious names would be effected by a person unknown to the registrar or if the registrar happened to be " partially blind " the ward leader might himself fill out the registration form for the phantom person. On election day " floaters " would be used to cast the vote represented by the false names. Since the voter might be called on to show his tax receipts and registration certificates, these were furnished him before he went to the poll. Although it was against the law to pay another person's poll tax the law was generally violated up to 1913. Behrman recalls that Governor Sanders paid the poll taxes of many of his supporters and that it was the practice of many business concerns to pay those of their employees.[36] With the enactment

[35] The precinct worker sometimes kept the money collected for poll taxes. The Organization would then have to pay for the poll tax receipts issued.

[36] *New Orleans Item*, Nov. 8, 1922, " Behrman Tells."

of the Corrupt Practices Act in 1912, which carried heavy penalties, open violations ceased. Whenever there was an opposition faction in the field, false counts and stuffing ballot boxes were almost impossible because such faction was represented at every polling place. When there was no opposition the practice was unnecessary. There seemed to be no evidence and few accusations of these latter practices in recent years. The more subtle and refined practice of padding registration rolls and voting " floaters " had taken the place of the cruder methods. Even this practice had greatly declined although accusations alleging them were made in the elections of 1920 and 1925.[37]

The New Orleans police have been active at election time for many years. Some of their activities have been legitimate and natural; while others have been open to question. The strongest evidence that they had been unduly influential for the Choctaws and against the opposing factions was that in every bitterly contested election an effort was made to prevent their use in policing the polls. In 1912 when the Good Government League faction seemed to have a chance to win, its leaders sought to have a citizen committee representing both factions to keep order at polling places instead of the police.[38] The charge was made that the police were in the habit of intimidating opposition voters and that they frequently arrested and held for the day precinct workers of those opposed to the Choctaws. Again in 1920 the same charges were made but the City government refused to allow the substitution on the grounds that the charges were false and that the state election laws required that the City police keep order. So bitter was the feeling in 1912 concerning the alleged activities of the police that the Good Govern-

[37] In the elections held in 1934 there was strong evidence brought out that the practice had been revived again.

[38] *New Orleans Times Picayune*, Aug. 29, 1912.

ment League held in readiness an armed squad of volunteers
to rush to polling places should trouble with the police
develop. The squad answered one call in the third ward
during the day but no major difficulties were reported.

Another criticism levelled against the Choctaw controlled
police was that before election they called on all the small
business men and " urged " that they vote " right ". It was
charged that in effect the police could make it very unpleasant
if the person visited failed to take the hint. Although these
practices by the police were officially denied by the mayor
and the Organization there seems to be no doubt that there
was some truth in the charges.[39]

The official attitude toward these evils was what would be
expected from realistic politicians schooled in ward politics.
The caucus had nothing to do with them. It denied their
existence. The mayor would have preferred that such
things did not happen.[40] He did not approve them but for
the most part he ignored them. When charges were made
he urged court action; he always expressed a willingness to
see the guilty punished. These were sins of ward and precinct politics and the leader of the Choctaws and mayor of
the City took no part in them. He knew there were some
over-zealous ward leaders who erred at election time but
the rules of the game were that what happened in the ward
was of little concern to those at the top provided the leader
delivered his ward on election day. No official effort was
made to prevent prosecution when the charges were indi-

[39] Specific instances were related to the writer by small store-keepers.

[40] An amusing story is related about Behrman which involved election
practices. At an election in the early days the returns in an uncontested
election showed that there had been a hundred more votes reported in the
count than there were registered voters in the ward. Behrman is reported to have called the leader in and chided him about such tactics in an
uncontested election. The leader's explanation was he had received no
orders not to stuff the boxes, so he had acted as usual.

vidual and specific but owing to the difficulty of proving charges in court and the fact that all officials concerned in election cases were friendly to the Organization, prosecution was seldom instituted. Election irregularities were confined to the Democratic primary since there was never a contest at the general election except perhaps when a controversial constitutional amendment was up for consideration by the voters.

CAMPAIGN FUNDS

Campaign funds came from various sources. In order to get the Choctaw Club nomination for an elective office a candidate was required to pledge ten per cent of the salary he would receive from the office sought in case of election. If the candidate was a man of means a higher " contribution " might be suggested. Every office holder was solicited, by the head of his department, for a contribution. It is needless to say that the method was effective. Dues for membership in the Choctaw Club were used so far as not needed for routine expenses of the Club. Probably the greatest source of campaign money were the business interests. Before 1915 corporations were allowed to contribute directly but after that date no corporation was permitted to make a donation by any method. Reports filed in the Clerk of the Court's office, as required by the Corrupt Practices Act of 1912, are general in character and do not reveal any unusual facts concerning the source of the money or the character of the expenses. These statements neither substantiate nor refute the charges that the Machine had on occasions received money for campaign purposes on which the letter of the law frowned.[41]

In considering the use of money in campaigns it was necessary to turn to sources for information which permit of no documentary proof.

41 Statements made by opponents of the Choctaws are of like character.

The investigator must sift and weigh as best he can information obtained from personal interviews, campaign charges, newspapers, and general observations which appear to show that money was used in New Orleans elections which came from unreported sources and was used for unexplained purposes. The " big stick " was not used on business men and corporation heads to force contributions. Mayor Behrman was far too diplomatic for such a practice. Several months before the campaign he would have the person from whom a large contribution was expected to lunch and after an oyster poullette, shrimp arnaud or other French delicacy the subject of campaign funds would be raised. While the guest was enjoying one of the mayor's mellow cigars and sipping cointreau or absinthe, the chief of the Choctaw Club would suggest a contribution. Usually the personal charm of the mayor, the incomparable lunch, the wine, the cigar, together with the memory of past favors on the part of the Choctaws produced the desired result and the contribution was promised. No political promises were made and none were asked on such occasions. The relationship of business and the Machine had grown so close that agreements were unnecessary. Had not the Choctaws always had the " interests " of New Orleans at heart? After all was business not as much a part of the Machine as Behrman? The answer to these questions was always in the affirmative. Small business was solicited by leaders who seemed to be best fitted to approach particular people. It is not to be inferred from this statement that building up a " war chest " was always easy. New Orleans business men paid only what seemed necessary and in adverse years the Organization often had difficulty in raising what it felt was needed.

Another source of campaign money was from the vice elements in the City, such as gambling, prostitution, racing and liquor.[42] The two latter, during most of the period under discussion, were legal and perhaps should not be classed in the category of vice. When gambling, prostitution and saloons were legal these interests might legitimately be expected to contribute to campaigns. When laws at various times outlawed some of these activities they continued operation by virtue of the tolerance of the City Hall. It is, therefore, not unnatural that such privileges were paid for. There is no evidence of any relation between Mayor Behrman and vice elements. Such money as passed in consideration for tolerance was handled through ward leaders and other workers without his official knowledge. Here was a practical situation dealt with in a practical way. In general the same motives moved these interests to contribute that moved others. They too sought political favors. Unused, except when necessary, were the powerful weapons of assessment, influence of Baton Rouge, and control of the City government. The mere knowledge that the Machine could help or punish almost any interest with one or more of these powers must have exercised a strong if silent persuasion.

Money received from sources approved by law was accounted for and used to defray ordinary campaign expenses. As previously indicated there was in most campaigns some money available to the ward leaders for election day " expenses ". The source of this money remained unrevealed as did its uses. The money received and the purposes for which it was used appeared to be about the same with the factions opposing the Choctaws. The chief difference was that because of the power it possessed the Choctaw Club ordinarily had more sources on which to draw.

In summarizing the influence and work of the Choctaw Club, it is well to remember that political organization is undoubtedly as inevitable as it is indispensable in a democ-

---

[42] A discussion of the relation of the Machine and vice is given in the next chapter.

racy. It is particularly essential and is necessarily more elaborate in a metropolitan city such as New Orleans. Much voluntary work is needed for the functioning of the democratic process. The government must depend on party organization to nominate and select many of its officials. No adequate substitute as yet has been found for many of the functions that the party organization performs. The Choctaw Club, when first organized, had a clear field and performed these voluntary and essential political services. In return it expected and obtained the right to dispense the spoils. By the time factional opposition arose to question its power the Club was firmly entrenched. The Choctaws had developed all the essentials necessary to gain and hold political powers. They gradually attained the reputation of being winners and drew to their support the " high siders " who always wanted to be on the " band wagon ". There were many reasons for their continued success. Some small business men may have voted the " Regular " ticket because of fear of punishment. Big business supported the Machine because it was friendly and seemed " safer " for business than the reformers.[43] Mayor Behrman was popular with all classes. He was a hard worker and astutely looked after the interests of the City in Baton Rouge. There was newspaper opposition but this only seemed to confirm the already general belief in the Machine's power, and more people, as a result, went to it for favors. For the higher positions, good public servants were often selected or appointed. True, the Machine sometimes delayed picking its ticket until the opposition was announced and if it were formidable, the leaders chose stronger men than they might otherwise have selected. In 1912 when the issues were economy and efficiency, the Machine drafted business men for the first commission council. Behrman was thoroughly alert to the fact that

[43] A full discussion of the relation of the Machine and business will be found in the next chapter.

there was a growing demand for adequate, effectual City government and he sought to produce this result, subject, of course, to the inherent limitations of the spoils system.   The fact that Behrman was mayor as well as the leader tended to produce a feeling of responsibility on the part of the Choctaw Club for the welfare of the City government that an organization whose rulers hold no office probably could not have had.   He was faced daily with the responsibility of the highest public official and this brought home to Boss Behrman, Ward Leader Behrman and Legislative Lobbyist Behrman that good city government was almost as useful in perpetuating the Machine as was ward and precinct politics. When the interests of efficiency and politics conflicted Behrman sought a compromise but since he was not absolute boss and what he did was not always of his own making, efficiency was frequently sacrificed to political expediency. Organization was the keynote of Boss Behrman's political technique and he well knew that patronage was the foundation on which the Choctaw Club was founded.

In hotly contested primaries the proportion of votes actually cast to the number of people legally qualified to vote was high.   Often not more than 10,000 of those registered failed to vote.   Choctaw majorities usually exceeded this number and hence election results would not have been changed in the event that all had voted.   Had all persons of voting age, exclusive of Negroes, participated and voted against the Organization it would have lost some elections that it won.   It is fair to assume, however, in both of the cases mentioned above that those who did not vote would have been subject more or less to the same influences as those who did vote and would have divided their vote among the factions.   If this assumption be correct the Machine in New Orleans would still have ruled very much as it did.[44]

[44] The above analysis is based on reports of election returns and registrations for 1904, 1908, 1912, 1916 and 1920 and the appropriate census reports.

CHAPTER VI

RELATIONS WITH BUSINESS—LEGITIMATE AND ILLEGITIMATE

In the first chapter attention was directed to the chief economic forces present in New Orleans and Louisiana. The relationship between these interests and the politics of the City was close, even crucial. The long period of uninterrupted power which the Choctaws experienced from 1900 to 1920 was one of constant economic expansion and growth. With exception of the panic of 1907 there was little to interrupt progress. The return of the Choctaws to power in 1925 was also in an era of prosperity. Through these years a friendly business community furnished campaign funds for the Machine and in gratitude the favor was returned in the form of political privileges. This was an epoch in which the pronouncements of the business man and the Chamber of Commerce were considered to contain the wisdom of the ages. Their declarations regarding what would help or hinder the economic, industrial and commercial advancement of New Orleans was not subjected to any critical analysis, least of all by Choctaw politicians. Were not they business men who made these statements, and should they not know? If the factories and the commercial associations opposed the workman's compensation law, did not that mean it was a bad law which should be defeated by the Choctaws in the legislature? If the utilities, the banks and the investment houses said a proposed bill regulating utilities would destroy the value of securities surely it must be true. Were not these people experts in stocks and finance—certainly they would not misinform the Machine. Business and industry in New

Orleans, as elsewhere, in addition to its rights, sought privilege, special favors, and protection against taxation and regulation. Any political organization which could furnish these services in so far as the City government was concerned and which could deliver the influence of the City delegation in the state legislature automatically became the choice of the business interests.

The relationship between business and the Machine was, in fact, extremely close. Mayor Behrman made a practice of calling in individual business men and groups for advice. He boasted that when commercial interests were under consideration he called on business men; when legal matters arose he called in lawyers; when politics was the order of the day he consulted politicians. He was for anything that would advance New Orleans industrially or commercially and usually opposed anything that would hinder progress in these lines. The fundamental point, however, was that his decisions and those of the Machine were based on what the business interests said was good or bad. New Orleans business men, as elsewhere, had difficulty in seeing the difference between their personal profits and the general welfare of the City. Thus, what the banks, textile mills, light and gas companies, shipping interests, exchanges, and factories said was good, so far as the Machine was concerned, was good. Behrman was a booster of everything that the economic philosophy of his day taught him would foster " progress ". He believed in " giving business its head " except where political strategy absolutely dictated the opposite. He fully realized that political power followed economic power and he handled the political Machine in New Orleans so as to tie the major economic groups to it. Although distrusted in his first administration by business he soon proved that it had nothing to fear from the Machine and that by cooperation it had much to gain.

In discussing the relationship between economic interests and the Machine, it is well to note at the outset that no documentary evidence can be cited. The writer interviewed men representing a cross section of New Orleans citizenship to determine, as far as such a method could, the connection between business and the Choctaws. With practically no exception all those interviewed agreed that there was, no doubt, a general understanding and spirit of cooperation. Some were hesitant to admit that there was any more than a casual, necessary and legitimate connection. Some few denied that business had anything to do with politics but when asked concerning specific occurrences gave assurance that no ulterior motive was involved. For the most part, however, politicians and business men in New Orleans were very realistic concerning the matter and discussed it with frankness. To them these mutually beneficial relationships were normal, necessary and in the interest of the City. It is not to be implied that many of them were not perfectly normal and legitimate, but it is believed that in some cases the relationship was something less than beneficial to the average citizen whose vote the Choctaws controlled.

One prominent politician stated that there was no " understanding " between business and government but that they " got along." An outstanding business man who had also been close to politics said the Machine let the business interests control its position on matters coming before the state legislature. A former floor leader of the Orleans delegation stated the matter very delicately by saying that the Organization was interested in the commercial growth of the City and that it " just agreed to do nothing that would hurt business and that business was to be the judge." He added that there was a practical arrangement but no definite agreement. A high state official, formerly active in the Choctaw Club, said business knew if it put its proposal up to Behrman and the Machine, and if it was within reason politically, it could count on support. This idea was also expressed by several others. A prominent attorney, long identified with City and state politics, made the statement that the Machine was " hand in glove with business on everything and that was the reason the Choctaws stayed in power so long and were almost invincible at elections."

These statements were made freely by men who for the most part are still active in New Orleans political and business life. The circumstances under which they talked prevent the use of their names. But these very conditions seem to make their opinions even more impressive. The fact that some hesitated to bring out the full implications involved seems to this observer to give weight to their statements.

With this background given by persons who were actually participants in the politico-business relationship it now remains to point out a number of specific illustrations which tend to substantiate these general remarks. To understand how the City Machine could have so much influence with business and commercial interests it must be kept constantly in mind that the Orleans delegation was large, well organized, and completely controlled by the Choctaw Club. Its trading leverage at Baton Rouge made it valuable.

The bosses of the Machine and their clients were in an enviable position in state politics, lawmaking and administration because New Orleans was the one great City of the state and possessed over one-fourth of the votes which could be delivered in a block. If the country vote on a given issue was divided, and it frequently was because of the varying economic interests, the Choctaws did not find it difficult to prevent action in the legislature or constitutional conventions. Positive action, although more difficult, was not uncommon. With twenty-five votes in the house and nine in the senate to offer to the governor or to the country interests in exchange for what was wanted in New Orleans, the City Machine had at hand powerful incentives for an exchange of "courtesies." Since the governor in Louisiana was picked by the country with the consent of New Orleans, and since he often needed the City vote to carry out his legislative program, the political mechanics of the Machine's power become ever clearer.

The Orleans delegation frequently voted against bills which were at the same time being opposed by powerful business forces from New Orleans. In 1912, during the administration of Governor Hall, an employers' liability law was passed without the support of the Machine. Mr. Generelly, who had long been floor leader of the Choctaw Delegation at Baton Rouge, stated that it had cooperated for years with the employers to defeat this measure.[1] The protracted obstruction of this measure, of course, cannot be wholly attributed to the New Orleans Organization. Louisiana was largely an agricultural state and labor was only slightly organized. These two facts were at least as important as the pressure brought by employers. Here at any rate was a clear instance in which the Machine lent its influence to business interests against the welfare of a great mass of the people of the City.

Two considerations seemed to count heavily with the Choctaw Club in determining the attitude toward utilities. One was that it usually followed the course urged by the business interests whenever regulation was under consideration and the second was that it opposed any plan calculated to take the New Orleans utilities from under the control of

---

[1] An examination of the House roll calls for the sessions of 1906, 1908 and 1910 on a proposed bill confirms this statement. *House Journal,* 1906, p. 240; *House Journal,* 1908 and 1910, pp. 121 and 374 respectively. See *New Orleans Times Picayune,* Sept. 8, 1912. Mr. Generelly had broken with the Machine in August, 1912, but having been floor leader he was familiar with its previous position.

the City government.   In the session of 1912 a law was
proposed to establish a public utility commission to regulate
street railways, light, gas and water companies throughout
the state.   It was defeated with the aid of every member
except one of the Orleans delegation.[2]   A powerful lobby,
representing the New Orleans Public Service Company, the
leading banks of the City, and other financial interests, was
active against the bill.   The claim was made that it would
deflate the value of the public utility securities.   The two
largest banks (The Hibernia and The Canal) organized the
country banks against the measure and these in turn brought
pressure on their senators and representatives.   In a hearing
on the bill it was brought out from the testimony of the
country bankers that they were opposing it only because
they had been asked to do so by the big banks in New
Orleans.[3]

The proposal was undoubtedly defeated by influences from
the City.   The Choctaws stated they were against the bill
because it would have transferred the regulation of New
Orleans utilities from the City council to a state commission.
Even if it be conceded that this was the major reason for
their stand it may be assumed that the solid opposition of
finance in the City also had its weight.   Another case where
the Machine could plead its desire to retain its powers over
the utilities in the name of home rule occurred when a bill
providing for the segregating of property for state and local
taxation was being considered.   The proposal was made to
assign the public utility properties in New Orleans for exclusive taxation by the state government.   This the New
Orleans delegation refused to permit and in order to get the
bill passed, it was necessary to allocate the utilities to the

[2] *New Orleans Times Picayune*, July 3, 1912.   The member voting for
the proposed law was a member of the Citizens League.

[3] *House Journal*, 1912, p. 209.

City government for its exclusive tax purposes.[4]   The tax segregation program was submitted in the form of a constitutional amendment but failed to carry at the November elections.   Of the seventeen proposals submitted the Choctaw caucus endorsed eleven and opposed six.   It is in point to add that one of the amendments opposed on this occasion both by the Choctaws and the financial interests of New Orleans provided for the exemption from taxation of homes and farms having a value of less than $2,000.[5]   Here again the position of the Choctaw Club and big business corresponded and the small owner was forgotten.   In this instance there also might have been a dual reason for the action taken by the Machine.   To have exempted property valued at less than $2,000 would have cut the tax receipts of the City.   It would have been necessary then to increase the taxes on the more valuable property, raise assessed values, or cut government expenses.   To have done either of the first two mentioned would have exposed it to the attack of a very articulate and powerful element and the latter would have meant fewer jobs with which to keep the Machine going. Being realistic it chose to use its influence against the well being of the group in the community least able to bear taxation.

The utility question appeared again in the constitutional convention of 1921.   Renewed effort was made to take the regulation of New Orleans utilities out of the hands of the City government.   Although the Choctaws had suffered defeat in 1920 some of their number were delegates to the convention.   Among them was Martin Behrman, representing the fifteenth ward.   The Choctaws again opposed the move and were joined by the City reform elements that were dominant in the convention.   An ordinance was also in-

[4] *New Orleans Times Picayune*, Aug. 22, 1912.
[5] *New Orleans Times Picayune*, Oct. 31, 1912.

troduced authorizing municipalities to operate public utilities and ice plants. Most of the delegates from New Orleans, including the Choctaws, consistently opposed the measure.[6] When it became evident that it would pass, an amendment was introduced by a Choctaw member of the convention requiring the holding of an election to obtain the consent of a majority of the duly qualified taxpayers before a municipality could embark on a municipal utility program.[7] Under this amendment the Organization knew when it returned to power that it could control any election involving utilities as well as the City council.[8]

When the ratification of the federal income tax amendment was before the legislature, the City delegation voted against ratification. It was undoubtedly influenced in this not only by the financial interests in New Orleans but also by the sugar planters and refiners who feared the repeal of the sugar tariff if the federal government should adopt the new form of taxation.[9] The amendment was defeated in 1910 but ratified in 1912. On both occasions the sugar interests were active opponents and representatives from the sugar producing parishes voted against it almost solidly.

[6] The Choctaw delegation also voted against Ordinance 494 authorizing municipalities to own and operate street railways and Ordinance 455 exempting homesteads from tax sales. *Official Journal*, Constitutional Convention of 1921, pp. 672 and 897 respectively.

[7] *Ibid.*, pp. 487 and 516.

[8] The writer is not unaware that besides the possible political considerations probably involved, the whole controversial question of public ownership of utilities was involved in these decisions. The amendment forced in the measure by the Choctaws requiring an election before the adoption of a municipal ownership plan was in line with almost universal practice.

[9] The New Orleans Machine was sensitive to the wishes of the sugar planters because the congressional districts of which New Orleans forms a part include several sugar producing parishes. The refineries are centered in and near the City. *House Journal*, 1910, pp. 204 and 334; *House Journal*, 1912, p. 178 and *Senate Journal*, pp. 540 and 554.

During the 1912 session of the legislature when many bills involving the regulation of business were under advisement, Judge Farrar and Mr. Sol Wexler representing the corporations succeeded in making an agreement with Governor Hall to postpone so-called " anti-corporation " bills until the next session of the legislature.   The agreement reached provided that all proposals should be considered by a committee of legislators and business men who were to recommend the bills they considered desirable for action by the next session. Sol Wexler was a wealthy New Orleans capitalist.   In working out the agreement Wexler had the political support of the Choctaw Club.[10]   Although the Choctaws had not supported Governor Hall in his campaign in 1912 a friendly relation had subsequently been established, as was Behrman's custom. Any legislative program as controversial as corporate regulation had little chance of success if the solid Orleans delegation was against it.   During the 1912 session a bill regulating legislative lobbies was defeated with the assistance of the Choctaws.   Behrman in his fight on the bill remarked that lobbying could not be controlled and that the only way to remedy its evil influences was to send honest, intelligent men to the legislature.[11]

An extra session of the legislature was called in 1915 primarily to enact laws relating to corporations and monopoly.   The Wexler advisory committee in 1912 had been merely a means of delay.   The promised agreement had not been reached.   The corporations were no more anxious to be regulated in 1915 than in 1912.   The only thing that the financial interests could agree on was opposition to any proposals for regulation and further postponement.   The

[10] New Orleans Item, June 18, 1912.

[11] Ibid., June 18, 1912.   A bill requiring lobbyists active before certain state boards to register with the secretary of state and give their employers' names was passed, Acts of Louisiana, 1912, no. 144.

tide of reform was running high, however, and procrastination proved impossible. A further dilemma presented itself in the conflict of the various interests. Behrman sensing the impending storm trimmed his sails and sought to compromise discordant friends within his own domains.

The legislative contest centered around several different sets of bills all having the general purpose of regulating monopoly. The ones given major consideration were sponsored by Representatives Fontenot and Vincent. One from each set was for the specific purpose of regulating sugar refining; another, to protect trade from unlawful restraints, combinations and conspiracies; and a third to provide for preliminary investigation of alleged trusts. The laws were advocated principally by the sugar growers who were feeling the pinch of monopoly. They were joined by the other agricultural interests and by small business. Opposed to the bills were the American Sugar Refining Company, the New Orleans Association of Commerce, the New Orleans Clearing House Association (the banks), the Sugar Exchange and labor in the sugar refineries.[12] The latter had been frightened by threats of the corporations to leave the state if the laws were passed. The Association of Commerce opposed the bills as being the first inroads on private business, which would eventually lead to socialism.[13] It was particularly opposed to the provision in the sugar bill which declared the business of refining a public utility. The New Orleans Clearing House showed much originality in a resolution that condemned the bills as " an unwarranted interference with private business, antagonistic to capital, causing it to flee from the state." It appointed a special committee to lobby against the bill.

[12] *New Orleans Times Picayune*, May 20–June 10, 1915.

[13] At the Senate hearings the Association was charged with bad faith, i. e., with bringing in a weak bill to protect the sugar monopoly.

The New Orleans Machine found itself in a delicate situation. For the most part its financial friends in the City were against the bills. On the other hand the sugar growers within the congressional districts favored them. Besides there was real sentiment in the state and in New Orleans for legislative curbs on monopoly generally. To have followed the financial elements might have been bad politics. Furthermore Behrman considered that the interests had failed to carry out the plan adopted in 1912 and had nothing satisfactory to propose. Behrman announced the Orleans delegation would take no united stand on the Fontenot bills which were the most stringent—each member would be free to vote as he pleased. Regarding the Vincent bills, Behrman said: " The local (New Orleans) commercial interests have made no effort apparently to show that the anti-trust bills are objectionable to them so the representatives of the City organization will vote for the passage of the bills." The New Orleans Association of Commerce immediately had introduced substitute bills which would have been harmless to the monopolies. This did not, however, change Behrman's announced decision, and the Choctaw delegates voted to regulate monopoly against the wishes of business in New Orleans but in accordance with the wishes of their friends in the sugar districts. Three bills regulating monopolies were passed.[14]

[14] *Acts of Louisiana*, 1915, nos. 10, 11 and 12. The first applied only to the business of sugar refining. It declared sugar refining a public utility, prohibited certain irregular practices of the business, provided for the sale of properties of refineries held idle for reasons of monopoly, created the office of state sugar inspector and levied a tax on refining to pay the expense of administering the law. The second bill was general in its application and designed to protect all trade against unlawful restraints, combinations and conspiracies. It forbade consolidations that would lessen competition; provided for the sale of plants kept idle for more than one year in order to lessen competition; and fixed penalties for violation. The third bill established legal proceedings for preliminary

In 1924, Henry L. Fuqua was elected governor with the support of Martin Behrman and the Choctaw Club. In fact he owed his election to the Machine. Behrman therefore had large influence with him. A bridge across Lake Pontchartrain as an outlet to New Orleans was greatly needed. In 1918 an amendment to the constitution had authorized the building of a free bridge at a given point across the lake but had provided no funds.[15] In 1924 there were strong interests that desired to build a toll bridge across the lake and also one across the Mississippi at New Orleans. These interests had the ear of the Machine and, though not leading in the move, it supported a law passed in 1924, authorizing the building of toll bridges anywhere in the state at the discretion of the highway commission.[16] The law was designed to commit the state to a toll-bridge policy. Under its terms the state highway commission let a contract to the Watson-Williams Syndicate of New Orleans to build a toll bridge across the lake at the same point authorized by the law of 1918. The contract permitted an excessive charge for toll.[17] Huey Long immediately began to fight the toll bridge plan itself. He first brought suit to require a change to the free bridge policy of the 1918 law. The courts decided that the contract made with the Watson-Williams Syndicate did not violate the constitutional amendment of 1918, since its terms did not exclude other bridges across the lake. The amendment was also declared unaffected by the later law.[18] Hence the state could still build a free bridge across the lake at the point designated in the amendment. Failing

investigations of alleged trusts. The three bills were regarded as complimentary and the same forces had opposed or supported all three.

[15] *Acts of Louisiana*, 1918, no. 18.

[16] *Ibid.*, 1924, no. 141.

[17] The Company might charge as high as $3.50 per car to cross the bridge.

[18] *Talbot* v. *Louisiana Highway Commission*, 159 La. 909.

to stop the building of the toll bridge, Long then sought to regulate the Pontchartrain toll bridges as a public utility and again the courts decided against him.[19]   Meanwhile the bridge was built and opened.   Behrman died in January, 1926 and Fuqua a few months later.   Governor Simpson who succeeded him announced a free bridge policy, sensing that it was both the wisest and also the most popular course. Efforts were then made to sell the toll bridge to the state for an amount far in excess of the cost, but the whole matter had been proved unsavory and the state refused to buy. Throughout this episode the New Orleans Organization had not played a major hand but it had lent itself to a policy and supported a specific application of it which were hardly in the public interest.   Private enterprise had been backed in a matter which plainly should have been undertaken by the state.

These illustrations serve to show how the Machine was of service in the state legislature to its chief business backers. Although City government does not have the broad economic favors to confer that state government has at its disposal, it nevertheless does many things in which business interests are involved.   The task of dealing with economic interests in the City was more complicated than in the legislature.   On legislative issues relating to the regulation of business, labor and taxation, the economic forces of the City were for the most part at one; hence the Choctaws could lend a hand and were seldom sniped from the rear.   In contrast, in City affairs there were conflicting counter-currents within the economic groups.   Further, the purposes of the City government and the Machine did not always coincide with those

---

[19] *Louisiana Public Service Commission* v. *Louisiana Highway Commission*, 159 La. 932.   After the court decision upholding the state's right to build a free bridge not withstanding the private contract, Long boasted he would make a buzzard roost out of the toll bridge.   A free bridge was later built by the state and the private company was ruined.

of private business.   It was frequently necessary for Behrman and his Organization to make common cause with one
group against another or to force through a City policy
against powerful opposition.   Behrman once stated that
during his long service as mayor and City leader he had come
in conflict with every major business interest in New Orleans.
This was undoubtedly true but the conflict usually involved
more than simply public policy versus private interest.   Such
a case was the building of the public-belt railway.

In 1898 the state dock board had been created to hold
and administer the docks in the public interest.   Access to
and from the docks, however, was in the hands of the railroads.   The carriers were fighting among themselves, each
seeking a monopoly along the water front.   Service was bad.
There was no arrangement for the interchange of cars among
the lines.   Shippers and merchants were required to pay
heavy drayage costs between points on the docks and the
different railways touching them.   There had long been
agitation for a belt line that would connect all docks and
railways.   A franchise to build such a line had been acquired
at different times by several roads, but rivalries, legal questions and other difficulties had prevented building.   It was
proposed in 1904 that the City establish the belt line and
that it be under public ownership and control.   There was
immediate favorable response from the merchants and all
local business.   The railroads did everything in their power
to prevent the City from carrying out the plan.   The lines
of conflict were thus drawn between local business and the
railroads.[20]   Mayor Behrman and the Machine chose to build

[20] In the Constitutional Convention of 1921 Behrman fought the continuation of the provision of the two previous constitutions forbidding
public officials to accept or common carriers to grant passes or free
transportation to public officials.   He argued that such favors in no way
affected the action of politicians.   He stated that if this form of favor
was controlling, the Railroad Commission and the dock board would not

the line. Public interest as well as political expedience was on their side. Here two economic groups, each with a great deal at stake, engaged in a conflict the outcome of which depended on the side the government supported and the ability of the latter successfully to carry out the decision made. The persistence and skill Martin Behrman showed in overcoming all obstacles and completing and putting into operation the belt line was a notable tribute to his ability. An independent board was established to manage the enterprise and the technical operation was put in the hands of experienced railroad men. Shippers and merchants were saved from eight to ten dollars on each car load of goods moved. The construction of the public belt line, together with the state-controlled docks, put the public in complete control of the port of New Orleans. In officially opening the line, Mayor Behrman said: " This enterprise establishes the fact that the river front and its vast opportunities of commerce belong to the people and should be owned by them." [21]

In connection with the development of the Dock Board's policies for public ownership, Behrman threw the support of the Choctaws in favor of state owned and operated warehouses and rice elevators. To do this he had to go against strong private interests in the City but he had the support of other influential groups who felt private warehouse and elevator rates were too high. In this connection Behrman said: " Whenever government wants to do something some private interest always says it is unjustly injured. Some-

have been established in 1898 and the public belt line would never have been built. He pointed out that during these years practically every politician could get free transportation on the railroads. In the convention of 1898 Behrman opposed the establishing of the railroad commission because he had been requested to do so by a large number of his constituents who were employed in the shops of the Southern Pacific Railroad located in Algiers. *New Orleans Item*, Nov. 6, 1922.

[21] *New Orleans Item*, Jan. 19, 1923, " Behrman Tells."

times they are right but most of the time they are wrong." [22]
In many ways Behrman was socially minded. In most instances, however, his support of public ownership or control
occurred where the public interest corresponded with the
interests of a large part of the business community. In
clear-cut instances of public versus private ownership, as
for example in the utility field, he voted with the private
interests. On occasions when political and governmental interests were at stake, he opposed private enterprise. His
inclination was toward public enterprise in many fields as his
fight for the public belt line shows, but his lack of social
education and the extent to which he uncritically reflected
the general outlook of the era in which he lived caused him
to stop short of broader and perhaps wiser political action in
this field. There were several situations in which political
considerations seemed to outweigh the claims of private enterprise and in which Behrman threw the weight of the
Machine decisively in favor of public interest. In the building of water lines and drainage canals great pressure was
brought on the Sewage and Water Board to contract the
work to private companies. This Behrman successfully
opposed.[23] Against the opposition of a number of interests
he built and operated a City paving plant.[24] As a member
of the Board of Liquidation of the City Debt he forced
upon it a policy requiring bids from fiscal agents for the
custody of public funds and the payment of interest on City
balances held by such agents. The business men on the
Board, who were bankers, consistently voted against the
proposals and for several years prevented their enactment.[25]
The politicians on the board finally forced adoption. Here

[22] *Ibid.*, Jan. 27, 1923.
[23] *New Orleans Item*, Dec. 11, 14, 16, 21 and 24, 1922.
[24] *Ibid.*, Dec. 30, 1922.
[25] *Ibid.*, Jan. 2, 1923.

is a case where business men as public officials considered private before public interest—not perhaps an unusual phenomenon.

In 1915 the Choctaw-controlled City government forced the New Orleans Light and Power Company to lower its rates by threatening to build its own plant. This occured under the administration of the first commission council. The lead was taken by the commissioner of public utilities, one of the business men drafted by the Machine after the charter election of 1912. Rates before the reduction were twelve to fourteen cents per kilowatt hour; the cost of producing electricity, according to the commissioner, was about one cent a kilowatt hour. The threat of public ownership brought the rates down to a level that ranged from six to ten cents. The reduction proved to be short-lived, however; the charges were raised again when the United States entered the War. The writer was informed that the move on the part of the City was purely a bluff, as none of those in power had any intention of carrying out the threat made.[26] It, nevertheless, had the desired effect. It should be noted that

[26] The facts concerning the rate controversy were made available to the writer by a former City official identified with the fight and from the New Orleans newspapers for 1915. Another instance where Behrman forced the street car company against its will was in the development of a City park in the west end. The company refused to run a car line to the park. Behrman threatened to grant a franchise to a rival concern and give it the privilege of operating the park. A compromise with the light company resulted in a " loan " to the City of $175,000 to be spent in the development of the park so that the car line to be built would have an assured revenue from increased traffic. A clause in the act by which the state granted the site to the City had stipulated that the returns from the operation of the park should be used for improvements and that such claims should take precedence over all others. The contract between the public service company and the City provided that the $175,000 " loan " should be paid back only out of proceeds from the operation of the park. By this device the " loan " was made worthless to the company except as a part of its rate base. *New Orleans Item*, Dec. 29, 1922.

here again the Machine had the support of large economic interests as well as the electrical consumers generally who wanted cheaper power rates. The City government itself saved on its own light bills by the action.

New Orleans did not get natural gas from the vast North Louisiana fields until 1928. In various campaigns it was alleged that the Machine had connived with the local artificial gas company, which controlled all the utilities, to keep natural gas out of the City. There was at least one occasion on which the City government seemed to have made a sincere effort to secure for its citizens the cheaper and more efficient fuel from the Monroe fields. A franchise was actually granted in 1919 to a responsible concern.[27] The rates agreed on were half of what was then being paid for artificial gas. A $50,000 bond was posted with the City to insure the fulfillment of the contract. Later the company decided it could not furnish the gas at that price and forfeited its bond.[28] The evidence that the Machine subsequently thwarted efforts to bring in natural gas is negative. The circumstances might well have evoked more constructive zeal than was shown. The natural gas supply had been available for twenty years in North Louisiana. The rates charged for artificial gas in the City were generally regarded as exorbitant. Other cities nearby as far from the Monroe field as New Orleans had been able to secure natural gas at rates considerably below those charged by the local company. None of these communities had a consumption that approached the potential demand in the metropolis. When gas was finally brought to the City in 1928 it was with the reluctant consent of the City government.[29] It is difficult to give a satisfactory explana-

[27] *New Orleans Item*, Jan. 22, 1923.

[28] *Ibid.*, Jan. 22, 1923, " Behrman Tells."

[29] Governor Long had a hand in forcing the issue and focusing public attention on the matter. *New Orleans Item*, Feb. 16, 1928.

tion for this long delay if the government was really trying to serve the public interest and not the local utilities.[30]

The instances thus far mentioned in this chapter have related to what is regarded as legitimate business, and the evidence seems to point to an intimate association between the Club and these interests.   There was prevalent in New Orleans through the period under discussion what is generally regarded as illegitimate business.   Since vice was rather flagrant, its political ramifications were of necessity important or many practices after being outlawed could not have continued so openly.

To understand the problems that arose and the relationships that grew up between vice and City government, it is necessary to recall some of the background of the City.   New Orleans was settled by the Spanish and French and for years the moral habits brought in by these people were those of the City.   This influence has by no means ended.   In addition, during the nineteenth century there was considerable foreign immigration and the moral attitudes of that drawn from Italy and other places further accentuated those of the earlier settlers, which were anything but puritanic.   Furthermore it must be recalled that New Orleans is located in a semi-tropical climate.   The early intermingling of the French, Spanish and other races was in part a result of easy colonial morals and in part a cause of conditions that later developed.   The fact that New Orleans was a port city and became a widely visited resort center also fostered the continuation of the age-old vices of gambling, prostitution and drinking.   When the Choctaws came to power in 1900 Storyville (the red-light district) was the most glamorous

[30] The writer is conscious of the weakness of this evidence since no documentary proof is available.   Interviews with well informed people in New Orleans, however, lend substance to the charges that the Machine and the utilities were mutually serving each other.

resort of courtezans in the country. It was in the day when Tom Anderson was king of the tenderloin and when fortunes were being made in the district by madames who had taken a page from the business methods of the robber barons of the gilded age. The Louisiana lottery had gone out of existence only five years before but the passion of the people for gambling was being well supplied by under-cover lotteries, gambling houses, cock pits, and the race tracks. Liquor of all descriptions was considered as essential to the maintenance of life as air, water and food. In fact it would have been difficult to convince the average Creole that wine was not food. To have insisted that gambling was a social evil would have been received with contempt. As for the "district", this native in reply to criticism would have felt that after all did it not rival Paris and could laws make such places unpopular? These then were the sinful conditions the Choctaw Club inherited when it went to the City Hall to govern New Orleans. They found no majority sentiment among the citizens for altering the *status quo*. Such constituted a challenge, however, which has continued to the present time. Their regulation has been an issue in practically every political campaign since 1900 and perhaps one of the decisive elements in at least one City election.

The exposure of vice conditions made during political campaigns was inspired less by shocked moral sensibilities than by the belief of the opposition that here was one of the sources of power being used by the Machine. Reformers knew that the mere exposure of the existence of gambling, prostitution, and lotteries would cause no revolt but they believed if they could prove that tribute was being paid the Choctaws by these elements it would be good election strategy. Although the opposition promised to abolish all these evils, it had only one opportunity to prove its sincerity and on that occasion followed the time-honored policy of being officially blind to law violations in these fields. The Parker-Sullivan machine which won the City Hall in 1920 were no less realists than the Behrman-Choctaw faction they had defeated.

The Choctaw Club had a consistent record in favoring a restricted district. When Storyville was legally established, men later prominent in the Club voted for the City ordinance. Behrman recalled that it was opposed by some real estate interests, not owning property in the proposed area, because it would mean the loss of tenants who would be forced to move to the new district. During Behrman's first term as mayor there was little opposition to segregation. Beginning in 1910 a crusade was started to abolish it. The attack was led by Philip Werlein, a prominent business man, and Miss Jean Gordon, a social worker and leader of the Era Club, a woman's organization.[31] In 1914 a bill to abolish the district was introduced in the legislature. The Choctaw-led Orleans delegation opposed and defeated it. It was not until the World War that the move became strong enough to affect seriously an election. Martin Behrman continued to favor the segregation policy. He believed there was no way of stopping prostitution and that in a great City like New Orleans the chances of graft could be minimized and the regulation of the evil could be better handled by frankly recognizing its existence and dealing with it openly. It is probable that in this he had the average citizen with him. His personal life was above reproach and his attitude was interpreted wholly from an official standpoint. In 1917 because of the presence of military and naval units in New Orleans, the War Department ordered the district closed. Behrman refused to comply and went to Washington to see Secretary Baker in an effort to get the order changed. He proposed that military and naval guards, as well as police, be

[31] *New Orleans Item*, Mar. 16, 1923, " Behrman Tells."

kept on duty at the points of access to the district to keep
out soldiers and sailors.   His point was that by segregation
it would be possible to protect the morals of the troops much
more effectively than to close the area and allow the women
to scatter over the City.   Secretary Baker agreed to allow
the experiment proposed by Mayor Behrman to proceed until
further notice.   No later action was taken by the War Department and guards were maintained in accordance with the
plan.   Later, however, Secretary Daniels of the Navy Department, ordered the area closed.   Behrman submitted and
the council passed the proper ordinance.   In the election of
1920, Behrman's 1917 effort to retain the segregated district
was one of the issues effectively used by the opposition in
defeating him.   Shortly after the election of 1920, however,
the new reform City officials without legal action allowed and
even encouraged segregation.   When the Choctaws returned
to power in 1925, a similar policy was followed.   The police
were instructed to order women of known unsavory reputation to return to the old district.

Gambling on horse races during most of the period was
legalized by state law.   The Choctaw Club consistently
opposed all anti-racing bills introduced in the legislature and
with the exception of the Locke Anti-Racing Bill, passed by
one vote during the administration of Governor Sanders,
was successful.   Governor Sanders was elected in 1908 with
the support of the Choctaw Club and his action in putting
through this bill was resented by Behrman.[32]   It forbade
legalized betting which Behrman predicted would ruin racing
and substitute irresponsible bookmakers for a system of
regulated betting.[33]   Racing attracted tourists to New

[32] See chapter VIII.

[33] *New Orleans Item*, Jan. 11 and 12, 1923, "Behrman Tells." The
Locke Law was passed by the country influences.   The bill permitted
individual betting at country fairs.   Betting on horse racing, according
to rural standards, was wicked only in New Orleans and not at home.

Orleans and officials and business men wanted it continued. They also knew that unless gambling was permitted racing would soon die out. In spite of the law it did not die out. Gambling was permitted unofficially by the sufferance of the City government. The parish officers, being Organization men, caused no difficulty. The racing men were active in politics and could be counted on to contribute and occasionally furnish jobs at the track for deserving political workers.[34]

It is difficult to appraise the relationship between the gambling interests and the Machine. Here again the evidence is of a negative character. Gambling establishments of all kinds were tolerated. It certainly was a privilege well worth paying for in New Orleans. It was learned from creditable sources that gambling houses paid regularly for police protection and were assessed additional amounts during campaign periods.[35] Undoubtedly petty police graft was practiced in New Orleans as in other large cities. It was the opinion of many people that Mayor Behrman took no part in these arrangements and officially knew nothing of them. As stated in a previous chapter, these matters were handled by the ward leaders. At times one particular leader might have connections with the underworld that enabled him to make all the necessary arrangements. The leaders in the two wards where prostitution was rife usually dealt with this element as they saw fit. Enemies of the Machine charged that during the era of legalized prostitution an assessment of one dollar a night was collected by the police from each prostitute and that after the district was made illegal the same assessment was levied but was collected by a special agent or as extra rent by the landlord. The money, it was alleged, reached the campaign chest of the Machine, not

[34] *New Orleans Item*, Jan. 14, 1923.

[35] People making these statements were both friends and foes of the Choctaw Club.

perhaps at headquarters, but rather in the wards. The writer encountered no concrete evidence to indicate the truth of these statements except that it was general knowledge that prostitution was openly practiced in well-known establishments after it became illegal.

The relation of the Choctaws with the liquor and brewing interests was similar to that with other major economic interests. The Choctaws consistently supported local option and opposed state-wide and national prohibition.[36] In this position they were undoubtedly correctly representing the majority of people in New Orleans. Behrman, in commenting on the prohibition controversy, very aptly observed that the people from the country were for prohibition at home but when they came to New Orleans they were wet and wanted New Orleans to be saturated. The Machine showed no hesitancy in increasing the City license tax on the saloons in 1904 and 1909 even when the brewers alleged it would deprive the poor man of his beer. Here, as in other cases involving a clash with business, political need for revenue outweighed the desire to serve the ends of business. In regulating the saloons the laws were enforced about as the citizens desired "Unobtrusive non-observance" was the keynote of the enforcement of Sunday closing laws. This meant that such citizens as desired to gather over a glass of beer on Sunday could do so provided the front door remained closed, the blinds pulled, and order maintained. The charge was made that Behrman was ruled by the liquor people, but the more reasonable statement seems to be that he followed the course desired by most of New Orleans, where drinking was never considered out of order.

[36] In 1908 the Choctaws supported the Gay-Shattuck Bill regulating liquor because they believed it would eliminate the liquor issue in the coming state elections. *New Orleans Item,* Jan. 30, 1922.

CHAPTER VII

THE DISTRIBUTION OF PATRONAGE—THE CITY-STATE RELATION

PATRONAGE

THAT the New Orleans Machine considered patronage the primary essential and an indispensable element in building its power is clearly indicated by its consistent opposition to civil service, the many statements of its leader Martin Behrman and actual practices of the Organization over a period of thirty years.[1] Inheriting the spoils system from its predecessor, the Crescent Democratic Club, the Organization attained power in 1900 by a succession of fortunate circumstances, not the least of which was the state patronage furnished by Governor Foster. The fact that its leaders were professional politicians of the old school was a further reason for the flowering of the patronage system under the Choctaws. Machines in New Orleans had in the past held power by leaders building up about them loyal workers who owed their appointment, nomination, or jobs to the ward leaders and whose hope of advancement in politics depended upon them. Having before them the experience of the past they considered patronage as the *sine qua non* for building a machine. The brief introduction of civil service in some of the City departments from 1896 to 1900 had made no great decrease in the spoils and had not at all affected the thinking of the politicians. A contributing cause in the growth of the patronage system was the strong opinion on

---

[1] For an account of the Machine's action in changing civil service laws to serve its ends, see chapter II.

the subject held by Martin Behrman. He had utter contempt for the " reformers." He doubted their sincerity, frequently with good reason. He believed that their attacks on the spoils system were motivated wholly by their desire to get into office. He noted that their promises of civil service reform always outran their performances, once they were in power. When he became mayor in 1904, after sixteen years of practical experience in New Orleans politics, he could not conceive of putting any one in the City Hall except an Organization man. He said he believed that unless the employees of the City were of the same political faction as the elected officials they might cause the program of the faction to fail. That there could be developed a neutral public service that would serve efficiently whatever faction was in power was at least doubted by Martin Behrman, if not wholly disbelieved. Certainly there had been nothing in his experience to indicate that such a thing was possible. Perhaps in New Orleans in 1904 it would have been hard to find enough qualified, non-partisan people to supply the administrative personnel. At least a long-range program was involved in civil service and practical politicians are not interested in innovations for which there is no great demand. The patronage policy was tried and true, and so it was continued.

Behrman's experience in office had convinced him that the appointive system, unhampered by civil service, was the best. He said it gave the executive in charge more control over his subordinates. He insisted that appointments were made because of what a man had already done in a campaign and not for what he would do in the future. " You appoint a man," said Behrman, " not to get control of his vote, but because you already have his support." It is to be supposed, however, that the Choctaws expected those who were given jobs to be " faithful to the cause." Behrman had great faith in the professional politician.   In fact he felt that he had developed a " merit " system among elective and appointive public officials, who, he believed, should be professional politicians.   He proudly pointed to the fact that many City employees advanced in their departments and held jobs for twenty years.   These men he contended became experts and served the City well.   Speaking of the professional politician, he said : " All things being equal, the voters should support the professional politician.   Nine times out of ten, perhaps oftener than that, he makes a better official.   He is not concerning himself only with the job he has at the time, but is looking forward to reelection or another job and that gives him a good reason to do the best he can.   The amateur or ' now and then ' politician who usually comes out for office when he thinks there is a wave on against the professional, seldom expects more than one term.   He seldom gets more than one.   He lacks experience and isn't looking for promotion." [2]   Here Behrman shows that he realized the professional character of public service but had no appreciation of the possibilities of well-operated civil service. He combined elective and appointive positions in one category and regarded the problems involved in dealing with both as identical.   It did not seem to have occurred to him that when advancement depended on political activity both elective and appointive officers might use their position to further their personal interests at the expense of efficient public service.   He boasted that, after all, it was the professional politicians who really had done the big things in Louisiana and pointed to the fact that Governor McEnery had built the levee system; Governor Foster had abolished the lottery, eliminated the Negro vote and established the

[2] *New Orleans Item*, Oct. 24, 1922.   Most of the material concerning Behrman's attitude on patronage was obtained from the *Item*, Oct. 24, 1922, to Mar. 15, 1923, " Behrman Tells ".   Here he expressed his position very frankly.

Dock Board; and that Governor Blanchard had restored the credit of the state. It may be seen that he made no clear distinction between policy-making and administration. Because these governors were brokers of successful ideas and had carried out important policies, Behrman was convinced that all phases of government should be in the hands of professional politicians.

His other observations on the professional politician are less open to question. He noticed that successful business men did not often succeed in politics.[3] He believed that no democratic government could be operated without professional (experienced) politicians. He pointed out that when business men or other amateurs were in power " invisible " government was more common. This, he said, was true because they were inexperienced and someone not in office had to tell them what to do. He does not seem to have regarded the frequent determination of the position of the Machine in the legislature by business interests as coming in the same category. Perhaps the latter could hardly be called " invisible " or outside influence as it was so openly practiced. Behrman observed also that professional politicians were as honest as any other group—" as honest as merchants and bankers." In this he was probably correct but he was paying the politicians no great compliment in his specific comparisons. " When a bank clerk steals," said Behrman, " the president is not tainted but when a city clerk steals the mayor and all the rest of the city officials are accused of dishonesty." It was a source of pride to him that in his sixteen years as mayor there had been only two cases of shortage in the handling of money. He wondered what large business concern could show as good a record.[4]   What

[3] This was said during the abortive administration of Mayor Andrew McShane, a successful business man. *New Orleans Item*, Oct. 24, 1922.

[4] John Fitzpatrick a famous New Orleans politician paid to the state money stolen by an employee in the state tax office whom he had recom-

are called sound business standards are undoubtedly desirable in government but a political organization that would base its claims to competence and morality on those of business from 1900 to 1926 hardly deserved the complete confidence of the voters. At least its ethics would be open to question.

The method used in distributing City and parish patronage among the wards was originally designed to prevent bickerings among the ward leaders over which one should get the disposal of certain jobs. Each leader was assigned the patronage of a whole City or parish department, board or office. It was his exclusive property and a kind of " vested interest " in particular branches of patronage developed. This tendency was so marked that the same wards have controlled a specific aspect of the spoils for as long as forty-five years.[5] There were few shifts of jurisdiction made once a ward considered it had authority in a particular area. A leader seeking additional patronage for his ward might look with envy on his neighbors' " greener fields " but seldom question a right of long standing. It was in the expansion of governmental functions that the more aggressive leaders got a lion's share. In general the leaders and the caucus, keeping in mind the votes involved and the political situations in the ward, sought to divide patronage as equitably as possible. Inevitably, however, the system broke down, and the more powerful leaders garnered more and more. The inequalities developed more rapidly after the appointive power was concentrated in the mayor and five commissioners

mended and bonded. Although his liability held only for the amount of the bond he made good the entire amount stolen. Behrman wondered how many business men would have done this. *New Orleans Item,* Oct. 24, 1922.

[5] For example, the patronage of the coroner's office belonged to the tenth ward, that of the criminal sheriff to the third, and that of the civil sheriff to the seventh.

in 1912.[6] The City officials had favorites among the ward leaders and were naturally influenced by the more aggressive. Under the aldermanic system it had been easier for the ward leaders, through the ward-elected council, to secure a more equal share. There seems to be a general agreement in New Orleans that Col. Bob Ewing, leader of the tenth ward, was the most insatiable patronage " grabber " among the leaders. He was above the average in intellect, persistent, domineering, acquisitive and ambitious to be the one great boss. As he grew wealthy and his business interests expanded he had less and less time to devote to his ward. He therefore resorted more and more to the use of patronage to hold his leadership. He bought his support with City, state and federal jobs and was not popular with the mass of his followers. At one time he controlled nearly one-fourth of all the patronage in the hands of the Choctaws.[7] Behrman regarded Ewing as one of his closest advisers for sixteen years but said on one occasion that they always got along better " when I was agreeing with him." [8] Ewing could not follow and unless he got what he wanted he broke with Behrman and tried to take the Machine with him. His political judgment was less astute than Behrman's and usually he failed to gauge public sentiment correctly. Except on one occasion Behrman was the victor in these disputes. In spite of his deflections and the defeat of those he backed, Ewing remained much of a power in New Orleans and Louisiana politics until his death.[9] Other leaders secured above the

[6] The defeat of the Machine in 1920 was attributed by some to inequalities of patronage among the leaders which caused jealousies and desertions. A Choctaw ward leader remarked in September, 1934, that the success of the Long City machine in the congressional elections of that month was due to the fact that Long distributed the state patronage on which his organizaion was built with no favoritism.

[7] *New Orleans Times Picayune*, Aug. 16, 1912.

[8] *New Orleans Times Picayune*, Jan. 6, 1925.

[9] See chapter VIII.

average amount of patronage because of their prestige, long service, intelligence, popularity or because they ruled in doubtful wards.   Among these were Capt. John Fitzpatrick, onetime mayor, Col. John P. Sullivan and John Mauberret.[10]

The caucus settled disputes which arose over patronage jurisdiction and when a new agency was created, it was assigned to a given ward.   In this matter, as in the case of nominating, the more important leaders were in control.

The question of state patronage depended on the governor, but since New Orleans was such a power in elections, the Choctaws usually controlled all available patronage in New Orleans except a few appointments the governor might wish to make for personal reasons.[11]

A large amount of state patronage was available in New Orleans.   Besides the Dock Board, there was the Conservation Department, tax administration, a number of state courts including the Supreme Court, a charity hospital, and a few other agencies centered in the City.   In addition to the patronage in the state agencies having offices in New Orleans, the Machine got its share of the appointments at the state capitol in the offices of the Highway Commission, the Tax Commission, the Attorney General, the Board of Health, the Supervisor of Public Accounts and others.   State patronage was not divided through the allocation of particular departments to particular wards as was the case with City and parish offices.   The State Dock Board, for example, employed hundreds of men and no one ward was ever in control of such a large single agency.   The state jobs were parcelled out where they were most needed.   Each ward

---

[10] All of these men were also aggressive.   Fitzpatrick had been Mayor and was a sort of patriarch of the Machine.   Sullivan was a well-to-do lawyer and Mauberret had acquired wealth and was a hard worker.

[11] From 1900 to 1926, only one governor completely withheld control of state patronage from the Machine in New Orleans.   He was John M. Parker, 1920-1924.

leader would be given a certain number, as the caucus might decide. Behrman would then notify the appointing authority in the state office concerned that he was to recognize the recommendations of certain ward leaders for so many jobs in the department, board or office.[12]

During the period when the Democrats were in power in Washington, the Machine was in control of federal patronage in New Orleans and in the first and second congressional districts. The large influence of the City vote in electing United States Senators caused both Senators to defer to the Machine. About half of New Orleans is included in the first congressional district and the other half is in the second. Both districts embrace a number of country parishes. In order to control these districts it was only necessary to split the vote of the country parishes and to carry the City. The Choctaws divided the country vote by the use of federal patronage when it was available; otherwise an arrangement was made with local leaders or with the governor. For the most part the parishes in these districts were sparsely populated and contained a large proportion of illiterate people. As parish bosses were in control it was not difficult for the City leaders to make trades with them by using either federal or state patronage or other political " currency." The fact that New Orleans was the second largest port in the country added to the number of federal jobs available. When the Republican party was in power, the patronage was

[12] In the 1925 City election letters written by Behrman to the Dock Board concerning patronage were published and he was roundly condemned by the opposition for this "wicked" practice. Later during the campaign copies of similar letters written by the Parker-Sullivan faction were uncovered by the Behrman forces. Behrman then observed that it appeared that what was "crooked politics" for the "Regulars" was regarded as statesmanship when done by his opponents. He added that the only difference he could see was that their letters "were of inferior literary composition". *New Orleans Item*, Jan. 10, 1920.

used throughout the state by the President to build up his influence in the next national convention.   At no time after 1900 was a serious effort made to build up the strength of the party locally with the idea of contesting the supremacy of the Democrats.   Occasionally a Republican could not be found for some federal office in the state and a Democrat would be named.   The Republican leader would approach Behrman to get him to secure the consent of the Louisiana senators for confirmation.   Behrman was always friendly with the Republican leaders and occasionally they exchanged favors.[13]

Whenever an agency was proposed either in the state or City that would add new functions to government, the Machine ordinarily favored it.[14]   It seldom approved measures which proposed to combine or consolidate offices.   The everincreasing activities of City and state government ordinarily served to increase the hold of the Choctaws.   Many new functions undertaken by government required technical personnel and hence limited somewhat their value as patronage.   Because of the one-party system and the fact that most Democrats in New Orleans were also Choctaws, it was not difficult to fill these positions with engineers, doctors, lawyers, chemists, railroad managers, and other professional people who were sympathetic with the Organization.   The only difficulty was that ward and precinct workers were not

[13] Sometimes the Republican vote was effective and was in opposition to a program sponsored by the "Regulars."   In 1908 there were 2,000 Republican votes in New Orleans.   An amendment to the state constitution voted on at the general election and opposed by the "Regulars" was carried by 1,800 votes.   The Republican vote had been decisive.   The amendment abolished the seven tax collectors in Orleans Parish and created an office to be held by one collector.   Ewing, who was one of the collectors, opposed the change.   *New Orleans Item*, Jan. 11, 1908.

[14] See Chapter VI concerning the creation of the Dock Board and the public belt railway, which the Machine favored, and public ownership of utilities, which it opposed.

often found in these classes. Civil service was nominally applied to some of the new agencies created, but its emasculation in 1900 had rendered the law of little value as a means of improving personnel administration. The good sense of the leaders and public demand for efficient City services could be counted on to prevent the appointment of a hod-carrier or a barkeeper to the position of city engineer. The pressure of the professional societies also tended to require the appointment of well-qualified technical men to the more important posts. Behrman had a real appreciation for the value of good technical men particularly in engineering and promoted their work and backed them in experimental improvements.[15] The vast drainage and flood protection problems of New Orleans would have permitted no other course than the use of technical skill.

Behrman encouraged the ward leaders to engage in reciprocal exchanges of patronage so that better-fitted persons might be secured. For example, if the first ward had control of the patronage in the City engineer's office and a draftsman was needed there and there was no well-qualified man in the first ward but there was in the seventh, the man in the seventh would be appointed. Later the leader of the seventh ward would give a job to some one named by the leader of the first ward. Behrman would do his best to get a worker a job but he would not insist that he be kept if he loafed or was inefficient. He felt that a man who did not do his work well would do the Organization no good and would cause criticism of his administration as mayor. Here his dual capacity as mayor and leader probably made the service better than it might otherwise have been under the spoils system. Although the test for jobs was factional and personal he expected his "professional politicians,"

---

[15] *New Orleans Item*, Dec. 11, 1922. The chief engineers of the Sewage and Water Board held their jobs for twenty years.

whether in elective or appointive offices, to perform their duties so as to avoid public complaint.[16] Because the Choctaw Club remained in power for twenty years without interruption there was no complete turn-over of job holders every four years. However, dissension within, desertion of ward leaders in the more bitter elections, the change in the form of City government and the other exigencies of politics had their constant effect in bringing about personnel changes. Behrman himself was in power sixteen years of the twenty referred to but no other appointing official remained in office more than two terms. The frequent change of principals had its effect even though their appointments were largely made on the recommendation of ward leaders whose lease of power was indefinite. As conditions in a ward changed it was often necessary for the leader to put new people in the places under his control. Even the combination of the long tenure enjoyed by the faction, Behrman's dual responsibilities and his development of a " merit " system among the professionals did not constitute an adequate substitute for an intelligent, well-trained and carefully selected permanent civil service. The City government not only had to employ enough people to perform its proper governmental functions but also had to carry on its payroll a large number of party workers much of whose time was devoted to the political interests of the faction to whom they owed their jobs.

[16] After the defeat of the Choctaws the personnel of most City departments was changed. In one or two the "amateurs" bungled affairs badly and there was much public complaint. Behrman chided Parker and Sullivan for failure to select competent men. He did not blame them for discharging the Behrmanites but argued that his system of professional politicians was better. It did not seem to occur to him that if, during his long lease of power, New Orleans had built up, by civil service, a trained permanent personnel, such complaints of inefficiency would not have arisen. *New Orleans Item*, Mar. 3, 1923.

Ward leaders were careful to distribute the patronage of their wards so as to establish effective influence with the various social and economic groups. The Irish, the Italians, the Germans, the French, the Spanish, all had to be included in the spoils, and care had to be exercised to select the leaders of racial groups for the better places.[17] Since the Negro had no political influence after 1900 his chances of getting anything but common labor were slight. In seeking to keep labor friendly, leaders or influential members of labor unions were given City jobs.[18] Veterans' groups were given special consideration even though they were avowedly non-political. There is little or no Jewish prejudice in New Orleans and there have been a number of successful politicians who were Jews. Religion was not a test for patronage; Protestant or Catholic, Jew or Gentile, had equal chance so long as he could " deliver " votes, work, or influence in return for his appointment.

Reference has already been made to favors other than patronage which the Machine had at its disposal. Among them were the use of legislative power for the benefit of special interests; tolerance of open vice; the policy of " unob-

[17] This was also true in building the Choctaw election slate. Since 1920 special consideration has been given to the Italian population in this connection. Every ticket usually included a creole name.

[18] There was no evidence found that the endorsement of labor organizations was bought outright by the use of patronage among the leaders. It may have been influenced but patronage did not seem to be the decisive factor. The labor vote was often divided when there was a strong faction in opposition. This might be interpreted as meaning that the leaders in control had sold the endorsement and then could not deliver the vote. Opinion of politicians and labor leaders in New Orleans was that the work of the precinct leaders, lack of class solidarity and interests of these people aside from trade union membership were more decisive than the formal recommendation of their hierarchy-controlled organizations. The labor record of the Choctaws will be discussed in Chapter VIII in connection with the 1920 campaign in which it was most clearly brought out.

trusive non-observance " of Sunday closing laws; leniency in law enforcement promised by the police for votes; the influence of ward leaders in Recorders' Courts; " friendly " regulation of utilities; control of the election machinery; and the manipulation of assessments.[19] It was the use made of these sources of power around which election conflicts most frequently turned. Through its complete power over legislative, administrative, and court machinery in the City and parish, the Machine had other spoils which it could and did use to advantage. The other sources of spoils than patronage were not often campaign issues. Some would be classified as " honest graft " and were participated in by the " best " people. Among those favored were: " insiders " who profited by having advance knowledge of the City's intention to acquire certain real estate for public improvement;[20] lawyers and others who were granted " judicial plums " in connection with receiverships, bankruptcies, and guardianships; a heterogeneous array who profited by administrative laxity or liberality in the enforcement, interpretation and prosecution of contracts, health regulations, building codes, and factory regulations.

Judges in the Louisiana courts after 1898 were elected by popular vote. District judges were elected for a period of six years except in Orleans Parish, where the term was twelve years. Judges of the Appeal Court and the Supreme Court were elected for terms of twelve years. The longer term

[19] See chapters V and VI.

[20] In 1912 persons close to the City Hall were accused of having purchased land at a very low figure and then selling it to the City, in less than a year, at a much higher price. The implication, though not proved, was that the purchaser, who was a Choctaw, knew of the City's plans in advance of the public announcement. The opposition did establish that either the City paid too high a price for the land or the owner was favored with an extremely low assessment. *New Orleans Times Picayune,* Aug. 16, 1912.

for District Judges in the Parish of Orleans was designed to make them less subject to political influences. The chief service of the courts was the patronage the judge assigned to friends of the Machine. Since the judges owed their election to the Organization they were active in party work, contributed to campaigns, and often served as election orators. If it seemed that they handed out more " judicial plums " to Choctaw lawyers and friends than to others, the explanation given was that this faction was more numerous and its lawyers were just as able as those of any other group. Charges of Choctaw bias in the judiciary were seldom made. The term " Ring Judge " was rarely heard and then only during bitter campaigns in which election controversies had gone before the courts. Behrman wisely insisted on the nomination of able men to the courts.

Through the process described the Choctaw Club insinuated its influence into every part of government. Thus every geographic section, social class and economic force within its political domain, was tied to its support by bonds of patronage, favor and privilege.

RELATIONS WITH THE STATE—SELECTING THE GOVERNOR

" In every state where there is a city large enough to be a decisive factor in most elections there is always some sentiment in the country to oppose whatever organization dominates that city." [21] This observation was made by Martin Behrman after thirty-five years of participation in New Orleans and Louisiana politics. No politician in the state was more familiar with the City-state relation and none was more successful than he in manipulating the relation to serve the City and the Machine. The political power of New Orleans was felt in every phase of state politics and government. In the legislative and constitutional conven-

[21] *New Orleans Item*, Mar. 11, 1923, " Behrman Tells ".

tions and in state administration the normal influence of the City, by virtue of its population, was greatly accentuated by reason of the dominance of the City by the Machine.   In elections, a majority could be delivered to the candidates endorsed by the Choctaws; in party councils the Orleans delegation was a solid block; in the legislature and constitutional convention the large City group was a unit on the major issues and on all matters relating particularly to the City. There was no other large city and no block of country votes that could hope to match this concentrated power of New Orleans.   Tending to balance this extraordinary influence was the governor who held large appointing power within the City.   Affecting it also was the disposition of the country voters to look with suspicion on the City Organization and to oppose it.   It was therefore the task of Behrman and the Choctaw Club to divide and rule.   The Organization must keep the peace with the governor and prevent the country factions from uniting against the City Organization either in elections, in the legislature, or in party councils.   The strategy of course lay wholly within the framework of the Democratic party since the Republican party had lost its power with the disfranchisement of the Negro in 1898.

The process of selecting a governor clearly reveals some of the practices of the Machine in state political affairs.   The Machine did not put forward a candidate for governor.   To have done so might have caused the country to unite and make common cause against the candidate of the " wicked " City Machine.   Behrman and his associates played a waiting game.   Men ambitious to be governor announced their candidacy a few months before the primary and began preparations for the active campaign which ordinarily lasted six weeks.   These various candidates made their contacts with parish leaders throughout the state seeking support. Through all this preliminary work, Berhman and his Machine kept in close touch with the progress made by each candidate in lining up the country votes. The Monteleone Hotel on Royal Street in the French Quarter became the mecca of the country politicians who came to town to discuss the political situation among themselves and with the City Organization. The question on every side was " whom are the Choctaws going to endorse for governor? " The answer was that the Choctaws were going to endorse and deliver New Orleans to the candidate who seemed to have the best chance of winning in the country and who did not propose war on the Machine.[22] With rare exceptions men desiring the governor's office sought privately the support of the Choctaw Club. The Organization might encourage a candidate by telling him it would look with favor on him if he gained more strength in the country, but no public endorsement was given until the caucus felt sure of the political strength of their man in the country; nor would they approve unless they had assurance that at least he would not fight the Machine in the City if elected. The candidate receiving the endorsement of the Club could feel certain of election if he had substantial support in the country because he could count definitely on carrying the City by a big majority. Candidates endorsed by the Machine always sought to minimize the importance of this approval while campaigning among the country people in order not to be labeled the " tool of the bosses." As little publicity as possible was given to the endorsement outside of New Orleans. Opposing candidates made capital of the fact even though they had sought and failed to get the support of the City Organization.[23] The candidate receiving the Choctaw endorsement would tell the country voters he had not sought the support of the Machine but that seeing him to be the winning candidate it

[22] *New Orleans Item*, Feb. 25, 1923, " Behrman Tells ".
[23] *New Orleans Item*, Jan. 6, 1923.

had gotten on the " band wagon." He would add that he was under no obligations to the " Ring " and would not be controlled by it.

The Governors of Louisiana from 1900 to 1926 were W. W. Heard, H. C. Blanchard, J. Y. Sanders, Luther E. Hall, Ruffin G. Pleasant, John M. Parker and Henry L. Fuqua. All save Hall and Parker were elected with the endorsement and support of the Choctaw Club and only Parker used his office to fight the Machine in the City. The interplay of state and City politics can be more clearly seen by reviewing the forces that carried certain of these men into the governorship.

J. Y. Sanders had been lieutenant-governor under Blanchard and by the time the latter's term was drawing to a close had made himself more influential than the governor. He announced his candidacy and began his campaign in the summer of 1908. Governor Blanchard favored his friend, Mr. Wilkinson, who also desired the office. Very shrewdly the Governor called a special session during the midst of the campaign partly to keep Sanders at his place in the Senate and thus prevent his work in the field. Before the session assembled the Governor left the state to attend the Jamestown Exposition and Sanders became acting governor. He quickly seized on the impending legislative session and made political capital of an event by means of which his opponents hoped to handicap him. None of the items in the call issued by Governor Blanchard had any special popular appeal. As soon as Blanchard was out of the state Sanders added several items calculated to bring him popular support.[24] On his return to the state, Governor Blanchard disclaimed all responsibility for the additions and said if the legislature

---

[24] Regulation of the railroads and of public utilities were the more popular items Sanders added. *New Orleans Item*, Jan. 6, 1923, "Behrman Tells '. *Proceedings of Senate and House Extra Session*, 1907.

failed to act Sanders was to blame. Sanders succeeded in pushing through the legislative program including the items he had added to the call.[25] This had demonstrated the strength Sanders possessed in the state. Seeing that he was popular in the country, the Choctaws had endorsed him early in the campaign and practically assured his election. A very close relationship grew up between the Governor and the Machine until Sanders was defeated for the United States Senate in 1912.[26] This case illustrates the general practice of the Machine of not putting forward a candidate but of choosing the one who had demonstrated his country following.

The election of 1912 demonstrates the conduct of the Machine when it picked a losing candidate. There were three candidates in the field, Luther E. Hall, John T. Michel and James B. Aswell. A reform wave had been started in the City and state under the name of Good Government League. It centered in New Orleans and made much noise about the close relations of Sanders and Behrman. This group agreed on Hall who was popular in the country and a man of high reputation. James B. Aswell was an educator with an inclination to politics; he had not been on good terms with the New Orleans Organization.[27] John T. Michel had long been friendly toward the Choctaws and therefore seemed

---

[25] *Acts of Louisiana Extra Session*, 1907.

[26] The break occurred because Sanders thought the Machine had deserted him in the election. Behrman denies that this occurred, attributing Sanders' defeat in New Orleans to his general unpopularity and the anti-racing bill which he put through the legislature. Behrman carried his ward for Sanders. *New Orleans Item*, Feb. 21, 1912, "Behrman Tells".

[27] Aswell was offered a $10,000 position as superintendent of the Orleans Parish schools by the Machine-controlled School Board in 1910. It was alleged by opponents of the Machine that this was a "plot" by Behrman and Sanders to eliminate Aswell from the race in 1912, because he was opposed to them in state politics.

the logical candidate for them to endorse. The political pot had started boiling earlier than usual in this race due to the fact that United States Senator McEnery had died in the summer of 1910 and Governor Sanders had been elected by the legislature to succeed him.[28] This had brought announcements from gubernatorial candidates. Lieutenant Governor Labremont wanted to be governor and expected the endorsement of the Choctaws. On failing to get it he announced that when Sanders went to the senate he would call a special session of the legislature and enact laws that would curb the power of the New Orleans " Ring." [29] At this time New Orleans was making efforts to get the Panama Pacific Exposition. At the request of the directors of the local exposition company, Governor Sanders resigned the senatorship to which he had just been elected in order to devote his time and influence to securing the exposition.[30] It was in the interval between Sanders' election to the Senate and his resignation that Hall, Michel and Aswell had made their announcements for office. The City failed to get the exposition; a bitter fight over the schools in New Orleans was dragged into the governor's race; the Machine became divided; and Hall won.[31] In spite of the fact that Behrman had opposed the election of Governor Hall, he was soon on cordial terms with him. Hall was a man who could work with all factions. Behrman needed Hall in order to get the New Orleans patronage and the Governor needed Behrman if his legislative program was to succeed. Furthermore, John M. Parker had abandoned the Good Government

[28] *Proceedings of the House and Senate*, July 5, 1910, pp. 940 and 704 respectively.

[29] *New Orleans Item*, July 31, 1922, and August 1, 1910.

[30] Denial was made that Labremont's threats had influenced his decision.

[31] For an account of the school fight and the division of the Machine see chapter VIII.

League to support the Progressive party ticket in the national election and there was no outstanding leader left in the League whose influence Governor Hall cared to build up in the City through the use of patronage.[32]   He could hardly have afforded to turn patronage over to Parker since his Democratic standing was then open to question.   Governor Hall also knew Behrman's ability as a politician.   They had joined forces in the Democratic State Convention in June, 1912 and secured its endorsement of Champ Clark's candidacy against the efforts of Col. Bob Ewing to have the Louisiana delegation instructed for Woodrow Wilson.[33]

These facts all made a working arrangement between the governor and the New Orleans Organization seem wise. Behrman's influence with the governor became so great before the end of the latter's term that he was accused of conniving with the bosses against the interests of those who had elected him.   Behrman's " rapprochement " with Governor Hall was in accordance with his frequently expressed belief that since the primary was a family quarrel, all elements should " get together " after it was over and work for the good of the party, the state and the City.

A struggle in the legislature occurring in 1915 over the holding of a constitutional convention, in a large measure, determined the state political alignment in the election of 1916.   A constitutional convention had been held in 1913 to refund the state debt.   The powers of the convention had been severely limited by the call.   The convention, in spite

---

[32] John M. Parker was named as vice-presidential candidate on the Progressive ticket in 1916.

[33] *New Orleans Times Picayne*, June 4, 1912. The position of the Choctaw Club on presidential candidates was dominated by the small coterie of leaders. The average ward leader was not interested. The delegation at the state convention of the party, of course, acted as a unit under Behrman's direction. Both Behrman and Ewing were delegates to all Democratic National Conventions from 1908 through 1924.

of this fact, made changes in the constitution not authorized. Litigation followed and the courts declared parts of the 1913 constitution inoperative on the ground that they were not within the scope of the convention's authority under the call.[34] This naturally caused uncertainty. Another reason given for the necessity of a new convention was that the " grandfather clause " of the suffrage article had been nullified by a decision of the Supreme Court of the United States and a substitute had to be found. The plan for the convention was worked out between Mayor Behrman, Governor Hall, Mr. Sol Wexler and Col. Bob Ewing. As soon as the plan of this group became known, L. E. Thomas, Speaker of the House, and Ruffin G. Pleasant, Attorney General, announced they would oppose the plan when the bill came before the legislature. They were soon joined by former Governor Jared Y. Sanders who, because of his belief that the Choctaw Club had failed to support him as promised in his campaign for the Senate in 1912, was opposed to any plan coming out of New Orleans. Furthermore, rumor had it that Martin Behrman was slated to preside over the convention. This rumor, together with the support of the bill given by the " Regulars " and the plan to hold the convention in New Orleans, gave the Pleasant-Sanders-Thomas faction a great opportunity to label it a plot on the part of the ward bosses, the governor, and big business in the person of Sol Wexler, to dictate a new constitution for the state. Involved also in the fight were the liquor interests of the state which had persuaded the proponents of the convention to provide in the proposed call that no change was to be made in liquor laws.[35] A bill submitting to the electorate the

[34] *State* vs. *American Sugar Refining Co.*, 137 La. 407 and *Foley* vs. *Democratic Parish Committee*, 138 La. 219.

[35] This was put in to make sure that statewide prohibition would not be adopted. Col. John P. Sullivan, prominent Choctaw, was the apostle of

question of a constitutional convention to be held in New Orleans, September 15, 1915, was finally passed in the legislature but was defeated at the polls through the efforts of Pleasant, Sanders and Thomas.[36] The issue was clearly drawn between the City and the country in this election. The proposal received a majority in New Orleans but lost heavily in the country.[37] This contest made Sanders a power in politics again and made Pleasant the leading candidate for governor. Lieutenant Governor Barrett had favored the convention plan and when he announced his candidacy for governor, he expected to have the support of the pro-convention groups. He failed, however, to secure the support of the Machine though he did secure the support of Governor Hall. The Machine followed its policy of watchful waiting. The convention election had indicated that Pleasant had great strength in the state and the Choctaws did not want to repeat the mistake of 1912 and pick the losing candidate even though the relations with Governor Hall had been friendly. They had failed to get as much patronage from Hall as they wanted. There also developed in the state the feeling that Barrett was " tainted " with Machine influence and that if elected he would be a tool of the New Orleans " Ring." His support of the convention plan had created this impression and the country fully expected the Choctaws to announce that he was their choice. These factors together with Sanders' support made Pleasant appear as the likely winner. The Club therefore came out in his

the brewers to the state legislature at the time. For full account see *New Orleans Item*, Feb. 21—March 4, 1923, " Behrman Tells ", and *New Orleans Times Picayune*, May 26—June 15, 1915.

[36] The proposal for the convention submitted to the voters gave the convention unlimited powers except that no change was to be made in the state debt and the liquor laws. *Acts of Louisiana*, no. 17, 1915.

[37] *Report of the Secretary of State*, 1916, p. 572.

favor and made his election practically certain.[38] Events seem to indicate that Pleasant had not sought the support of the Organization. He had opposed their convention plan in the legislature and was opposing its adoption before the people in his campaign. Nevertheless, there seems little doubt that he received the support of the Choctaw Club because of his strength as a candidate. In offering the Club's support, Governor Pleasant said Behrman made no demands; no definite agreement was reached and no promises were made on his part. He also added, however, that he knew the Organization would expect to handle state patronage in New Orleans.[39]

Pleasant was nominated in the Democratic primary and under ordinary circumstances there would have been no further question about the result of the general election. However, John M. Parker had announced his candidacy on the Progressive ticket and, as he had a large personal following in the state, the Choctaws and the Pleasant-Sanders-Thomas state faction maintained their organization until after the general election.[40] Pleasant was elected by a big majority but Parker polled a creditable number of votes.[41]

[38] *New Orleans Item*, Feb. 28, 1923. *New Orleans Times Picayune*, Aug. 25, 1915.

[39] The information concerning this campaign was obtained from Governor Pleasant, the New Orleans and Louisiana papers and from Behrman's story in the *New Orleans Item*, Oct., 1922—March, 1923.

[40] Some political observers thought Parker's candidacy had been inspired by Theodore Roosevelt. It was thought if a Roosevelt Progressive could break the solid south in a state campaign it would be a good test of the strength of Roosevelt in the country.

[41] Pleasant received 228,365 and Parker 41,280. *Report of the Secretary of State*, 1916. The Negro issue was raised in this campaign. The Democrats urged the defeat of Parker on the ground that if a permanent party opposed to the Democrats was established it would bring the Negro back into Louisiana politics. Another issue raised was whether a Democrat who had voted in the primary had a right to vote against the nominees of the party in the general election. *New Orleans Times Picayune*, Feb. 15, 1916.

After the election the Governor and Mayor Behrman continued friendly relations. Behrman stated that in the matter of appointments Governor Pleasant gave the Choctaw Club more complete cooperation than any other governor with whom he had dealt.[42] This election emphasizes the fact that the Choctaws got behind the winner if they could. The fact that the person endorsed was opposing them in state affairs and was supported by their political opponents did not deter their action. If the country was going to elect Pleasant Governor, the Machine could be counted on to " second the motion ".

In 1920 the Machine had little difficulty in deciding which of the leading candidates to support. John M. Parker had returned from his " Progressive wanderings " and was again in the Democratic party and was an avowed candidate for the governorship.[43] For twenty years he had fought the New Orleans " Ring " and with his announcement for the governorship, he began to pour out vitriolic denunciation of this " band of crooks." Under such circumstances it would have been difficult for the Machine to endorse Parker even though he appeared to be the strongest candidate in the country parishes. The other candidate was Colonel Stubbs of Monroe, who, with a brilliant war record to his credit, was also seeking the Democratic nomination. Since he was not making the New Orleans Machine an issue in the state election, he was the logical choice of that Organization. As Parker made the destruction of " bossism " the leading issue, Stubbs was charged with being a tool of the bosses when his

---

[42] *New Orleans Item*, Mar. 4, 1923. Behrman also stated that Governor Pleasant extended fair treatment to Sanders who had been a big factor in his election.

[43] It might be recalled that Parker had been nominated Vice-President on the Progressive ticket with Roosevelt in 1916. Since Roosevelt declined to accept the principal place, the party withdrew from the campaign.

endorsement by the Choctaw Club was made public.   Parker was elected in April, 1920, and built a City machine with state patronage that caused Behrman's defeat in the September election in New Orleans.   There was no " getting together " with Parker; he was out to destroy the Choctaw Club.[44]   In part the failure of the Choctaws to influence the course of events in 1920 more adroitly was due to the break that occurred between Governor Pleasant and the Machine in 1919.   United States Senator Broussard died that year. Colonel Bob Ewing wanted Governor Pleasant to appoint him Senator to fill Broussard's unexpired term.   This Pleasant refused to do as he desired to appoint Mr. Seth Guion, a close friend of his days in the attorney general's office.   This angered Ewing, who then undermined Pleasant's influence with the Machine.   As the election of 1920 approached, Governor Pleasant tried to agree with Behrman and the Organization on a candidate whom they could both support, but because Ewing fought the proposal, no agreement was reached.   Ewing then engineered a complete break between the Choctaws and Pleasant.[45]   After this occurrence Pleasant threw his support to Parker.

Endorsement of candidates for other state offices involved no great difficulty once it had been decided whom the Club would support for governor.   This was true because in most elections the minor candidates had indicated which of the candidates for governor they were supporting.   If this circumstance did not exist, the Choctaws would decide on the candidates individually or might make no specific declaration.   In deciding on a candidate for the United States Senate a number of considerations of course entered.   Chief among these was his attitude on local patronage and his

[44] For a complete account of this election, see chapter VIII.

[45] Shortly after these events Ewing deserted the Machine and went over to Parker. See chapter VIII.

chances of election in the country. As long as a Louisiana senator voted for tariff on sugar and regarded the Choctaw Club as representative of the highest traditions in New Orleans politics he could count on the continued support of that Organization. The average ward leader was not interested in the United States Senate, and Behrman and his chief advisers could endorse anybody they wished provided the Organization gave them the needed jobs for their wards. The choice of Congressmen in the first and second districts was not difficult to decide since the City could ordinarily contribute a majority sufficient to overcome the country vote of an opposing candidate. Furthermore close relations were built up with the country leaders through the use of state and federal patronage.[46]

THE CITY ORGANIZATION AND STATE LEGISLATION

The Orleans delegation in the legislature was large and a majority of the members owed their election to the Choctaw Club.[47] In order to make the influence of the delegation effective at Baton Rouge the Club provided for its organization, leadership, and discipline. Before the first session of the legislature, the City caucus of the Choctaw Club selected a floor leader for each branch of the legislature. A meeting of the legislative delegation would then be held to ratify the selection. Ordinarily men of previous legislative experience were chosen. The position of the Orleans delegation on important legislation was determined by the City caucus or

[46] Since Long has built a city machine in New Orleans, the situation has been changed. Long first took over the country parishes with state patronage and then the City fell under his sway in the Congressional election of 1934.

[47] Under the Constitutions of 1897 and 1913, New Orleans elected 25 of the 125 House members, and 9 of the 39 Senators. The Constitution of 1921 apportioned to the City 20 of the 100 members of the House and 9 of the 39 Senators.

by a caucus of the delegation itself. When either caucus had made its decision, the members of the delegation were obliged to vote as instructed. The City caucus took a hand in legislation more often in connection with laws directly affecting the City government or the control of the Machine. It might also issue instructions when certain economic forces in the City were being threatened. When the governor had outlined his program, the caucus met and decided which bills it would vote on as a unit and which it would allow members to vote on individually. It was quite common when uninstructed for the New Orleans members to vote on different sides of a question. Discipline, however, was perfectly maintained and on a signal from the floor leader the vote of the entire Choctaw group would be cast as directed.[48]

The floor leader made any necessary emergency decisions. He might designate another member to act in his stead when absent from the floor. Coordination between the work of the members of the House and Senate was effected in a joint caucus, by instructions from the City caucus, or by agreement of the leaders in the House and Senate. Since the Orleans group had a comparatively large block of votes it was in a position to make its support greatly sought after in organizing the House and Senate. It always demanded the chairmanship of the Committee on Affairs of the City of New Orleans and always wanted representation on the Committees on Parochial and Municipal Affairs and on Elections, Qualifications, Registration and Constitutional Amendments.[49] It was in these committees that blows were sometimes struck at the Machine or at some special power

[48] The floor leader ordinarily gave his instruction to the Choctaw member whose name came first in the roll call. Other members would then vote as this member voted.

[49] Except when the governor was opposed to the Machine a majority of the members of the Committee on Affairs of the City of New Orleans were from the City.

of the City government. If the Choctaw members of these committees failed to stifle an adverse proposal in committee, they could at least be forewarned of what was impending and prepare for the fight on the floor or arrange to defeat the unwelcome measure in the other house. It was also in these committes that legislation especially desired by the Machine or the City government was shaped, a further reason for the wish of the leaders for a voice in this work.

As will be indicated in specific instances in the following paragraphs, Martin Behrman was very active in legislative affairs. When extremely important laws affecting the City were under consideration, he spent much time in Baton Rouge as the chief lobbyist for such bills. As spokesman of the Organization, he carried much weight with the state legislative leaders and the governor. His personal qualities and his political ability also made him more effective than any of the delegation members could be. He knew what to do and how to do it in a legislative crisis and he never hesitated to use his power and prestige. Furthermore, he could make decisions without the necessity of consulting others. Once an objective had been agreed on by the City caucus, Behrman was authorized to work for it and to make such compromise as he might think wise to achieve the major purpose. Although the floor leader on occasion did similar work, his command of the situation never carried the weight that Behrman's did. During legislative sessions, Behrman kept in constant telephone communication with floor leaders and frequently issued the instructions of the Choctaw caucus on particular legislation by that means.

Considerable criticism has been leveled at the Machine for the caliber of men it sent to the legislature to represent New Orleans. One critic labeled the average Machine legislator as " a scarcely animate hunk of protoplasm, having the appetite of an elephant and the brains of a sparrow ". It was felt in some quarters in New Orleans that these men were below the average of country legislators in ability. If this were true, its possible adverse effects on the Machine were, to a large extent, overcome by the control exercised over the delegation by the leaders. There were always a few men of ability among the group, and the floor leader was selected from this number. The system undoubtedly put a greater premium on voting in accordance with instructions than on the thinking of individual members. An individual member whose constituents insisted on his voting on a particular measure, contrary to the decision of the Machine, might do so without loss of standing in the Organization. In 1912, for example, a member elected from the fifteenth ward where the Southern Pacific Railway shops are located voted for a fifty-four hour bill and a full crew law. In his campaign he had pledged support of such measures to a large number of his constituents who were railroad employees. Both of these bills had been opposed by the Machine.[50] A legislator might also vote at variance with instructions if his reelection might be endangered by not doing so even if he had made no election pledge concerning the issue involved. Information was that such a case must be very clear and have the tacit approval of the Choctaw floor leader. In general the practice in this matter was in accordance with the spirit of the rule now prevailing in the Democratic caucus of the United States House of Representatives.

The action of the Machine on various types of laws differed. The intent of the law and its subject matter usually determined its stand. When general legislation was before the body, the Machine was particularly alert. If the bill concerned the regulation of business or taxation, the Orleans delegation might be controlled in its position by the interests affected in New Orleans.[51] If the law dealt with

[50] *New Orleans Times Picayune*, July 3, 1912.
[51] See chapter V.

the election machinery its position depended on how the leaders thought the proposal would influence control of the City. Ordinarily if the country desired a particular measure that was not wanted in the City, the mere putting in of the words " the Parish of Orleans excepted" served to remove the opposition of the City representatives.[52] A good illustration of the action of the Machine on a particular bill affecting the whole state was its opposition to the " anti-assistance clause" in an election bill before the legislature in 1912.[53] Governor Hall had just been elected in April as a candidate for the Good Government faction. The City election was scheduled for September. The Good Government League planned to challenge the power of the Choctaws at that election. These men believed the provisions of the law allowing indiscriminate assistance to illiterates at the polls had been abused by the Choctaws and had helped to perpetuate their power. A bill was therefore introduced in the legislature, which met in May, to abolish all forms of assistance to voters. This would have been a blow to the " Regulars" since they controlled a large illiterate foreign vote. The provision would also have prevented many illiterate country voters from participating in the elections. The Machine under the floor leader in the House, Mr. Generelly, led the fight on the bill. The contest was so important that Behrman came to Baton Rouge. The Machine shrewdly based its opposition not on any possible loss of votes it might experience in New Orleans but on the appeal that it would deprive the ignorant white man of his vote. The Choctaws were determined that the bill should not pass in its original form. They began to filibuster and delay the whole legislative program of the governor. The advocates of the measure threatened an investigation of graft and

[52] See chapters II and III.
[53] *New Orleans Times Picayune*, July 2—July 20, 1912.

law enforcement in New Orleans if the Orleans group did not withdraw its opposition.[54]   They even agreed to insert a clause making the bill inoperative until after the coming City election.   To this Behrman replied: " When the proposition was conveyed to me and did not come from our side, I sent word to Mr. Generelly that I would not approve such a compromise.   We do not want any law that will not be effective in New Orleans at this coming election."   He was confident that the country legislators were not going to pass the law unless it allowed some sort of assistance to illiterate white voters on whom many depended for election.   He therefore took a bold stand.   The Choctaws continued to block the whole legislative process.   As a demonstration of their strength in blocking the legislative program and in retaliation to the threat of investigation, the Choctaw group in the Senate succeeded in permanently shelving an administration bill regulating the quality of commercial fertilizers.[55] Finally, through a conference between Governor Hall and the Mayor, a compromise acceptable to the City Organization was worked out which corrected the worst evils of the old law.[56]

[54] Behrman stated he would welcome such an investigation and assured the gentlemen that the Orleans delegates would support a resolution providing for it.   *New Orleans Times Picayune*, July 10, 1912.   No investigation was made and none occurred until Long's dominance of State politics.   The only time an investigation was politically possible was in the Parker administration but having beaten the Machine it was felt to be unnecessary at that time.

[55] *New Orleans Times Picayune*, July 10, 1912.

[56] Under the revised bill, which was passed, assistance could be furnished at the request of the voter by any election official but must be given in the presence of a second official.   Illiterate persons, those with physical disabilities which prevented writing and persons who had registered under the educational clause by being taught mechanically to write in order to register were allowed to ask for assistance.   An affidavit must be made by the person requiring assistance.   *Acts of Louisiana*, 1912, no. 12.

In the same session of the legislature, a bill proposed by Representative Sere to abolish the fee system for the compensation of public administrators and substitute a fixed salary was opposed by the Choctaw delegation. The Sere forces claimed the bosses wanted to keep the fee system as a source of patronage. The bill was finally passed over the opposition of the Choctaw Club.[57]

The Orleans delegation naturally took a major interest in all bills introduced which applied only to the City of New Orleans. Its action in such cases was illustrated by the charter controversy of 1912. The Good Government League, founded in 1910, had been steadily agitating for a commission charter and by 1912 had marshaled sentiment in favor of the change. The reformers insisted that the ward-elected council of the aldermanic system was the chief reason that the Machine continued to control the City. A proposed charter was introduced at the 1912 session by representatives of this group.[58] John M. Parker helped draft the Act. In addition to establishing the commission form of government, the bill also provided for reorganization of the parish government, proportional representation, initiative, referendum and recall.[59] The bill was opposed by the Choctaw Club, directed by Mayor Behrman, floor leader Generelly and City Attorney, I. D. Moore. Their tactics were simple. At the hearing they conclusively demonstrated that the Parker bill would require at least thirteen amendments to the Constitution before it could become effective.[60] The many constitutional changes were necessary because of

---

[57] *New Orleans Times Picayune*, July 21, 1912.

[58] The Good Government League had elected several representatives to the legislature at the election of 1912.

[59] *New Orleans Times Picayune*, June 14—June 28, 1912.

[60] This is in accordance with the views on the special legal and constitutional position of New Orleans brought out in chapter II.

the provisions which would have partially combined the City and parish governments.   This turned sentiment against the bill and its advocates then offered to eliminate the sections requiring constitutional changes.   Since their offer did not include the elimination of the proportional representation, the compromise was refused by the Choctaw delegation.   The club feared these provisions would destroy the party in New Orleans and certainly break its hold on the City.   Sensing that there was much sentiment in New Orleans in favor of the commission form of government, Behrman then had his attorneys draw a substitute bill providing the new form but containing no provisions for non-partisan elections and requiring no constitutional changes.   After considerable debate in the legislature it appeared that this was all that could be passed at the session.   Preferring the Behrman charter to no change at all, the Good Government League supported the bill and it was passed.   They did insist on an amendment requiring a referendum vote on the proposed charter at a special election.   This was included in the bill enacted and on August 28, 1912, the electors of New Orleans adopted the Choctaw written charter.[61]

A controversy occurring in 1910 over political influence in the schools in New Orleans brought a demand for a change in the organization of the school board.[62]   At that time the school board was elected by wards.   It was therefore large and lacked prestige.   To remedy this situation a bill was introduced in the legislative session of 1912 providing for a board of five members to be appointed by the governor.   The Choctaws opposed it and Behrman suggested that the mayor be allowed to appoint three of the members and that the governor name two.   This did not seem satis-

[61] *New Orleans Times Picayune*, Aug. 29, 1912. *Acts of Louisiana,* 1912, no. 159.
[62] See chapter VIII.

factory and the original bill was finally enacted providing for the election at large, of a school board of five members.[63] The aim of those who introduced the measure was to take the schools out of politics and by creating a small board elected at large to add to its prestige and thus secure more able men as members. The bill was passed and the improvements desired were achieved but the Choctaw candidates for the smaller school board succeeded in being elected as long as the Machine controlled the City. There were seldom any charges of undue political influence in school affairs made after the new board was created.

In voting on legislation which concerned some specific parish or city other than New Orleans, members from the City were ordinarily allowed freedom. In some instances where the controversy was important or where it was related in some way to the general political situation in the state, the delegation voted as a unit and frequently wielded the balance of power. Such an instance occurred in 1912. An attempt was being made to oust the mayor and other city officials of Monroe and provide for a change in the form of city government. The controversy was bitter and was of some general political concern. The country elements were divided and the City Machine was put in the position of having to make the decision in a local controversy.[64] This demonstrated very clearly that the City Organization was at times important in determining the fate of local issues. In fact, realizing this, country politicians often sought the Machine's support for their local bills in exchange for favorable votes by them on Choctaw-sponsored measures.

The Machine was little interested in what happened in Congress. Its political activities were almost wholly confined to the City and the state. It seldom sought to direct

[63] *New Orleans Times Picayune*, July 1, 1912.
[64] *New Orleans Times Picayune*, June 3—June 10, 1912.

the votes of the two Congressmen and the Senators with whose election it was concerned.   That Behrman's influence with these men was large was demonstrated by the effect of his request to Congressman Estopinal of the first district when the Greater Navy Bill of 1916 was under consideration.[65]   The bill had gone to a conference and one vote was needed for its adoption by the conferees.   Congressman Estopinal was one of the conferees and was opposing the adoption of two features greatly desired by big navy advocates.   B. T. Waldo, head of the Louisiana division of the Navy League, went to the City Hall to request that Behrman intercede with Estopinal.   The Mayor was in an important meeting of the Sewage and Water Board but because of the urgent request came out and talked with Waldo.   After having the situation explained to him he authorized the sending of the following telegram over his signature to the Congressman: " I urge on you your support, as a member of the House conference committee, of the construction program and the increase in the number of officers and men provisions in the Senate Navy Bill.   The sentiment here is, in my opinion, overwhelming for preparedness along all lines and I am sure you feel as we do about it ".   At this time Behrman's influence was at its height.   By some, he was regarded as the complete boss of politics in New Orleans. There is little wonder that the Louisiana Congressman from a New Orleans district dropped his opposition and voted for a big navy.   An interesting side-light on this case was that the headquarters of the Navy League in Washington had requested Waldo to seek Behrman's assistance.   The Washington office evidently knew by whom effective influence could be brought.

These cases are illustrations of the wide influence the Machine had in legislative affairs.   Because of its power

[65] *New Orleans Item*, Aug. 9, 1916, May 3, 1925.

in elections and the legislature it naturally was given a prominent place in the state administrative organization. It had charge of state tax administration in New Orleans under the supervision of the State Tax Commission and ordinarily had a member on that Commission. The headquarters of the Department of Conservation were located in New Orleans and the administrative personnel was largely drawn from the City. Every governor was tempted to favor unduly this great center of population with a disproportionate share of appointments in other administrative services and, as already mentioned, the Organization controlled the large supply of state patronage within New Orleans. In the Constitution of 1898 and the two subsequent constitutions a provision designed to overcome the inclination of governors to use their appointive power to build up influence was inserted. It stipulated that no governor should be eligible to succeed himself.[66] This had little effect since the governor was always identified with a faction and desired to perpetuate his group in power. His ambitions might also run toward Congress or the Senate and hence in the future he could capitalize personally the results of his activities as governor.

A state machine was never developed during the period from 1897 to 1926, though several attempts were made. In 1904 an effort was made to combine the City of New Orleans, the first, second and third congressional districts into a permanent faction to control the state. The City leaders and the parish leaders included in this territory believed if they could act as a unit while dividing the rest of the state they could elect the governor and dictate Louisiana policies. The combination had influence for several years but never was fully successful. It was really a union of the sugar-producing areas with the City of New Orleans which was also interested in sugar. The advocates of this

---

[66] *Constitutions of 1898, 1913 and 1921*; arts. 62, 63 and 65, respectively.

proposed state machine believed there was a community of economic interests that could cooperate.   In this their judgment proved wrong and issues arose which caused the combination to fall apart.   The friction involved the conflict of the producers and the refiners of sugar and of rural and urban interests.   Again from 1908 to 1912 during the period of cooperation between Mayor Behrman and Governor Sanders a state machine was believed to be in process of formation.   Their falling out and the election of Governor Hall brought to an end the possibility of state-wide unified faction.   Sanders had great influence in the country but did not achieve an organization that could be called a machine. The fact that he was unable to carry the country in his race for the United States Senate in 1912 is evidence that his faction was not a permanent organization.   The elections of 1920 put the Parker faction in control of the state and City, but its influence in both was short-lived.   No successful state machine was created until Huey P. Long built his now famous organization.   Two combinations were always possible; one was to unite the country solidly against the City; the other was to unite the City with influences controlling half of the country vote.   These contingencies were difficult and no leader arose who could accomplish either until Huey Long became the master of Louisiana politics.[67]

[67] Governor Long first achieved solidarity in the country and later through state patronage built up a city machine which succeeded in carrying New Orleans against the Choctaws in the Congressional elections of September, 1934.

CHAPTER VIII

CHARACTER AND METHODS OF FACTIONAL OPPONENTS OF REGULARS—DEFEAT IN 1920—RETURN TO POWER 1925 —THE LONG SHADOW DEEPENS

THAT the Choctaw Club had factional opposition in most elections has already been indicated. In discussing the political background of the Organization it was shown that the old New Orleans machine, which the Choctaw Club succeeded, was defeated in 1896. This defeat caused the organization of the Choctaw Club and, with the disfranchisement of the Negro, enabled the new Organization to achieve control of the City in 1900.[1] Since 1900 two major City factions have appeared with state support, and in addition two lesser factions have arisen, one with only partial state cooperation and the other with none at all. As contests between the Choctaws and these factions are analyzed it will be clearly shown that the Organization could be successfully opposed only when the governor cooperated fully and when other factors were favorable. The two major factions which had the support of the governor were the Good Government League of 1912 and the Orleans Democratic Association of 1920. The latter had the more wholehearted state support. Two factional contests of less importance occurred in 1904 and 1925. The opposing groups in these two instances were the Home Rulers of 1904 and the New Regulars of 1925. The former had no state support and the latter only such aid as Governor Parker had given it before he was succeeded by Fuqua in 1924. In

[1] Chapter I, p. 39.

1908 a potential faction died in embryo and in 1916 there was no contest. In considering the factional struggles in New Orleans particular attention is called to the fact that the state election always preceded the City election by several months.

A number of forces entered into the creation of the Home Rule faction in 1904, some of which have been discussed. The chief inspiration, as the name of the faction clearly indicates, was the interference of Governor Blanchard in local affairs when he forced the Choctaw caucus to substitute Porter Parker for C. C. Luzenberg as the candidate for District Attorney.[2]   Porter Parker was a brother of John M. Parker and the latter supported Blanchard's move.   This apparent high-handed action of the Governor served to rally all those opposed to Behrman and the Machine, the Governor, and the convention system.   The movement was the answer to Governor Blanchard's question: " Well, what are you going to do about it? "[3]   The " it " referred to his local interference.

Another force was the refusal of the Choctaw-controlled Orleans Parish Democratic Committee to nominate the Democratic candidates under the provisions of the optional primary law of 1900.   Still another was the reorganization and consolidation of the Sewage and Water Board with the Drainage Commission which was suspected by some to have been a " plot " of the Machine to control the funds of both.

The Choctaw Club at the time of the election seemed in an enviable position politically.   It had controlled state patronage for eight years and City patronage for the past four. Knowing the danger of attempting to oppose the wishes of

---

[2] See chapter IV.

[3] This is so reminiscent of William Tweed's remark that it may have been given a local habitation by the newspapers who quoted the Governor as having made the remark on this occasion.

the governor, it had accepted his dictation in the selection of a district attorney and had been assured of the right to continue to dispense state patronage in New Orleans. In view of this it was surprising that the Home Rulers were able to present such formidable opposition.

The movement was led by Page M. Baker, publisher of the *New Orleans Times Democrat,* who was opposed to organization politics and believed in the rule of the rich and well born. He undoubtedly carried with him most of those in his stratum of society. The candidate for mayor of the faction was Charles F. Buck, a prominent, well educated lawyer who had been active in politics for many years.[4] He had been candidate for mayor in 1896 when the Democrats were defeated by the Republican-Populist-Citizens' League combination.[5] He was highly regarded in all circles and was a brilliant campaigner. His presence as the head of the ticket explains much of the vote received by the faction. Behrman was elected, receiving 13,962 votes to 10,047 for Buck.[6] The defeat of the Home Rule faction was due to patronage in the hands of the Choctaws. There was a difference of less than four thousand votes, over half of which probably came from job holders in City and state governments. In commenting on the election, Behrman attributed his victory in part to the fact that the " silk stocking " element had failed to qualify under the new suffrage laws and to pay their poll tax and hence were not able to vote.[7] His position was that the very instrument designed to disfranchise the Negro and weaken the Machine had been oue of its greatest assets. This undoubtedly contributed to Buck's defeat but the decisive factor was the advantage in-

[4] *New Orleans Times Democrat,* Sept. 1, 1904.

[5] See Chapter I.

[6] *Report of the Secretary of State,* 1904.

[7] *New Orleans Item,* Nov. 19, 1922.

herent in control of the City government and State support. The Home Rule campaign speakers made charges which they could not prove and this had an unfavorable effect. The business interests were divided in the campaign to the disappointment of Page M. Baker and the so-called " better elements." Except for Charles F. Buck, the organization was composed of inexperienced politicians, which made its work less effective. Characteristic of " reform" movements, as soon as the election was over the organization disbanded and no effort was made to make the faction a permanent opponent to the Choctaw Club.[8] This was natural since it had no spoils on which to base a permanent existence. Unfortunately for New Orleans, it left the Machine with no organized faction to question its administration.

In 1908 the Independent Democratic League was formed to oppose the Machine but decided not to contest Mayor Behrman's nomination in the Democratic primary. Instead it planned to nominate candidates by petition and to enter the general election.[9] When the petition of nomination was

[8] *Ibid.*, Nov. 20, 1922.

[9] The League's reason for not entering the primary was that it felt that the primary election machinery was too firmly in the hands of the Choctaws. At the state election a few months before a contest over the lieutenant governor's office had taken place. The Democratic State Central Committee decided the contest in favor of the candidate supported by the Choctaws. The League contended that the Choctaws controlled the Committee and it therefore feared that if it entered the primary it might be cheated. The facts do not support the charge that the " Machine" controlled the State Committee. The winning contestant had not only received the support of the Orleans members of the Committee but also a majority of the country members. The influence of the Governor in this instance was important. Sanders had just been elected, with the support of the City Organization. A combination of City and state influence made the disputed decision. There was no evidence found to indicate the decision was wrong. *New Orleans Item*, Jan. 10, 1923. As a result of this contest the primary law was amended to provide review by the courts of the decisions of the State Central Committee in primary election disputes.

filed it was found that the papers did not contain the number of signatures of qualified voters required by law.[10] The League disputed the local registrar's decision and took the case to the election contest board in Baton Rouge composed of the governor, lieutenant governor and the speaker of the house. It lost before this board and also in the courts where the struggle finally ended. The Supreme Court refused to compel the secretary of state to place the names of candidates of the League on the ballot.[11] Behrman received 26,897 votes, a Socialist candidate polled 270, and an Independent, 89. The history of the faction fully explains its impotence. The Independent Democratic League, was headed by Rollo Tichinor and was made up of a number of former members of the Home Rulers of 1904. Its first meeting was not held until July 20, 1908. Newspaper accounts of the meeting indicate that there was no great interest in the movement. The chairman was authorized to appoint leaders for each of the seventeen wards to act as organizers and as an executive committee.[12] This effort was the outstanding example occurring in New Orleans politics of amateur politicians seeking overnight to organize to contest the supremacy of the powerful City Machine which not only had its own patronage but had just elected another friendly governor. The League never had a remote chance of success even if it had drawn to its support all the two thousand Republican voters in the City. Its own foundations were far too weak.

Events occurring between 1910 and the City election of 1912 both favored and hindered the chances of the success of the faction that was organized at this time in opposition to the Machine because it endorsed a candidate unacceptable

[10] See chapter III.

[11] *New Orleans Times Picayune*, Oct. 28, 1908.

[12] *New Orleans Times Picayune*, Aug. 1 and 2, 1908.

to the reform elements. The new faction, known as the Good Government League, had been organized two years before the election. Its early organization had been due to the fact that it appeared, in 1910, that Governor Sanders would leave his office and go to the United States Senate before the end of his term in 1912. Although this expected event did not take place, various candidates announced their intentions to run. This precipitated political alignments sooner than was usual.[13]

Colonel Lewis was made president of the League and John M. Parker, vice president. Both had been active opponents of the Machine for years. The League laid plans to force the adoption of the commission form of government and to secure the election of a governor who would support the League instead of the Choctaw Club. It hoped to be able then to elect the mayor and commissioners in 1912. A bitter controversy in New Orleans over the selection of a parish superintendent of schools helped the League's plans. In the first place Behrman chose the side of the school contest that proved to be unpopular and was accused of using the schools for political purposes. In the second place an apparent effort on the part of Behrman and Sanders to eliminate James B. Aswell from the governor's race by offering him the $10,000 superintendency in New Orleans failed. The Machine lost many votes as a result.

Aswell was thoroughly qualified for the school position. He had been in educational work all his life; hence the criticism of the action of the Behrman-controlled school board in offering him the position was not based on Aswell's lack of competence but on the supposed motives of Behrman in engineering the offer.[14]

13 For a full account of the incident, see chapter VII.

14 The contest in the school board was spirited and the board was about equally divided. John R. Conniff, the assistant superintendent, was fav-

Colonel Bob Ewing favored Aswell's candidacy for governor and when the Choctaw Club endorsed John T. Michel in place of James B. Aswell he broke with the Machine. Another important loss to the Machine occurred when Floor Leader Generelly of the Choctaw delegation went over to the Good Government League after he failed to secure the endorsement of the Club for district attorney.[15] Still another favorable sign for the League was the election of Governor Luther E. Hall in April, 1912, whom the organization had supported. Strong support was expected from the governor in the form of state patronage in New Orleans. Another factor of some significance was the defeat, at the same election, of Governor Sanders, who was running for the United States Senate. Because he felt he had been tricked by the Choctaws in his campaign such support as he had was used against the Organization in the City election. After the state election Ewing remained unreconciled and

ored for the place by many people, including some of the Choctaw ward leaders. Behrman opposed him for the place, claiming new blood was needed in the schools. He favored Professor Gwinn of Tulane University. During the contest one of the members of the school board resigned. Behrman was authorized by law to fill the vacancy and appointed a member favorable to Gwinn. This turned the tide and Gwinn was elected. Behrman was accused first of trying to use the schools to eliminate a candidate for governor by seeking the appointment of Aswell and second with naming a former bartender to the board so that he could control the election. After the election of Gwinn a mass meeting protesting the action was held. Behrman was accused of having tainted the schools with " the odor of the tenderloin, the barroom and the racetrack ". He appeared before the hostile mass meeting and explained his stand. Behrman insisted he was not playing politics because he had chosen the unpopular side of the controversy. *New Orleans Times Picayune*, Sept. 1 to Nov. 15, 1910, and *New Orleans Item*, Feb. 2-12, 1923, " Behrman Tells ".

[15] It will be recalled that Mr. Generelly had given the Choctaws valiant service in the charter contest in the legislature during the summer of 1912.

threw his support to the Good Government League in its fight for control of the City.[16]

Against these facts which gave the Good Government League hope of success were a number of others which indicated that its chances were perhaps less than even. It seems probable that the success of Mayor Behrman and the Machine in defeating the proposed City charter of the Good Government League in the legislature a few months before was the decisive influence in the election.[17] The Machine had then drawn a commission charter more to its liking and secured its passage by the Legislature and its adoption by the voters. This was a demonstration of the strength of the Machine in the legislature and in the City and naturally did not augur well for the League. It had in fact removed the leading issue which the League was advocating, the question of a new charter. The school controversy was also greatly allayed by the passage of a bill reorganizing the Orleans Parish School Board. The Good Government League during the summer suffered the loss of its most outstanding leader, when John M. Parker turned Progressive and supported Theodore Roosevelt. It appeared also that Governor Hall's support would not be over-zealous. During the summer session of the legislature a friendly relation had grown up between him and Mayor Behrman and the reformers looked on this with suspicion. It was believed by some observers that Governor Hall felt that he must have the co-operation of the City delegation if his legislative program was to pass. It was also obvious that Behrman was openly

---

[16] It is probable that had Aswell accepted the school position in New Orleans, Ewing would not have been opposed to the Machine in the City election. If Aswell had been out of the race, Michel might have won and strengthened the "Regulars" for the City fight. The break between Ewing and Behrman was accentuated by the Wilson-Clark contest in the Louisiana Democratic Convention. See chapter VII.

[17] For an account of this, see chapter VII.

courting his favor in order to prevent, if possible, the use of his power against the Organization in the coming election. Although Behrman secured no active support from Hall he succeeded in preventing him from assisting the League to any marked degree. Besides the elimination of the charter and the school issues and the neutralization of the governor's influence, the Choctaws were wise in the selection of candidates for the first commission council. The ward-elected council under the aldermanic form of government was said by the Good Government League to explain the Club's control of the City. Efficiency and business methods were supposed to characterize commission government. The Good Government League had popularized the idea that the new form of government would be a " board of directors " for the City, elected at large and much more efficient than the old system. In addition to showing their good faith in securing a new charter, the Choctaws now proceeded to " perfume " the ticket with business men—in fact they literally saturated it with " efficiency ".

Four business men of recognized standing were named on the ticket headed by Mayor Behrman. They were: A. B. Ricks, brewer, baker and hide-dealer; Harold W. Newman, banker; W. P. Thompson, cotton broker; and E. E. Lafaye, merchant. This tended to remove all doubt that the Choctaws were opposed to good government and eliminated still another issue from those on which the hopes of the Good Government League were based. It availed the League nothing that it named a business slate headed by Charles F. Claiborne.

The campaign proved to be a bitter one. " Down with the bosses ", was the cry of the Leaguers. Because they believed the police interfered with opposition voters, the League threatened to have armed men at the polls to insure fair play. The Choctaws accepted the challenge through

John P. Sullivan, who said the " Regulars " would meet the
League at the polls " gun for gun ".[18]   The " Ring " was
accused of permitting gambling, prostitution, and graft; it
was charged with wasting the City's money on useless jobs
and ill-planned projects.[19]   Behrman based his campaign on
his record and pointed to twenty-one new school buildings,
sixteen fire stations, seventy-five miles of paving, four
markets, the public belt railway, a city paving plant, and
other improvements.   His positive program was one of additional civic improvements.   Behrman had the endorsement
of organized labor while Claiborne's labor record was
brought into question.[20]   When the votes were counted
Behrman had 27,371 and Claiborne, 13,917, and an entire
Choctaw ticket was also elected.

THE CHOCTAW CLUB DEFEATED—ROLE OF THE
GOVERNOR IN CITY POLITICS

John M. Parker's long experience in Louisiana politics
had taught him that the road to power in New Orleans was
by way of Baton Rouge.   There was no man more zealous for
political reform in the City and state.   In his opinion it followed that any man less zealous would be unable to resist the
flesh pots of politics offered by the Machine.   He therefore
decided to become governor of the state and use his power to
crush the Choctaw Club.   No other factional struggle so
clearly reveals the power of the governor in New Orleans
politics as the one occurring in 1920 between Mayor Behrman and his Choctaw Club and Governor Parker and his

[18] *New Orleans Times Picayune*, Aug. 16, 1912. Behrman refused the
request for neutral police. He stated that the opposing ward leaders had
agreed to peace plans.

[19] *Ibid.*, Aug. 20, 1912.

[20] Claiborne was charged with voting against semi-monthly pay and
increased wages for City workers while a councilman from 1896-1900.
New Orleans Item, Sept. 27, 1922.

Sullivan-led state-supported City machine.   The contest also demonstrated that the power of the Machine was not broken by the righteous indignation of an outraged electorate, but by the work of a counter machine, which, at least momentarily, had superior strength.   Policies of the Choctaw Club, long in semi-obscurity because of the absence of alert opposition, were brought into question.

The World War served to bring a reaction in Louisiana politics just as it did in national politics.   The people wanted change and John M. Parker was proposing change.   His candidacy therefore fitted the temper of the times.   There were other more important influences that led to his election. As stated in the previous chapter, a break had occurred between Governor Pleasant and Mayor Behrman under the inspiration of Colonel Bob Ewing.[21]   The efforts of the Governor and the Machine to agree on state candidates therefore failed.   This was probably the fatal mistake as the Governor then joined the Parker faction in its war on the Machine.   The candidate opposing Parker was Colonel Stubbs of Monroe.   Since he was not fighting the Organization he received its endorsement.   Former Governor J. Y. Sanders, still at odds with Behrman, came out for Parker. He did not believe a soldier could be elected in the post-war reaction.

Huey P. Long was just beginning his political career.   He had been elected to the State Public Service Commission in 1918 and had begun a campaign against the Standard Oil Company, the railroads, and the utilities.   Supposing John M. Parker to be a crusader for economic reform, as well as political purity, he supported him for Governor.   Long's campaign efforts in the country in the interest of Parker's candidacy were most effective.   Though believing mildly in curbing economic privilege, Parker was by no means ready

[21] See chapter VII.

to move as fast or as far as Long wanted him to move.[22] During the course of the campaign it became evident that Parker was fairly sure of election.   Some of Behrman's advisers tried to get him to switch to Parker and to seek a compromise before it was too late.   Having given Stubbs the promise of the Choctaw caucus, Behrman refused even though he knew his candidate had no chance.   Parker won the election by a large majority.

Colonel John P. Sullivan, a former Choctaw leader who had joined the Reformers in 1919, had been manager of the Parker campaign in New Orleans.   On election night, as soon as the returns showed Parker had won, a parade was held which marched to the steps of the City Hall.   In a rally held then and there the Parker leaders announced the beginning of an eight months' campaign to capture the City Hall.   The Parker faction was known as the Orleans Democratic Association and began perfecting the machine already started in the governor's race.   Governor Parker took office in May and immediately put all state patronage in the City at the disposal of his City organization.   At last the Choctaw Club was faced with an opposition with jobs on which to build effective precinct and ward units.   All the newspapers supported Parker's move to break the hold of the Machine.[23] No opportunity was missed, from January to September, to impress the people with the mistakes, shortcomings, and " corruption " of the Machine.

All factional quarrels in New Orleans had been bitter but this one proved more personal and violent than any since the elections of the Nineties.   The " Regulars " were charged

---

[22] Later as a result of Parker's deference to the Standard Oil Company in the Constitutional Convention of 1921, Long broke with Parker and announced he would run for governor in 1924.

[23] Behrman remarked in 1922 that he " was slaughtered in 1920 to make a newspaper holiday." *New Orleans Item*, Oct. 30, 1922.

with every known evil of city government.   The opposition
evidently had a research staff comb the newspapers, legislative proceedings, and City records for the past twenty years.
Nothing was overlooked that might prove the incompetence
or corruptness of the Organization or any individual office
holder connected with it.   In some ways this was very unfair
and unreasonable.   Many of the things charged to the door
of the Choctaws as being " evil and wicked " had been done
during the time some of the very men who were making the
charges had been equally responsible with Behrman for what
the Machine had done.   Sullivan and Ewing had long been
Choctaw politicians and had never before shown any unusual evidence of " righteousness " in politics.   Their association with the reformers seemed a little out of place.

The Machine was charged with saddling vast debt on the
City, tolerating open vice, padding the City payrolls, permitting violation of health laws, protecting the restricted district,
and working against the interests of labor.   The *New
Orleans Times Picayune* ran a column, entitled " Under the
Shadow of the Vulture's Wings ", which pictured lurid vice
conditions and described to the reader the visits of the enter-
prising reporter to " gambling hells and palaces of plea-
sure ".[24]   Specific names and addresses were given to prove
that vice went on with the knowledge of the police.   Mayor
Behrman's effort during the War to keep the restricted district was used effectively in the campaign.[25]

[24] *New Orleans Times Picayune*, Aug. 25–Sept. 12, 1920.   The *States*
and the *Item* carried similar stories; a series of cartoons entitled,
" Martin and Minnie " depicting Behrman and the Machine was also
published in the *Picayune*.   It was interesting to note that neither in the
election of 1920 nor of 1925 did the metropolitan press attack the
fundamental politico-business relationships of the Choctaw Club.   Its
labor record was exposed in 1920, but merely for election purposes and
not from a desire for reform.   The evils emphasized concerned election
irregularities and privileged vice.   Privileged business was undisturbed.

[25] See chapter VI.

The Orleans Democratic Association had named as its candidate for mayor, Andrew J. McShane, an outstanding business man, with little experience in politics. Neither he nor his running mates were prominent in the campaign. Behrman and bossism were the issues. McShane and his mates were presented to the voters as respectable, honest men, who had been drafted for public service to save the City from ruin. They advocated the stock commonplaces of politics, efficiency, economy, and progress and for the most part opposed only the obvious forms of graft, corruption, and waste. Parker and Sullivan promised that an efficient civil service system would be provided for the City.

Because labor in New Orleans was very active at this time, the Parker forces investigated the labor record of the Choctaw Club carefully. The revelations made and for the most part substantiated by legislative records were anything but complimentary to the Choctaw Club.[26] Attention was called to the fact that the City authorities during the past twenty years had broken strikes of the public belt railway and dock workers, using the police against strikers and blacklisting the leaders. This was not denied by the Choctaws. Behrman's explanation was that these were instances of strikes against government which no city could permit. He charged that Governor Parker had broken the dock workers' strike successfully in 1920 with even harsher methods.[27] This could not be successfully denied by the Parker forces. The position taken by the Machine in the wage controversy during the War involving the employees of the New Orleans Railway and Light Company could not be explained so easily.[28]

[26] *The New Orleans Item* of September 5, 1920, gave a complete summary of the labor record of the Organization and cited the proper House and Senate Proceedings to substantiate the statements made. The article also described the action taken by City officials in specific labor troubles.

[27] *New Orleans Times Picayune*, Sept. 6, 1920.

[28] *New Orleans States*, July 23, 1918.

In 1918 car-men were receiving from the company 24½ cents per hour. Because of the tremendous increase in the cost of living, the men asked for a wage of 45 cents per hour. The company offered to pay 31 cents which would have meant an average income of $69.50 per month for a man and his family. An appeal was made by the men to the War Labor Board and this Board ordered the increase. The company petitioned for an exception from the ruling and were supported by the City authorities. One of the City commissioners and the City attorney were sent to Washington to support the Company's claim. They urged the War Labor Board to allow the company to pay only 31 cents per hour on the ground that it was in financial difficulties and that the wage offered was fair and sufficient for a man and his family in New Orleans.[29]   The Labor Board wisely ruled in favor of labor and granted the higher wage.

By reference to the proceedings of the Louisiana House and Senate for the session of 1918, the opposition proved that the " Regular " delegation at Baton Rouge had voted against seventeen of twenty labor bills at that one session.[30] Among them were a minimum wage law for minors, a bill prohibiting the importation of strike breakers, a bill to prevent rent profiteering and a bill requiring street cars to carry both a motorman and a conductor. It was also shown that these same bills were being opposed by the large employers of the state and City. Particular attention was called to the action of the Machine on House Bill Number 362 of

[29] In an effort to bolster his labor record Behrman called attention to his action in the textile strike in 1906. In this strike he had sought to arbitrate the dispute and had been sympathetic to the cause of labor. The company had imported strike breakers and as soon as the strike was broken had turned them out. They immediately became public charges and Behrman insisted on the company sending them back to Georgia from which state they had been brought at the company's expense.

[30] *New Orleans Item*, Sept. 2, 1920.

1918, introduced by Representative Fortier. This bill provided for minimum wages and maximum hours for minors and women employed in factories. The record showed that the bill was passed on first reading and was sent to committee where it was approved and reported out. At this point Mayor Behrman sent for Representative Fortier and according to Fortier made the following statement: " Fortier, you understand, do you not, that the political organization of which I am the voice has grown to be more than a mere political organization. The manufacturers of this City have called upon me and look to me to see to it that no laws are passed that are inimical to their interests. You know or ought to know that having affiliated ourselves with big commercial interests in New Orleans that we have thereby eliminated the possibility of contests, because these are the people who have heretofore contributed large sums that permitted the organization of reform movements." Having said this, according to Fortier, Behrman urged that he let the bill go back to committee and that it be shelved. Fortier refused to do this. When the bill came up on the third reading Mr. Fortier moved its adoption. The floor leader of the Orleans delegation then moved that the bill be sent back to committee. Twenty-two of the twenty-four representatives from New Orleans voted to return the bill to committee. A simple command from the Mayor had changed the vote of the entire delegation which had previously voted for the bill. In spite of this opposition the bill passed the House. In the Senate it was defeated when a motion to indefinitely postpone, made by a " Ring " Senator, prevailed.[31] This was effectively played up as Behrman's 1918 record for women and children. The only aspect of the story

---

[31] *New Orleans Item*, Sept. 5, 1920. A check of the Proceedings for 1918 reveals the action described as substantially correct. See especially *Senate Journal*, p. 762; *House Journal*, pp. 343, 501, 703.

that seems doubtful was a part of Behrman's alleged statement to Fortier. Undoubtedly Behrman was asked by manufacturers to prevent the passage of labor bills. Being a believer in free enterprise and wanting the support of business, he marshaled the opposition of the Choctaws against such bills. If the manufacturers said a bill would hurt the commercial progress of New Orleans the Choctaws accepted their position and acted accordingly. It is doubtful whether Behrman made the last part of the statement as he knew the reform movements did not originate with the business interests. He was aware that these movements received little financial encouragement from business unless the strength of the reformers indicated it was advisable to " buy " a share in order to play safe.

The City election was held September 14, 1920, and resulted in the closest vote of more than thirty years. Behrman lost by only 1200 votes, which was less than the number of jobs furnished the Orleans Democratic Association by the state. Only one Choctaw candidate was elected to the commission council. Both organizations had maintained strict watch at every poll to assure a fair election.[32] For several days there was talk of a recount and it was not until September 23rd, that the campaign manager of the Choctaws conceded Behrman's defeat.[33]

Mayor Behrman attributed his defeat primarily to the state patronage furnished by Governor Parker particularly on the state docks. There seems little doubt that this was a major cause. He pointed out in further explanation that high prices during the War had made it impossible for the City to do many things it should have done. In his view failure to increase the pay of City workers was in part

[32] It was interesting to note that T. Semmes Walmsley, present mayor of New Orleans, was Behrman's assistant campaign manager.
[33] *New Orleans Item*, Sept. 23, 1920.

responsible. He frankly admitted he failed to gauge the
wave of discontent that arose in 1919 and 1920.[34] He
remarked that he had been elected on his record in 1908,
1912 and 1916, and had been defeated on what other people
said was his record in 1920. " Most people " he said, " remember what you did to them rather than what you did for
them." [35]

During Behrman's life time, this was the only City defeat
suffered by the Choctaw Club since its organization in 1897.
A determined governor, taking a lesson from the Choctaw
Club's own methods, had built a counter machine in the City
based on patronage. Favored by dissension within the old
Organization, an era of discontent and a vulnerable record
on the part of the opposition he had proved his thesis that
the road to power in New Orleans was by way of Baton
Rouge. Governor Parker was soon to learn that his own
machine was not different from the one he believed he had
just destroyed. In fact it turned out to contain many of
the less desirable members of the Choctaw Club who had
" fled the old ship with the rats when the water had reached
the upper deck."

In spite of its election victory the Orleans Democratic
Association failed. It was unable to consolidate its position
and maintain its unity. The elements constituting the organization were too discordant and it did not become the
permanent opposition to the Choctaw Club. This had been
Parker's aim and he was greatly disillusioned when the
organization fell apart. Its failure was due to the political
ineptness of Mayor McShane, the bickerings among the

---

[34] *New Orleans Item*, Mar. 11, 1923.

[35] *Ibid.* A further comment at this time also reveals his understanding
of politics. " No matter what you do in public life you will make enemies.
Sixteen years of enemies is a lot of them." *New Orleans Item*, Jan. 13,
1926.

leaders, and a serious division within the commission council. In 1922 John P. Sullivan formed a new faction made up largely of ex-Choctaws and former members of the Orleans Democratic Association. This faction he called the " New Regulars ".[36]

BEHRMAN AND THE CHOCTAW CLUB RETURN TO POWER

Unlike the reform organizations that had opposed it in the past, the Choctaw Club after its defeat began at once to prepare for a return to power. Former Mayor Behrman, in bad health following the campaign, had gone to the sea coast for a rest but kept in constant touch with his Organization. His defeat and his failing health, together with the ambitions of some of the leaders, brought a move to retire him as the official head of the Club. When informed that there was sentiment for his retirement he called the chief ward leaders together and on hearing from their own lips that they felt he should resign, he did so. Behrman stated to the leaders on this occasion that his sole ambition was to see the Choctaw Club restored to power and prestige in the City and pledged himself to work unceasingly to achieve these ends. Commissioner Maloney, the only Choctaw named to high office in the election of 1920, was chosen as City leader in Behrman's stead.[37] The political events of the next four years proved these men were wrong in thinking Behrman was done for politically because of his defeat in 1920. He went into business but never ceased his work of rebuilding and restoring his own political and personal popularity and that of the Organization.

[36] This faction never carried the City but succeeded in electing Francis Williams to the Public Service Commission and filled one judgeship.

[37] In selecting Maloney the caucus was following the precedent of naming the highest City official, who was a Club member, to the leadership.

Slowly Behrman rebuilt the Machine and on several occasions demonstrated its growing strength. In 1921, he was elected to the constitutional convention as the representative of the fifteenth ward of which he was still leader. In 1922 a Choctaw candidate was elected to the Public Service Commission and Charles Rosen, a foe of the old Machine, was defeated for a judgeship.[38] Behrman's influence helped reelect Senator Ransdall during the same period. By 1924 the " Regulars " were in a position to play a leading role in the state election. Parker's machine in the City was gone and in its place was the " New Regular " faction. The Ku Klux Klan was powerful in the state, particularly in North Louisiana, but its reputation had been greatly injured by the famous Mer Rouge murder cases.[39] Because South Louisiana was largely Catholic a number of state leaders feared the election might result in making the religious issue paramount. The leading contenders were Henry L. Fuqua, a tolerant Protestant and of the old school of southern gentlemen, from South Louisiana; Henry Bauncand, a Catholic and also from South Louisiana; and Huey P. Long, a Protestant living in North Louisiana and a member of the State Public Service Commission who had gained a large following by attacking the great corporate interests. Long seemed the most popular in the country. If precedent had been followed he would have received the endorsement of th " Regulars ".[40] There were other considerations that apparently outweighed precedent on this occasion. The Choctaws endorsed Henry L. Fuqua. Behrman wanted to avoid a religious fight in the state and he believed Fuqua the more tolerant of the two Protestants and he knew that a Catholic had little chance of winning in 1924. A further

[38] *New Orleans Times Picayune*, Jan. 13, 1926.

[39] *New Orleans Item*, Feb. to June, 1923.

[40] For discussion on selecting the governor, see chapter VII.

consideration was that Long, in his war on big business, had offended interests in New Orleans on which Behrman counted for support. The New Regulars and the governor being opposed to Long endorsed Bauncand because Parker would not support a man who had accepted the endorsement of the Choctaw Club.[41] Behrman and his Machine threw all the strength possible into the race knowing if they were to return to power in the City in 1925 the support of the governor would be necessary in order to overcome the advantages held by those then in power at the City Hall. With the help of the weather, which kept many country voters away from the polls, and superior work in the City, Fuqua was elected by a small majority over Long.[42] As a reward for supporting Fuqua the Choctaws were given the state patronage in New Orleans. Behrman's work in this election conclusively demonstrated that he was in fact, if not in name, the leader of the Choctaw Club. The failure of the incumbent City administration and Parker's waning influence made Behrman more popular than ever. A demand for the return of " Papa " Behrman to the City Hall had arisen.

The Constitution of 1921 had moved the City election forward to 1925. As the contest drew near the Choctaw leaders began to prepare the slate. Logically the choice to lead the ticket would have fallen to Commissioner Maloney, who was then serving the Club as leader and was its highest ranking City official. On the other hand Behrman had been responsible for the rehabilitation of the Machine and its leaders considered that he was in reality the boss. Behrman was anxious to run for reelection and to vindicate his record

[41] Long, feeling that Parker was a tool of big business, had opposed his state administration for three years.

[42] Long believed the election had been stolen from him in the City. At this time the Sullivan-Parker faction controlled a majority of the Orleans Parish Democratic Committee. This defeat made Long a more determined enemy of the Machine than Parker.

which had been so severely criticized in 1920. The only question was his health. His doctors agreed to let him make the race provided he would give up cigars and go on a strict diet. When Behrman consented to make the race the Choctaw caucus immediately endorsed his candidacy. Commissioner Maloney, who had been led to expect the endorsement for mayor in 1925, bolted the " Regulars ". Taking advantage of this break in the ranks of the Choctaws, the New Regulars made Maloney its candidate for mayor. Andrew J. McShane decided to make the race in spite of the fact that he had only scattering support among what remained of the Orleans Democratic Association.

The real contest was between Behrman and Maloney—the Old Regulars against the New Regulars. It was a contest of machines as in 1920 and on this occasion the Choctaw Organization proved the superior. Mayor Behrman desired sincerely to round out his career in the interest of the City. He proposed a vast program of public improvements which included a $27,000,000 lake-shore development, a two-year paving program, a municipal auditorium, modernizing of garbage disposal, a criminal court building, the building of a bridge by the public belt railway across the Mississippi, and cooperation with the state in securing a bridge over Lake Pontchartrain.[43] He offered this program to the voters with telling effect. The *New Orleans Item* gave him most brilliant assistance in presenting his cause and in countering the charges of bossism, vice and corruption.[44] The *Item* pointed out that the old bosses had been Behrman, Fitzpatrick, Ewing, Sullivan and Mauberret and that the new ones were Sullivan, Ewing and Maloney. The *Item* successfully proved from the record of the past that these men had been

[43] *New Orleans Item*, Jan. 6, 1925.

[44] *Ibid.*, Jan. 5, 1925.

a part of all the things they were charging as evils of Behrmanism.[45]

Great capital was made of the Parker-Sullivan failure to provide civil service in the City as promised in the election of 1920. Behrman showed that his record on the matter was consistent and without hypocrisy. He had opposed it since 1896 and still was against it. With some truth he said if the reformers of 1920 had really wanted classified service they could easily have passed the necessary legislation. It is probable that Governor Parker wanted the reform but was convinced by his leaders in New Orleans that his machine could not be maintained without patronage until it was firmly established.

The *Item* admitted that the old Machine had been destroyed because of its low appeal to commerce and vice but insisted that Behrman had rid the Choctaw Club of these practices. It was insisted that the Sullivan-Ewing-Maloney combination had taken over some of the worst elements of the old Machine.[46] One of the papers in New Orleans that a few years before severely criticized the administration then in power, was now supporting Maloney and the New Regular faction. The *Item* quoted from the past statements of the other paper to show that what it had condemned two years before it was now supporting. The paper had stated that it believed both the Old and New Regulars were corrupt. In reply to this inconsistency the *Item* chided its contemporary, saying that: " There is no wickedness in politics but Behrmanism, no villain but Behrman, no salvation but Maloney, no saviour but Sullivan." [47] It was also shown that these men who were seeking to make capital of Behrman's fight for the

[45] *Ibid.*, Jan. 8, 1925.

[46] The " Behrmanism " of the past according to the *Item* had now become " Sullivanism ".

[47] *New Orleans Item*, Jan. 8, 1925.

red light district during the War had themselves favored similar action.[48]   In one of his speeches Mayor Behrman stated that Ewing had broken with him because he would not support Ewing's plan to return to the aldermanic form of government.   His break with Sullivan he attributed to his refusal to prostitute his influence in the legislature to Sullivan's brewer clients.   The break with Maloney, he said, had come when he refused to satisfy Maloney's political ambitions.[49]

The race proved close.   When the votes were counted Behrman had 35,911; Maloney, 33,471; and McShane was third.[50]   A second primary was in prospect but when the McShane supporters went over to the Behrman camp the fight was given up and Behrman was declared the Democratic nominee as were the commissioners running on the Choctaw ticket.[51]   Behrman took over the City Hall in May and at once launched his great program of public improvements. He was now complete master of the Machine.   The election had been fought on the issue of Behrmanism.

From then until his death on January 12, 1926, his decisions were unquestioned by the Choctaw Club.   In his inaugural address he promised to create no new City jobs and to devote all possible funds to the planned improvements. In the six months before he died he succeeded in getting many of these projects well under way and the others organized and planned.   The succeeding administration carried them to completion.[52]

This analysis of the factional struggles occurring in New Orleans from 1900 to 1926 shows all were greatly influenced

[48] *Ibid.*, Jan. 9, 1925.
[49] *Ibid.*, Jan. 10, 1925.
[50] *Ibid.*, Feb. 4, 1925.
[51] A lack of money was also a reason for giving up the fight.
[52] *New Orleans Item*, Jan. 13, 1926.

and that two at least were decided by support provided by
the governor. The Orleans Democratic Association had
won in 1920 because Governor Parker had used state power
without stint or limit. As a result the Choctaws found
themselves out of the City Hall for the first time in twenty
years. Behrman who had used the influence of every governor since 1900 knew that to recapture the City Hall he
must have state support. This he got by backing Henry L.
Fuqua in 1924. The two successful campaigns of the
" outs " against the " ins " therefore began in the state election several months preceding that of the City.

After Behrman's death internal dissension beset the Organization. No leader came forward to take his place. He
had reestablished the Choctaw Club but the unity which he
had created in his last years went with Martin Behrman to
the grave. The victory in the state over Huey P. Long was
to prove but brief and the end is not yet of its far-reaching
effects on City politics. Governor Fuqua died a few months
after Behrman. The state and City policies of these two
men and those of other governors were rich political factors
for the coming master of Louisiana politics to exploit. This
rising star in the political heaven combined Behrman's capacity for political organization and use of patronage with a
genius for mass appeal. He was destined not only to rule
at Baton Rouge but to even the score of 1924 and challenge
the Choctaw Club where its power was so long undisputed.
This man of unbounded energy lost no time in turning events
to serve his ends and the " Long Shadow " deepened over
the Louisiana political scene.

CHAPTER IX

CONCLUSION

THE Choctaw Club was a result of the political struggles of the Nineties, which had divided the whites and brought the Negro back into politics. It was organized in opposition to a combination of Republicans, Reform-Democrats and Negroes, who had elected the mayor in 1896. A fortunate series of events, including the union of the Democrats and Populists, patronage from the governor, and Negro disfranchisement, made its entry into New Orleans politics most timely. The experienced politicians leading the Choctaw Organization quickly took full advantage of the lack of effective opposition, the peculiar election machinery, the purged and united electorate, and the City-state relation to entrench the power of the newly organized Machine.

New Orleans was the one great city of the state, and the immense political influence resulting from this had created a general division between New Orleans and the rest of the state. This division was in part inherent in the conflicting rural and urban interests and needs. It was also due to the idea built up by reform groups that machine control, which had long existed in New Orleans, was harmful not only to the City but also to the state. This natural antagonism was frequently broken down by political necessities. Country and City factions found they must cooperate on many occasions.

The economic life of the City and state from 1897 to 1926 was marked by the rise of corporate control and the ever-increasing power of well organized commercial interests in political affairs. Particularly influential were the geographically and financially concentrated sugar interests, the lumber companies, oil and gas producers and a number

224

of other manufacturing groups. Shipping, the cotton and sugar exchanges and the large banks wielded much power. Manufacturing was related closely to the products of the soil, which tended to intensify the conflict between the producers of the raw materials and the manufacturers.

The heavy reconstruction debts and the vast drainage and flood control expenses limited the opportunities of the Machine in the expenditure of money. As a further result of the reconstruction struggles, the governor was given large appointing power and this in turn affected his influence in City politics. On coming to power, the Choctaw Club took advantage of all these conditions. It cooperated with the governors, served the chief economic interests, emasculated a recently passed civil service law, restored and perfected the long used patronage system, and made no attempt to reform the habits and morals of the cosmopolitan population.

The aldermanic system of government, which the Machine inherited, was well adapted to organization control. By the time a change was made to the commission form in 1912, the Choctaws were in a position to dictate the new charter and defeat efforts to incorporate proportional representation and other reform features. The elimination of a large ward elected council and the substitution of a small commission council, elected at large, failed to shake the control of the Organization. The natural decentralizing tendencies of commission government and the several boards were overcome by the fact that the charter and laws gave the mayor some legal supervision over the commissioners and the boards. However, centralized control was maintained principally because all officials owed their election to the Machine and because Martin Behrman was not only mayor but also spokesman of the Organization.

The special needs of a metropolitan city in a rural state had built up through the years a peculiar legal position for

New Orleans.   This natural need had been frequently recognized in the constitution and laws.   A further factor in the development of a special legal position was the effort of the City to protect itself from rural and local reform waves and from the activities of the governor and legislature in seeking to control it politically.

The suffrage and election laws designed to disfranchise the Negro proved valuable to the Machine.   Great power was lodged in the party committees, which resulted not only in the " white primary ", but also in the almost complete control of election patronage by the Organization.   Since the winning of the Democratic primary was equivalent to election, control of the primary election machinery was all-important.

The election laws put a premium on party regularity and required a pledge of those participating in the primary to support the nominees in the general election.   The adoption of the direct primary in 1906 did not weaken the Machine's control.   The great power of party committees immediately fell into its hands.   Because the one-party system prevailed, the independent voter was of no consequence.   He could not serve as a balance of power between the two major parties, as only one regularly offered candidates.   Since he could not participate in the primary, he had no choice between opposing Democrats.   So powerful did the Choctaw Club become that their endorsement of candidates in the Democratic primary practically assured election.   In reality, there was little choice even for the Democrats themselves in the City.   They merely ratified the choice made by the Organization.   The election laws clearly reveal that some of their provisions were directed at election abuses practiced in New Orleans.   A corrupt practices act applying to both primary and general elections was passed in 1912.   It was more notable for its non-observance than for its salutary effect.   A court decision in 1921 declaring it no longer applicable to the primary completely nullified even its potentialities.   Because of the Organization's complete control of all branches of City and parish government and its close connection with state politics, any kind of regulation was difficult.   The suffrage provisions designed to disfranchise the Negro are two-edged swords and might be used against the whites as well as the blacks.   The ruling class could employ the same devices to disfranchise white voters bent on so-called radical social and economic reform.   A radical's interpretation of the constitution could be judged as unsatisfactory as that of a Negro in times of stress.   Because of this, democracy in Louisiana may be less stable than many assume.

The leadership of the Organization was in the hands of a few of the more powerful ward leaders, headed by Martin Behrman.   His hard work, political ability, and the prestige of the mayor's office gradually made him the most outstanding man in the affairs of the Club and finally its sole master. His dual capacity as a leader and mayor was unusual in city politics.   He loved politics and desired not only power but also high position.   He held his unique position not only by common consent of the Choctaw caucus, but also by majority vote of the electorate.   His assumption of responsibility as well as power seems to have sharpened the interest of the Machine in the welfare and efficiency of city government. The fact that he daily handled the problems of actual administration certainly caused him to be more interested in good government than the ordinary type of back-room boss.   He possessed many of the characteristics listed by Merriam, Kent, Zink, Sait, and Gosnell in their studies of bosses. He had the ability to lead, to select loyal subordinates, and to effect group action and compromises.   He had personal charm, which enabled him to meet all types of men.   His judgment of the motives of men was correct to a remarkable degree.   He could divine the direction of community

sentiment and anticipate with much accuracy the strength
and course of economic, social and political trends. His
personal character lifted him above much that the Machine
did, and he avoided for the most part individual responsibility for its "sins". The expression was frequently
heard: "Martin Behrman is better than his crowd." His
social and economic background made him popular with the
mass of the people; while his apparent belief in the wisdom
and righteousness of business men made him acceptable to
them. His political and economic motivations were those of
his day. Behrman regarded party as an agency to provide
responsible government and as the coordinator of its legally
decentralized branches. In New Orleans the party, in
Behrman's mind, was the faction known as the Choctaw
Club.

City, ward and precinct organizations were maintained on
the firm rock of patronage. The leaders were thus sur-
rounded by a group of workers who owed their jobs to the
Machine and who, because they were in government service,
could devote much time to politics. Ward leaders were
selected by popular vote at the primary, and the fact that
they had to be elected to the office of State Central Com-
mitteemen brought them actively into state politics. The
precinct and ward leaders were continually doing favors for
all kinds of people. They helped to mitigate the annoyances
of bureaucracy and made the government seem more human.
Desired meetings were arranged with officials; traffic violations were "fixed"; administrative laxity secured; penalty
for breaches of the peace was made less severe; and in a
thousand ways the Organization made itself seem necessary
to the mass of voters. Machiavelli once said, " . . . A wise
Prince should devise means whereby his subjects may at all
times, whether favorable or adverse, feel the need of the
State and of him and then they will be faithful to him."

This advice of the Florentine realist was followed by the Choctaw Club though probably unknowingly. The caucus and the leaders selected men for nomination, determined the distribution of patronage and recommended major appointments. The advice of the ward leader was taken in most instances in selecting representatives for the City council, legislature, and parish Democratic committee. The caucus served as the general coordinating and policy determining agency of the Machine. It was particularly useful in unifying the strength of the Orleans legislative delegation at Baton Rouge.

The election methods of the Club varied. In a large measure they depended on minute ward and precinct organization and the work of these units throughout the year. The Club more than matched any attempts of an opposing faction in this respect. In the active campaigns, the Organization adapted its strategy to meet whatever effort was put forward to oppose it. Behrman was quick to adopt new devices, such as motion pictures and the radio. When women won the ballot the Club immediately organized a complete women's division. Party principle played practically no role in elections since the decisive fight was between the Democratic factions at the primary. Elections were won or lost over bitter personal and factional issues. Charges of corruption and maladministration were frequent. The state legislative record of the Organization was a prominent issue only in one election. Far-reaching civic policy was seldom a major issue. Campaign funds for elections were secured from business men, office seekers and government employees. In view of the factional and personal character of the primary election, control of the Democratic party funds as such was of little importance because practically no money was spent in the general election. Each candidate or each faction raised the campaign funds for the primary. A perfunctory report of campaign funds was filed by the candidates as required by law, but it was obvious that the Choctaws and opposing factions spent much more money in elections than was ever reported.   Both the source and the disposition of most of the money remains a mystery as far as the law is concerned.   Candidates were frequently careless about filing the perfunctory reports even before the court held the law no longer applied to the primaries.

The relation between business and the Choctaw Club may be most aptly summed up in the words of a former ward leader: "The Club just agreed to do nothing that would hurt business, and business was to be the judge." In pursuance of this policy, bills were defeated or advocated in the legislature as powerful economic groups might dictate.   In return for these and other favors, business could be counted on to support the Organization politically and to contribute campaign funds.   Graft was seldom a consideration.   The politico-business relation was an arrangement of mutual benefits.   Most of the ward leaders believed in the benign influences of progress fostered by free competition in business, and in supporting commercial interests they were doing no violence to such thoughts as they may have had. Where popular sentiment was aroused, the Machine followed public will, especially if there were also economic interests back of such sentiment.   This was illustrated in the anti-trust law controversy of 1915.   Here there was public demand, and the demand of the sugarcane growers for reform. Opposing were the commercial interests of New Orleans and the sugar refiners.   When the Machine fought a private interest, it was generally found that it was taking the side of another powerful interest that happened to be on the side of public welfare.   The building of the public belt railway was a clear illustration of such a case.   In most cases involving the simple choice of public versus private interest, the Machine supported private interest except when its own political welfare was involved. This point is illustrated on the one hand, by its unfavorable vote on public ownership of utilities and the Ponchartrain bridge and on the other hand by its favorable action on public operation of a City paving plant and its refusal to contract with private concerns for the building of City water and sewage lines. Whatever corruption existed in the Choctaw Machine was ordinarily due to its contacts with business and vice. This was particularly true in legislation. The morality of the Machine was as good as the general moral tone of business and of the society in which is existed.

In its relations with the underworld, the Machine assumed a practical attitude. Most of the evils were inherited. When vice was legal, its support was gained very much as that of so-called legitimate business. When laws made gambling, prostitution, and drinking illegal, the Machine took a tolerant attitude. In this it was following the spirit of a community that wanted a wide-open town. That the Machine in some manner received support from these elements in consideration for its unobtrusive non-observance of law is probable.

City, parish, state and federal (when the Democrats were in power) patronage was used by the Machine to build up its organization. Other " spoils ", such as judicial " plums " and administrative favors were also used. Through the wide use of patronage of every character and form, the Organization insinuated its influence into all parts of government and enlisted the support of all classes of people. Patronage and privilege were the chief commodities in which it dealt. Since no effective civil service provisions were in force, the increase of governmental functions only served to further entrench the Organization. The technical and professional character of some services limited their political usefulness but not to any marked degree.

The Machine's connection with elections, patronage, and legislation brought it into state politics. In elections the City cast one-fourth of the votes of the state. It was therefore powerful in the selection of the governor. Because of the antagonism in the country toward the Machine, its role here was largely negative. The governor was chosen by the country with the consent of the City. The Machine endorsed whichever candidate seemed to be the choice of the country and thus assured his election. With only one exception, a friendly relationship was established with the governor. The vast state patronage powers of the governor in New Orleans was needed by the Machine to nourish its organization. Above all, it had to prevent this source of power from falling into the hands of the reformers. The trading value possessed by the Machine was the majority vote, which it could deliver at elections, and its controlled block of votes in the legislature. The governor on his side had patronage powers that could help and might break the Machine. He might also use his control of the legislature against the City. In the legislature, the Machine pretended to speak for the people of New Orleans. Its voice for the leading economic interests was very clear but dropped to a whisper in comparison when it spoke for labor or fundamental mass interests. Because the latter were unorganized and inarticulate, the Machine often opposed laws favorable to them. It never initiated social legislation or business regulation.

The factional opposition to the Choctaw Club was for the most part impotent. Without the active, whole-hearted support of the governor, factions formed against the Machine had little chance of success. The leadership of these groups was often inexperienced and apparently not fully aware of the tremendous advantages possessed by the Machine. Only one opposing faction in the whole period from 1897-1926 was successful in wresting control of the City government from the Organization. This successful fight was led by Governor John M. Parker, long an uncompromising foe of machine politics. Favored by changed conditions following the World War, dissension within the Choctaw Club, and with the unstinted use of state patronage, Parker defeated the Choctaws. In doing this he had in turn created a machine having the same characteristics as the Choctaw Club. In fact the Parker City machine had been organized and managed by former Choctaw Club leaders. Parker saw only the political evils of the Machine. The corrupter of politics in the form of privileged business he did not see, or seeing, was unwilling to break its strangle hold. His reforms failed because they were not in reality carried out and because they did not remove the economic causes of machine control. He abandoned his civil service plans and did nothing to curb economic influences.

In many ways the Machine represented popular will. It inaugurated no great policies in the legislature but followed fairly well the demand for civic improvements in New Orleans. In Behrman's final campaign, he proposed a wide program of public works which aided greatly in his election. Graft seemed to be comparatively rare, but City funds were dissipated in jobs for party workers and in some ill-planned City improvements.

This study reveals that there are no great differences in machine politics in the North and South. The one-party system and other environmental conditions have brought about variations of detail, accentuating some features and making less prominent others. The characteristics of the New Orleans Machine, which resemble those of other sections as reported in several studies, are more numerous than the differences.

The one-party system, which crystallized in Louisiana following constitutional disfranchisement of the Negro, threw the major political decisions into the primary.   The peculiar election machinery, designed to eliminate the Negro question, entrenched not only the Democratic party, but its dominant faction.   The choice both of men and issues was therefore markedly limited by the system.   Politics became personal and the question of who should govern overshadowed the issue of how the City should be governed.   Since all candidates were Democrats, no fundamental cleavage appeared. Questions relating to major policy were left unanswered because in a large measure they were unasked.

The degree to which it was the custom to name the so-called bosses to responsible elective office seems a distinctive feature of machine politics as developed in New Orleans. Martin Behrman was not only willing but anxious to hold the most responsible office in the City.   Under the aldermanic system of government the council contained many ward bosses.   After the adoption of the commission form, at least one commissioner was usually chosen from among the ward leaders.   The ward leaders all served as members of the Democratic State Central Committee, being elected at the primary.   This tended to identify responsible Machine leadership with responsible official leadership.   For the leadership of the Machine to be in high office was the rule in New Orleans; while it was the exception in the North and East.

Another difference to be observed was the absence of large scale graft from the City treasury.   This was due in part to the limited funds available because of heavy debt charges and unusual drainage and flood control expenses and to the responsible place held by Martin Behrman.   The rewards received from commercial interests for legislative and other privileges were returned to the Machine for the most part in the form of political support and campaign contributions.   Personal graft from this source was rare.   Such graft as existed was used by the leaders in political activities for the benefit of the Organization. With two exceptions, the ward leaders died poor. In both cases, outside commercial interests provided their wealth. The business of only one was closely related to political influences. The chief reward for the leaders of the Machine was to hold the better City offices. Petty police graft, minor rewards for special favors, existed, but built up no great fortunes.

An enumeration of the principal points of similarity reveals more clearly that in most respects, the Choctaw Machine resembled that of other localities. Its City caucus, ward and precinct organizations were essentially like those of other cities. Leaders won their places by hard work, and election was a mere formality which confirmed an already accepted fact. A dominant oligarchy ruled the Machine, a condition not uncommon elsewhere. Election methods were not greatly different. The New Orleans Machine served to select the personnel of government, determine policy, administer, act as intermediary between the government and the citizen and furnish the moving force for political action. Like the Northern machine, its sources of power were patronage, office, mass organization, and special favors and privileges granted to all classes of society. It was the force which marshalled the mass base for effective political action and, contrary to opinion in some quarters, did not use the power thus obtained against the business and commercial interests. The machine system in fact enabled the dominant economic class in New Orleans to have political power far beyond that justified by its numbers. The Machine did not sell out to the interests, but only " loaned " or " rented " its political power to them for a consideration—the consideration being in most cases political and financial support of the Organization. The favors asked from government by New Orleans business were not fundamentally different from those sought elsewhere. They had little mass appeal and hence it was wiser to deal with a political machine which already had the necessary power. When economic interests clashed, the Choctaw Club like its kinsmen in the North effected the most politically expedient compromise.

Favors and privileges dispensed by the Choctaw Club likewise were by no means confined to the large business interests. In some manner, every class was served. The difference lay in the economic value of the service. The Machine might help kill a labor bill in the legislature for the big employers, but it also let the middle-class housewife off for a traffic violation, got a job for a poor fellow who needed it, and obtained a suspended sentence for the man who had celebrated Saturday night in a riotous manner. As in the East and North, the Machine's essential characteristic was its humaneness, its knowledge of the needs and weaknesses of all classes and its willingness to lend its power to help when called upon, without any great consideration of ultimate results. Tammany Hall was once characterized as a political organization one day in the year and a charitable, social, and benevolent organization three hundred and sixty-five days in the year. The same may be said of the Choctaw Club. It served to allay the worst discontent of the masses and although first took what it gave, it nevertheless gave. The reform organizations which opposed the Machine centered their attacks on its granting of small privilege and its tolerance of vice, but failed to bring to a clear issue the politico-economic alliance which was the foundation of the whole system. They were willing to condemn petty graft, but lacked the courage to censure the leaders of business and finance who influenced the Machine against the public interest in more important matters.

In bringing together the scattered powers of government and focusing them for effective political action, the Organization did a real service. Since effective centralization was not provided by law, it was necessary for it to be achieved through party control. The custom which grew up for Organization leaders to hold high office was a wise policy. Such faults as the Machine showed lay in the use to which it devoted its power. Its natural tendency was to serve any powerful interest and to extend small privileges when requested even when such action was against the public interest.

All these facts and comparisons point to the conclusion that the machine pattern so often outlined by political writers and statesmen repeats itself even more emphatically in the South due to the one-party system, Negro disfranchisement, and the peculiar party machinery. It seems clear that the interpretation here given of the New Orleans Machine falls in line with that given of political machines elsewhere in the country; i. e., it represents the dominant economic interests of its locality. Political results in the South seem to have the same fundamental economic causes as in the North and East. The Machine did nothing daring; it was not an innovator, and its social vision was limited by that of the most powerful and articulate groups.

The Choctaw Club furnished in its government of New Orleans about what was desired by those elements in the community that had become conscious and articulate politically and socially. Its failure to represent labor and other mass needs on many occasions indicated that there were potentialities of demand not reflected by the Organization. Improvement seems to lie in a more intelligent understanding of the economic realities of politics. Abolition of the Choctaw Club, if it were possible, would not bring better government in New Orleans. Many of the leaders of the Organization are capable. The Club is experienced in politics and if its efforts could be confined within the bounds of public interest, it could be of great service in the City and State. In a democracy, the best way known to secure public responsibility from rulers is to provide an opposing force which will present a choice of issues and rulers. No such

permanent force has existed hitherto in New Orleans.   The
one party system, the presence of the Negro and the City-
State relationship present many difficulties in this respect.
However, they do not seem insurmountable.

Short of a social revolution or a complete change of attitude on the part of the Republican Party, Louisiana will for
a long time to come probably maintain the one-party system.
The problem of a permanent opposition to the Choctaw Club,
for the present, seems to lie within the Democratic party
where no differences of opinion on the Negro question exist.
The history of the past thirty years indicates that two permanent factions in New Orleans can not be maintained when
one faction possesses both state and city patronage.   Even
when one faction was in control of the City and another in
the State no opposition developed to challenge permanently
the Choctaw Club.   The interplay of State and City politics,
as now constituted, offers too many opportunties of cooperation and consolidation.   Patronage alone cannot furnish
a permanent basis of division.   The adoption of civil service
in both state and city governments would be a step forward
but would not of itself vitalize politics.   There is lacking an
alignment on fundamental issues that will at once crystallize
the factions within and demark the one from the other.
Until politics in the City is affected by the vital cleavages
which lie dormant in the larger fields of state and national
politics, opposition to the Machine will likely continue to be
transient and spasmodic just as in the past.

Social and economic conditions in Louisiana afford ample
promise for real political division.   The necessity of main-
taining a united front against the Negro has long prevented
fundamental issues from becoming the bases of political
cleavage.   Such state policies as taxation, public utilities, business regulation, social legislation and conservation could be
the back logs of division.   Such problems as relief, hospitals,
schools, local and state government reform, would serve for

a time at least as added issues. The natural alignment of state factions based on these issues would probably be about as follows: on the one side would be the small farmers and merchants and the laboring classes in the cities; on the other would be the large property owners and financial interests, the middle class and perhaps white collar workers in the cities. The latter combination would be smaller in numbers, but its superior leadership and economic power would tend to make it politically equal to the other. Should such issues be drawn and the formation of these factions appear likely, those in power would undoubtedly avow that they would bring the Negro back into politics. Since there is no radical leadership in the state which might bring to the fore extremely radical issues, the return of the Negro seems unlikely. The conflict would concern such matters as child labor, maternity protection, health insurance, old age pensions, labor legislation, unemployment insurance, income and inheritance tax increases, and problems of similar character. In other states, these issues in politics have not brought violent upheavals, and there is no reason to believe that the struggle produced by them would be so violently fought in Louisiana as to bring the Negro back to the polls.

Since the policies of City government offer less opportunity for real political division than state government, hope for permanent opposition in New Orleans depends on what may happen in the state. Because of its weakness in New Orleans, organized labor offers no base as yet for beginning new political alignment within the City. It can only serve to strengthen the broader state division if it comes. It is probable if factions based on real issues arise, they will tend to reflect themselves in New Orleans politics. The issues exist, and if they can be drawn in such a way as to avoid the Negro question, there is some hope of more realistic politics and better government both for Louisiana and New Orleans.

BIBLIOGRAPHY

PUBLIC DOCUMENTS

Acts of Louisiana, 1870-1926.
Annual Reports of Louisiana Public Service Commission, 1920-1926.
Compilation of the Constitutions of Louisiana—Long, 1930.
Proceedings of the Constitutional Conventions, 1898, 1913, 1921.
Laws and Statutes of the State of Louisiana, as amended to January, 1926, Marr. (Indianapolis, 1926).
Official Journal Proceedings of Louisiana House of Representatives, 1890-1926.
Official Journal Proceedings of Louisiana Senate, 1890-1926.
Debates, Constitutional Conventions of 1864-1867.
U. S. Census Reports, 1850-1930.
Reports of the Secretary of State, 1890-1930.

NEWSPAPERS

New Orleans Times Picayune.
New Orleans States.
New Orleans Item.
New Orleans Times Democrat.

BOOKS

Fortier, Alec, *A History of Louisiana* (New York, 1928).
Rightor, Henry, *History of New Orleans* (Chicago, 1900).
Gronest, T. G., "The Louisiana Constitutional Convention of 1913 and 1921," *Southwestern Political Science Review*, vol. iv, no. 4.
Ficklen, John R., "History of Reconstruction in Louisiana," *Johns Hopkins Studies in History and Political Science*, vol. 28, no. 1.
Marr, R. H., "Historical Review of Louisiana Constitutions," *Proceedings, Louisiana Bar Association*, 1912.
Hicks, *The Populist Revolt* (Minneapolis, 1931).
Lonn, *Reconstruction in Louisiana* (New York, 1919).
White, "Populism in Louisiana," *Mississippi Valley Historical Review*, vol. v, no. 1.
Gosnell, *Boss Platt and His New York Machine* (Chicago, 1924).
Taussig, *Tariff History of Louisiana* (New York, 1933).

Lewinson, *Race, Class and Party* (New York, 1933).
Myers, *The History of Tammany Hall* (New York, 1917).
Lynch, *" Boss" Tweed* (New York, 1927).
Kent, F. R., *The Great Game of Politics* (New York, 1924).
Steffens, *Autobiography* (New York, 1929).
Sait, *American Parties and Elections* (New York, 1927).
Merriam and Gosnell, *The American Party System* (New York, 1929).
Meyers, *Politics in the South* (Dallas, 1934).
Couch, *Culture in the South* (Chapel Hill, 1934).
Zink, *City Bosses in the United States* (Durham, 1931).

INDEX